Adult Webcam Studio 101

A Money Making Guide for E-pimps

Darby Jones

ISBN-13: 978-1544293394
ISBN-10: 1544293399

CONTENTS

ACKNOWLEDGMENTS

My sincerest thanks to Jack for his advice and assistance. Special thanks to Joehoya, Maddog152fo and Hooligan Harry for their inspiration.

Porn has always been a hotbed for innovation, consistently advancing technology ever since Gutenberg invented the printing press. It is an incredibly competitive market that adopts innovation as early as possible. Webcamming has quickly grown into one of the adult industry's and the Internet's biggest cash cows. LiveJasmin.com, which is based in Luxembourg and has long been the most popular camming site on the Web, ranks as one of the 100 most popular websites in the world. According to Compete.com, LiveJasmin generates more than 9 million unique viewers a month. Similar camming sites such as Chaturbate.com, Cam4.com and MyFreeCams.com boast 4.1 million, 3.7 million and 2 million unique monthly visitors, respectively. LiveJasmin boasts 25 million unique visitors per month.

The money generated by cam sites is now counted in the billions of dollars annually. At its most basic level, the live webcam phenomenon is merely the next technological extension of the live phone sex craze that started in the 1980s. A recent internal study by one company estimates that the now global industry boasts an average of at least 12,500 cam models online at any given time and more than 240,000 users. Many of the industry's top models are said to make six figures a year, and the pay networks that host and produce the content are taking in millions. Among the most vibrant adult industry market segments, the live webcam industry provides fans with connection, customization, interactivity, and an emotional experience that "porn" simply cannot match — while providing opportunities for performers and studios, cam companies, their affiliates, and more.

Moreover, webcams are one of the few parts of the adult industry that has not been affected by the tube sites. Guys go to webcam models to pay for the interactive nature of the experience, which is much more difficult to bootleg than a formulaic porn DVD. Unlike pre-recorded pornography, cam shows happen in real time. While you can record a webcam show and share it, the true value is in its interactivity, which can not be replicated.

To any red-blooded male entrepreneur, a webcam studio would seem to be a natural marriage of interests; money and naked young women. While many women are in director/management roles in the adult video market, there are relatively few female owned cam studios today but this is not to say that they too can not cash in on this thriving new business.

The most important thing obviously is to have a local product, which means local models — female, male, and transgender — that will generate the needed conversions from local users. For newcomers, just starting out, there are tens of thousands of cam girls already out there and the competition is fierce. Unless the girls are spectacular, there is a great deal of work involved in promoting them and getting guys to spend their hard-earned dollars. It is definitely not an easy task. No business anywhere, let alone one in a third world country, is easy. There are a multitude of little challenges that you will have to deal with. You can anticipate and mitigate against some challenges. Others will simply pop up with no warning. That is why I have written this book, to help you prepare for as many eventualities as possible. The key thing to keep in mind is that you are running a business and you must at all times treat it as such. This means market research, financing, and employee management skills. You are not going to just fly to Colombia, pick up a girl, put her in front of your laptop webcam, and become the next Larry

Flynt/Hugh Hefner overnight. It is a surprisingly complicated process, and part of that process is learning about the market and what sells. Another, even more important part is learning how to start and run a business like this in the country you intend operating in. As with analysing any other segment of the online adult entertainment industry, providing an accurate estimate of the size of today's live cam market, which is overwhelmingly made up of privately held companies that have no beneficial reason to report actual revenues, is problematic. While many numbers are tossed about, quantifying porn's revenues is impossible. With that being said, anecdotal reports indicate that live webcam revenues may account for as much as a third or more of online adult revenues today — making cams a multi-billion dollar business. It is recession resistant. No matter how bad the economy gets, there will always be lonely people who need to satisfy their needs.

What is a Webcam Studio?

Just to be clear from the beginning, a webcam studio is not a website like MyFreeCams, Cams.com, LiveJasmine, etc. where guys go to pay to watch girls masturbate. There are already several large players in this segment of the industry who have the massive traffic, servers and other infrastructure needed to sell video chat services to their clients. Cam sites of this size require connections of several gigabits per second, something that simply cannot be accomplished on a single server. This means that there are some pretty hefty upfront costs including advertising, hardware, bandwidth expenses, etc. which equate to rather high entry barriers in that particular market. If you want to start your own webcam site, you will need a team of really good programmers, smart marketing people, and at least $10 million that you are willing to risk on the world's acceptance of your dream product. Most independently run cam sites fail within their first six months. New sites have to compete with sites that have been around for twenty years and have thousands of models — and in most cases, there is no grace period before the comparisons are made to older, well-established sites. These new sites will usually begin with only a few models on-line at a time. Visitors come to the site and fail to see large numbers of models on-line, and so they never come back. When the models do come on-line, they wonder where all the traffic is — and then they defect to other larger sites. It is for this reason that the big webcam sites usually have multiple affiliate marketing plans in place to drive traffic, so the focus is on attracting customers and delivering content to them.

The basic premise of the cam girl game is a simple one: The internet viewer pays the girl for her time, and in exchange, she will chat, take off her clothes and play with herself (and others), or any combination thereof. The studios and their models are creating the content, which the website then sells to their clients (the traffic). If a client 'takes them private,' that means that he begins paying an ungodly amount each minute to watch the model in private. So for example, if a client is 'private' with a girl for ten minutes and she charges three dollars per minute, then thirty dollars is deducted from the client's account. That thirty dollars is then split between the website (for the traffic) and the model (or the studio, if she works for one).

Camsites rely on two main types of performers, home cammers and studio cammers. Home camming refers to broadcasting from home, and there are now vast numbers of cam girls broadcasting from the safety and security of their own bedrooms. These models have their own working equipment including internet access, computer, webcam, and working space. There is a huge push towards going independent. More and more models are performing shows exclusively on Skype and are seeking their own payment processors. On Chaturbate, for example the majority of cam girls and cam guys are broadcasting from their homes. Home camming is very popular throughout the Western World and Africa, especially in Western European and North American countries. African countries such as Kenya, South Sudan, Tunisia, Ghana, South Africa are also home camming strongholds. There definitely is a trend for girls doing the cam shows on their own. This will be accelerated as the access to broadband increases and the price decreases.

Studio camming on the other hand is the act of broadcasting from a 'studio'. In the adult cam world, a studio is a central location where girls or models can use equipment like computers, webcams and physical rooms for their sex chat job. The studios usually subtract the utility fees from the overall earnings of the models. Studios normally take part of the payment made by clients who tip the models, to cover the costs of promoting the models and or the supply of essential accessories. Apart from being a brick and mortar physical location equipped with camming equipment, a cam studio is also a company that recruits people to be webcam chatters, although it is definitely not a modelling agency. They may try to recruit aspiring models, but they generally have no connection with the regular modelling world. Most studios offer a contract that commits the model to a certain time frame. They usually offer a percentage of the token income ranging from about 10% up to 70%, sometimes even more. In some cases the studio will not allow performers to work without them for a considerable period after they quit. Occasionally models will accidentally sign up for a cam site through a studio only to find out later when they do the maths, at which point it is too late because the contracts have already been, signed complete with the non-compete clause (usually in effect for one year after the account is closed). In Colombia, many of the studios in cities like Medellin are only in business because they are able to receive payments on-line, while the girls cannot. At one time, that was the only value the studios provided.

America is starting to outsource an impressive amount of its hands-off sex trade to the third world webcam industry. Solitary men are swapping tables at strip clubs for laptops in bed, which actually makes a lot of sense. It is private, reliable, and arguably more intimate: members are able to check back in with their favourite models whenever they like. Webcam studios are to bedroom masturbators what brothels are to Johns. Webcams are completely virtual, meaning they do not have to drive anywhere or interact with anyone who's not on a screen.

Much of the behind the scenes information regarding sites and studios is kept very close to the chest, and many new models do not even know that they should be doing research about the studio they are joining ahead of time. This puts models at a considerable disadvantage when picking a studio to work for, and some studios will resort to aggressive tactics and even threaten models who eventually realize that the studio is not providing enough of a benefit for the percentage that they are taking. Generally speaking, studio models are averaging more money per pay period than independent models. Whether it is the room décor, superior webcams, internet connections, lighting or training, they simply make more.

The manager or administrator of a studio is often informally known as an E-pimp. Studio camming tends to be very popular in Poland, Romania, Russia, Ukraine, as well as in other Eastern European countries. In addition, there are large numbers of studio models in South America, especially in Colombia and Brazil, but there are also cam studios as far afield as Kazakhstan and the Philippines in the Far East. Generally speaking, a cam studio offers its girls (and sometimes boys) an agreement where they offer the use of their facilities for a number of hours per day, and a number of specified days. In return, they keep a percentage of whatever the models earn and they will often also set a minimum amount of money needed to be bought in per day or per week. Models who do not make that target are simply not paid and in some cases even left with a debt.

Some cam studios do not really add much in terms of real value, especially when the chat sites employed are accessible for everybody. Others offer a great deal to girls who have little experience in either performing or marketing. For those who are not technical, the studio will help them in setting up chat rooms or even Skype accounts. Many girls are referred by a newspaper or website listing. Maybe a friend suggested they try it out. Maybe they are shifting from traditional strip club work to the on-line equivalent, a popular trend in wealthier countries. Maybe they are working in a brothel where web camming is just another expectation.

One of the main advantages of studio camming, is that a model can hide her 'dirty job' from her family and friends. Some offer privacy that may not be available at the model's cramped and crowded home. Perhaps they simply want to keep their relatives away from the cam, especially if they plan to do more than just chat. Some girls will claim that they are simply 'not that kind of girl' and only do this because it is their job, but really, who are they trying to fool but themselves. Others simply do not have the disposable income to invest in a PC, working space, high speed internet or even a web cam. In some countries, it is much easier to obtain a work card from the studio than trying to do the same thing as a self-employed freelancer, so that they can get a loan to buy a car or an apartment. An experienced cam studio will generally have a plan for each model, detailing how or when they will be featured on various websites.

One of the most visual examples of the growing maturity and success of today's live webcam industry is found in the emergence of professional cam studios. These facilities evolved from simple locations that offered high-performance cams, computers, and internet connections, and now provide a broad range of essential services that are building and guiding webcamming's future. Some look like a film set, with a cardboard back-drop and a bed in it. Some studios provide hotel rooms where broadcasters have privacy. The degree of privacy broadcasters have differs. In some studios, every broadcaster is alone in a room behind a closed door. In others, broadcasters are crammed in like sardines, with barely enough room to move without bumping into each other. Studios can be located in office buildings, apartments, factory halls, hotels, in fact just about anywhere. Some have a luxurious modern looking set-ups with classy looking couches or artful backgrounds. Others have high speed Internet connections, high definition webcams and a variety of individual studios catering to all sorts of themes (including bedrooms, showers and dungeons). Some are really shabby places in old flats with ripped off wallpaper and worn furniture. Girls working in rooms with bright/gaudy wallpaper or big visible curtains that serve as dividers used to be a tell-tale sign of lower end studios, but more and more are now recreating a facsimile of what looks like a normal bedroom or living room.
Just to complicate matters further a webcam studio is different from a virtual webcam studio. The virtual studio owner, (e-pimps trying to sign up models to jerk off on camera in their own homes) are paid a percentage of what the model earns. An on-line or virtual cam studio is basically just a website trying to recruit wannabe performers to work on camsites. They do not provide equipment or opportunity at all. They may provide some support and may help with some practical issues, but basically all they do is take a percentage. There is no way of telling who or what is behind the website. They offer no guarantee at all to any service, including minimal support or coaching and timely payouts. Wannabe performers may stumble upon an on-line studio and erroneously subscribe to it thinking it is an actual camsite. This business model works only where there are a lot of women who already have the hardware/privacy to do the cam shows. These guys have no control over when and how often their models get on-line and hit the track. What is more, since there is very little value added working for the virtual e-pimp, most of these girls eventually smarten up and figure out how to cut out the middle man completely and work directly for the website. There is constant employee leakage with this type of business model. Webcam sites are filled with high school drop-out strippers that have set up their own webcams. If she is capable of setting up a computer at home, she could probably set up a fully working webcam studio.

Physical studios differ significantly from digital studios. A digital studio is more of an agent, who is basically an affiliate marketer with a model referral program. The agent earns a commission or revenue-share when models sign up through a special tracking link. Based in Geneva, Switzerland, and part of on-line marketing firm DAgency, Xmodels for example is active across all European countries, boasting a roster of more than 25,000 registered models. Physical studios provide an actual place for the models to perform while digital studios only provide promotion and consultation for the models. Both kinds of studios can be highly successful. A studio manages the models. The studio helps the models out with many things ranging from getting started and learning the industry to promotion and driving customers. Studios have a much more active role in the model's career than an agent does, and much more responsibility as well. Being an agent is nothing but affiliate marketing. Digital studios are learner operations that can operate more efficiently, but physical studios can provide everything models need to perform. This can be a major service for models who does not have all the required equipment or a place to perform. Both kinds of studios are responsible for a wide range of other services including promotion and consultation. Digital studios often have a bad rap in the camming community for doing "nothing but taking models money." Sadly many digital studios are guilty of just that. If you are going to start a digital studio, please try to have some integrity and provide value to your models.

An actual brick and mortar studio is basically a location with cameras and computers and, more importantly, the privacy where models can do their thing. Your job is to provide them with the tools, site, hardware, tech support, etc. The webcam studio is actually producing the content that the websites will sell to their clients. The website and studio split the gross sale from the client. The website then pays the model their salary. In third world countries, if you pay the girl $5 an hour she will think it is the greatest deal she has ever seen. Meanwhile, you as the studio owner, are earning $2-$3 per minute whenever she is in a private show. With just ten or 10-12 models earning 200 dollars every two weeks means the studio manager gets a hefty cut for sitting around in an office monitoring (perving) over the girls' cam feeds and doing very little else but supply the network connection and the machines.

Overall investment varies from country to country, but a studio can be set up in a less expensive part of the world for as little as USD 15,000 or less for streaming video 24/7 on a dozen separate stages. Companies like Odysseycam will happily fly directly to your current location and set up rooms for you at $1500 a pop (http://www.odysseycam.com/studiostartup.htm), but really all you need to get started is a webcam and some downloadable software. There are many parts of the world where it is still possible to get everything started for under $5,000. If you fill the place with girls (say, five work PCs) in the first month, you will have an instant cash flow. Assuming the average gross from each girl is around $2k, meaning $1.2k to her and $800 for the studio, minus all expenses such as PCs, ISP, cleaning, etc. you should be able to break even in just a couple of months. The ideal situation is where your models work directly for you, in your own studio. This is better for a whole lot of reasons; you set their hours, you set what they charge per minute of private chat, you make sure they are on line when their clients are looking for them, etc. The models work for you. The website (LiveJasmine for example) cuts you a check for their work. From that you pay the models, either hourly or a percentage of what they earn. Most websites, including LiveJasmine, will let you set it up this way but some others will not.

Although I have seen some models describe studios as "scum piggybacking off girls" hard-earned money, the role of studios transcends simply providing inventory, to being a competitive advantage for both cam companies and performers alike. To say all studios are bad is an unfair umbrella statement that simply does not hold water. There are now more and more studios that offer a great deal of value in return for that cut in commission. Cam sites themselves do not tend to offer very much in the way of personal support and training, but there are now studios that spend weeks training their models on how to be successful, so they can get ahead without the beginner's curve that models working from home often have. I know of at least one studio in Russia where new models receive guidance from an experienced model who has now moved into administration. These studios want to transform ignorant country girls into high class internet courtesans, which often involves an awful lot of work. In fact, there are a growing number of VIP studios, which offer personal trainers, sports facilities, tanning machines etc. Models enjoy regular breaks, conditions are clean, and they are free to joke around with members and each other. These are mainly in St Petersburg and Moscow, where operations are easily scalable: studios often have a high turnover and in most of the smaller Russian cities there simply are not enough suitable girls. The thing to remember, is that in many of these countries, being a cam girl is one of the best ways possible to make money. This is why there seems to be a never ending supply of Russian cam girls. Compared to a normal job in such countries, these girls have the potential to earn far more than if they worked a regular job.

Good studios offer a wide range of services to their webcam models.

Equipment and Location – Physical studios offer studio space to models. This includes all the equipment needed to perform, a location, outfits, toys, props and anything else the models require to perform their shows.

Help Getting Started – Some models might require some assisted getting started. This could include setting up their account and getting verified, signing up for payment processors such as Paxum or Payoneer and best practices for performing on live cam.

Driving Traffic – Most studios have a bunch of web properties, either social media accounts or websites. These web properties are used to generate traffic for all the models working with the studio.

Building / Hosting Websites – Managing a model's website is a very important task. SEO is mission critical in the adult industry and the model's website is the main hub where she links to all the different networks on which she performs.

Model Promotion – The main task of the studio is helping the model with promotion and acquiring customers. A successful studio must be able to generate more revenue for the model than she would get working independently and that requires help with promotion.

Both studios and agencies offer a multitude of benefits to models, especially those new to camming. Studios for example are better equipped to offer high quality service with a professional technical background. Many reputable and knowledgeable studios and agencies provide training, technical support, promotion, advertising and general encouragement to help models succeed. In many cases there are fees involved, and it really is up to the model to determine a balance between cost and benefit. The advantage of the studio system is based on what the studio is able to offer the performer over and above what they could normally have or achieve by themselves. For example, a studio may be able to offer training for the performer both in regard to their performance and to their chosen web platform. A studio may be able to provide better marketing and traffic, with designers and affiliate deals, and they may also be able to offer the model something in the physical sense such as equipment, luxurious rooms and outfits, or make-up. For many performers, the assistance and structure of a studio is a very important confidence builder.

Studio owners enjoy the added benefit of not necessarily being tied to one specific cam site. This allows studio managers to cherry-pick the sites that convert the best, which can be very profitable. Sites such as Stripchat actually prefer working with studio models. LiveJasmin has a very high proportion of girls working in studios. Site owners obviously prefer dealing with heads of studios that monitor hundreds of models, rather than policing thousands of individual models themselves. Many models, especially in developing countries, now have access to crucial tools because of studios — tools that they normally would not otherwise be able to afford. Some studios are investing in language lessons for their models, self development courses, high-tech equipment, new VR cameras, and much more. Performers can definitely increase their earnings as well as the quality of their broadcasts by obtaining this kind of assistance. There are now studios who provide resources such as photographers and make-up artists, so a model's profile looks professional and her appearance is at its best. Other studios also manage the model's Twitter account and promote them more than the model themselves might have time to or be able to do. All of the major players in the industry have established their own E.U. studios, mainly in Romania and some former U.S.S.R. countries. This was in order to be able to better control the studio performances, and in order to improve their own product. Flirt4Free for example, keen to integrate vertically has opened a training centre in Prague that has become a great resource for European broadcasters to learn the ins and outs of the network and what it takes to be successful.

Studios provide a consistent location from which a model can cam, because not every model has a spare bedroom that they can turn into a studio, or afford professional grade lighting. There is also a certain amount of benefit to leaving the house to go to work. Working from home can cause stagnation, feelings of isolation, and the line between a model's 'work' and 'home' lives can blur. It is important for models to maintain that compartmentalization between the two. It can be hard to keep people working on a regular schedule. And in order to make any real money you will need to keep them working around the clock. A studio gives girls a regular schedule, but once they start working alone from home, they tend to become sloppy, working less and less, or only when it suits them. Some studios have introduced minimum monthly earnings as well as requiring a minimum amount of time on-line (for example at least six hours a day, five days a week) and then fine models who do not follow the program. Models need to treat camming as a normal job and be consistent and disciplined. They need to put the time and energy into learning and growing in their profession (English and acting skills, performance techniques, etc.) and invest more money on their appearance and tools (clothing, toys, accessories, decorations). While many models might complain that they are camming in order to make money, not spend it, in Colombia for example, a good model could make more money than a doctor, lawyer, or someone else that spent many years in higher education. Many studios have models making more than $40K per month.

The best studios provide the highest technology and beautiful rooms to work from. Studios also provide up-to-date hardware, industrial level bandwidth, and technical support for models who are not as tech savvy. Some even offer daily payout options. There is a constant support group of professional, specialized support staff to help models; such as photographers, web designers, tech help and community managers, broadcast assistants, lawyers, psychologists etc. that would be very hard for them to afford on their own. Studios and other companies provide models with services and tools in several areas to help develop their careers. In terms of marketing, administering their own website, experience, photo/video accessibility, providing traffic, advice, faster internet speeds and high performance computers etc., it is almost impossible for an individual performer to do the same things at the same level of quality without such a dedicated team of people supporting and working for them. Best of all, all of this is happening while the model is both on-line and off-line, and even sleeping.

Training is one important aspect, but there are often other services to make their lives easier, such as contact with other professionals, including accountants, plastic surgeons, gyms, etc. that help the models focus on their jobs and perform better. Other services include professional training by high-earning models, instant technical support, in-house webmasters, foreign language classes, and personal development courses, for team building and friendship development. Additional perks include weekly and advanced payments, weekly contests, incentives and prizes, plus benefits from participating cam sites due to their relationship with the studio add to the reasons models choose to work with a studio.

Often times the largest benefit from working with a studio is personal attention matched with network-level exposure. This includes mentorship and guidance along with the big traffic in their rooms that only a network can provide. While girls working from home typically use their holiday snaps as profile pictures, studios can help them greatly increase their level of professionalism.

There are webcam studios popping up all over the US. Less ethical webcam pimps will bring in girls on a false premise, saying they can get them a job as a personal assistant then call them back for the second interview saying something completely different. And this is not taking place only on deprived ghetto areas. Even in America's most liveable cities, there are mercenary young women with an ambitious drive for money.

In the early years of the new millennium, I had two very close friends that both decided to go a work full time in the adult industry. The three of us had been working together in South Korea and all wanted a change of scene. The first was an Australian who decided to become part owner of a brothel located in the notorious Filipino red light destination, Angeles city. When I spoke to him recently, he explained that after ten years of living the Tony Soprano lifestyle, he had eventually returned Australia to bring up his son in the relatively sanitary environment of Cairns in the Northern Territories. Although he did make decent money as a pimp and a papasan, he had most definitely gone the George Best route, saying that most of it he had spent on women and booze. The rest he had just wasted. He rarely mentions some of the less glamorous perks that came with the job, such as TB, malaria and syphilis.

The second friend was an American who returned to Texas to open a twenty room warehouse cam studio. There was a break room with flat screen TVs and XBoxes, a pantry full of snacks, and free soda machines. One day he gave me a virtual tour of the working areas while some of his girls were working. All I saw were smiles, and all I could hear was lots of laughing. They were having fun and he was having fun too. Most of his girls pocketed $2000 for a couple hours per week, while he pulled in about $40k+ per month.

The Changing Face of Pornography

The modern view is that porn is as much a part of our society's infrastructure as electricity or air conditioning. After all, it is now claimed to be a global industry that is worth $97 billion. There was a time when even top shelf girlie magazines were household names. Who had not heard of Playboy, Penthouse or Hustler? This format created many multi-millionaires including Bob Guccione, Paul Raymond and Hugh Hefner. Sales of pornographic magazines in the U.S. Declined significantly since 1979, with a nearly 50% reduction in circulation between 1980 and 1989. This medium has all but disappeared thanks to DVDs and the internet. Fortunately porn is quite a resilient industry and has shown itself able to weather previous technological developments in the past. How many times have we seen the porn industry completely metamorphosed, emerging bigger and stronger than before?

Porn has historically positioned itself as an early adopter of and leader in tech trends. In 1897, just two years after the first ever commercial screening of a film, bawdy Victorian-era boys began setting sex onto celluloid. Somewhat later, printed magazines peaked in the seventies while VHS unashamedly bought fornication into the front room. The adult industry pioneered VHS distribution in the 1980s, allowing a copy of Debbie Does Dallas to find its way into every sock drawer in America. They also perfected most of the tools (and banes) of e-commerce in the 1990s, from electronic billing to on-line encryption.
The internet has lowered the threshold even further and we are now seeing the mass dis-intermediation of the market, as webcams displace the low budget movie studios that have been churning out boatloads of DVDs for the last decade. Just as Uber hopes to replace all the taxi companies with self-employed owner drivers, sites such as Myfreecams have witnessed a mass migration of video performers from the seedy studios of the San Fernando Valley. Santa Monica and New York have seen a growing number of porn shoots but Miami and Vegas are also popular locations. Vegas in particular has many advantages over LA for the industry. Porn stars are actually just prostitutes with a camera rolling, and that business model is already legal in Vegas. Lower real estate prices, partying caution-to-the-wind lifestyle, and lots of new customers rolling into town every week (especially during conventions) to sell themselves to. Not to mention the warm weather which helps if you like to wear skimpy clothing and a that city pays millions for their TV promos: What happens in Vegas stays in Vegas. The hardest thing is getting the performers to leave once the shoots are over.

A drastic drop in porn production follows the passage of Measure B, a controversial condom-only porn measure approved by voters in Los Angeles. The law requires adult film producers in the city to obtain a health permit before filming and performers to use condoms while engaged in sex. It also calls for health officials to be present on working sets and makes violators subject to fines and criminal charges. Ironically, Professional porn actors are 80 percent less likely to have an STD than members of the public of the same age. Not to mention all the other STDs such as herpes, hepatitis and HPVs which a condom will not block? Currently it takes $60 - 90 thousand dollars to buy the effective Hepatitis C treatment. With Obamacare, only the very poor and the very rich will be able to afford it. So when these people are finally done in the industry, do they take their Hepatitis and go flip burgers? Not likely, Once infected with Hepatitis C, that is $60-90 thousand each that the rest of us will be paying to help out, and that is just one example of the impact to society.

As Hollywood battles to keep movie and TV shows from moving to other cities and states offering tax breaks and rebates, filmed fornication has already fled Los Angeles. The number of permits issued for X-rated productions plummeted about 90% to just forty in 2013. Although critics say it is unclear how many companies may be filming illegally without permits, porn producers say they are taking their business to other counties in Southern California, as well as Nevada, Florida and Eastern Europe, where they say they face fewer regulations. Penthouse Entertainment in Chatsworth for example, which has ten television channels and produces up to 80 movies a year, has stopped all local film shoots and is now shooting ten movies a month in Brazil. Although porn production accounts for less than 5% of all film permits, the industry has traditionally been an important contributor to the local economy. A decade ago, local economists estimated that the porn industry in the San Fernando Valley generated 10,000 to 20,000 jobs annually and had $4 billion in annual sales. The Measure B ordinance was advocated by AIDS activists, who argued that it would protect performers from disease outbreaks. But the measure has been assailed in the porn industry, which has argued that mandatory actor testing for HIV was already effective, and that the law's real intent was to drive them out of business. Industry advocates also have argued there is little market demand for condom porn and that many performers object to wearing condoms. Vivid Entertainment and others sued the county last year to prevent implementation of the condom requirement. Production crew members, from videographers to make-up artists, most of whom are independent contractors, suffer the most in a shut-down. But at the same time, there seems to be very little thinking outside the box. They have talented people with unique insights could be using their equipment to do documentary films, such as short features autobiographical features. These are all kinds of things related to their unique insight into a society and culture which a whole different stratum of the population would find interesting, and some of it might even find a larger market than their primary product. London-based Customs4U, a video site that enables consumers to request bespoke adult content and performers to create it, found the moratorium actually increased their business.

And it is not just porno that is taking a hit. Employees in all sex related industries are feeling the pinch. Although the American worker has never been so efficient in terms of output over hours worked, real wages and benefits have plummeted. Prospects are appalling for college graduates and non-graduates alike. Lay-offs and cutbacks in previously solid industries protect the profits of an ever-smaller class at the expense of those who produce value. In standard stripper terms, lap dances in many places still start at $20, the same price they were in 1990. Customers expect ever-higher levels of contact and performance skill, meaning strippers work harder to earn the $20 tip that is worth a lot less than it used to be. At the same time, clubs charge dancers higher stage fees and tip outs, especially as customer counts and tabs drop and dancers become a primary source of income for the clubs. There are no lay-offs when your workers pay you, so instead of cutbacks, clubs hire more and more dancers, resulting in more competition for a smaller customer pool. The Great Recession has especially impacted the legalized prostitution industry in Nevada: more hookers, fewer johns.

Contrary to popular belief, porn is not recession-proof and the industry has now been on the decline for at least five years. Insiders claim the business has gone limp, metaphorically speaking. Actors and actresses in the adult porn industry still make money selling merchandise and going to photo shoots. The adult porn business reminds me of the head in the sand attitude of the music business. They did everything in their power to stop digital downloads but they still make money booking tours and selling merchandise. Porn, like the music industry before it, became so corrupt and debauched through the greed and incompetence of its executives. Playboy is an excellent example. When the stockholders began telling Hefner that his ideas sucked and were costing the company money, he threw a fit and took the company private again. He took is bat and balls and simply went home. By this time the combination of his senility and the fact that he ran the magazine with final editorial control, meant that Playboy was subject to one awful business decision after another. One great example was the annual 'contest' the magazine and website held to have readers vote for Playmate of the Year. Hefner and Hefner alone picked the winner, which is why for a long time they were all the same blondes, and why he had three of them at once as girlfriends. This was just blatant disregard for the readers and the company. In 2015, Hefner was so out of it that he put a new "feminist editor" in change who immediately dumped the nudes and people suddenly stopped buying. GQ and Esquire have also for the last couple of years, been pulling the "It's all white mens' faults" BS and needless to say they are not doing very well either. Male readers do not want identity politics, especially when they are told that they are responsible for all the world's ills and they are all rapists. This is why we have seen such a major Red Pill backlash.

Thanks to Hefner's incompetence, the company has spent decades ignoring massive IP they could have been monetizing, such as the bunny girl outfit. This costume is famous worldwide and is not considered nearly as adult as the magazine and yet all they do license is the rabbit head logo for unwearable colognes and tacky bumper stickers. Playboy Clubs should have been so entrenched in our culture by now that Hooters could have never happened. Maxim should have never launched, as any guy with a disposable income would have been reading Playboy Men's Health magazine at lunch, having dinner at a Playboy restaurant in the evening, going for drinks at a Playboy bar and then later on to a Playboy night club. And women should have had 'Playboy for women' (Not Playgirl) as a Cosmo-alternative to let them know 'Six tricks in bed to please your Playboy' or some such trash. So much marketing potential wasted on one man's ego.

Most of the old-school porn producers are suffering from Donald Trump Syndrome: they act like they are rolling in the dough, but when pressed they are incredibly cagey about their finances. The media, from highbrow think pieces to TV shows such as Silicon Valley, is quick to perpetuate these claims. American porn alone is often pegged as a $50 billion industry. It is not. Free tube sites have eviscerated traditional pornography. From 2007 to 2011, the industry collapsed by fifty per cent according to Vendo, an electronic pricing and billing platform serving a number of porn sites, with pay sites collectively making about $500 million a year. Studio producers alone used to churn out more than 10,000 skin flicks per year catering to these horny hordes, far outpacing Hollywood's 500-or-so offerings. A mid-level company that might have earned $350,000 a month in DVD sales before, was earning maybe $150,000 to $200,000 when the recession hit. That may have partly been due to the recession, but there has not been a bounce back like in other industries. Pornography has dominated the use of the internet since its inception until very recently. Social Networking has finally passed pornography as society's new internet habit.

In reality, it is hard to track how much money the porn industry has lost, because it is nearly impossible to figure how much it typically earns. It is still very difficult to secure funding for academic studies relating to porn. By some (albeit sketchy) estimates, porn adds up to 4 per cent of all sites, 14 per cent of all searches and 30 per cent of all data transfers on-line. Also, with the lack of benchmark data in the adult industry it is hard to support assumptions being made with the facts and data so many other industries provide. Adult Video News (AVN), a trade journal that covers the porn industry, estimated that the pornography business made $10 billion in 2012, but admits getting exact figures is close to impossible since many porn companies are privately owned and tend to inflate their figures. Best guesstimates are that the industry made as much as $13 to $15 billion during its peak in the mid-2000s, before the recession, but 80 percent of porn companies are now defunct or struggling. Even so, this is still a multi billion dollar industry where every second over 3000 dollars are spent and almost 30,000 people are watching porn. And to meet the vast demand of what has been termed 'gen XXX', a new porn video is still produced every 39 minutes. Twenty percent of men admit to accessing porn while at work. Also, 25 to 33 percent of the people who watch Internet porn are women, although only two percent of paying porn site subscribers are female.

And with all those men paying to watch, female porn performers are paid much better. While female performers often earn between $600 and $1,000 for a scene, men are usually only paid less than $150 for a scene. Even so, most female performers are not shooting that often, once or twice a month, maybe once a week, if they are very popular and in constant demand. Porn, like music and film, is having to adapt to the economic realities of the modern internet, yet most companies are still stuck in the 90s when it comes to their business model. Profits have plummeted, yet production companies have merely responded by lowering production budgets, rather than making genuine attempts to adapt their business model. The result is less work because there is less money to be made. For example, a single solo shoot may involve two or three photo sets and videos, so the girl gets paid once for two or three website updates worth of content. Male models have it a bit different, making very little per shoot but tending to work more often than female performers. Likewise, there are relatively few male performers compared to the number of female performers. Partly, this is because the male performers have an extremely difficult job, maintaining an erection in an artificial and entirely unsexy environment. When a guy cannot get hard, time is wasted, and when locations are generally rented per hour, the limited profitability of the scene dwindles. In other words, not many guys can actually do this job well, and those that can tend to find that producers want them back again and again. Furthermore, the focus of the scene is on the girl: what appeals to fans is the show the girl puts on, not the guy actually having sex with her. This means that a guy can be used fairly frequently, because as far as fans are concerned, he is almost in the background. The end result is that male models work much more frequently than female models, but do so for very low pay. Many adult actors also have to work as private companions, a polite term for hooker. Many people are probably under the misconception that porn is a lifestyle of partying and riches (and for a minority percentage it is) but this helps bring to light that most in this business are just hard-working individuals trying to make a living.

Porn's enterprising female performers have started to pursue other avenues for revenue. For example, a female performer who has scored fame starring in porn movies, can hit the road as a head-liner and make money feature dancing at strip clubs across the country. Female performers have numerous alternate income streams beyond shooting: strip club appearances, affiliate marketing, sex toy lines, their own web sites, etc. Other adult stars and companies are trying to make up for lost revenue by breaking into new products like sex toys or lingerie that cannot be digitally downloaded. However, the number one such alternate income stream which produces the largest share of the girl's income is escorting, i.e. going on paid dates with fans. We are talking about thousands of dollars per day here. That is where the money in the adult industry is. What porn becomes is brand creation and promotion so as to attract more escorting clients.

Producing and distributing porn is still punishable by death in countries such as In North Korea and Iran but in the US, most politicians know that it is wise to not touch the porn industry because of all its fans. However, the Republicans have made a call for more vigorous enforcement of pornography and obscenity laws, which is largely why industry folk are voting for the Democrats.

Over the past decade, revenue for on-line porn has plummeted because of the easy availability of free content on so-called "tube sites", video-sharing websites imitate YouTube and allow anyone to upload content but feature porn clips. Tube sites have doubled in a year to 1,000. Pornhub for example, has 2.4 million visitors per hour. Experts estimate on-line subscriptions and DVD sales have decreased from $10 billion to $12 billion in the mid-2000s to about $3 to $5 billion today. Even the big name studios are having to deal with a perfect storm: declining DVD sales, a complete misunderstanding of file sharing and a very weak economy. In addition, the rise of do-it-yourself porn is devastating the mainstream industry as increasing numbers of 'amateurs' use the internet to upload home-made sex videos. Telecommuting is shaking up the porn industry and traditional porn stars are being replaced by everyday people who upload porn to sites like Reddit or build up a fan following through live web cam sites such as Chaturbate. Which brings us nicely to the webcamming phenomenon.

A Brief History of Webcamming

Camgirl websites are basically digital peep shows, which became very popular during the 70s and 80s, but also existed previously and can still be seen advertised along the American interstates. They used to exist all over New York's Times Square and the notorious Soho in London. Essentially, it was a performer or two on a stage surrounded by glass which the audience sat behind. The name came from the idea that the audience would look through a slot which would close after their money had run out or after they had quit feeding coins into the viewer. Actually, peep shows go back even further than that.

Just a century before the arrival of the all pervasive internet, carnivals, circuses and sideshows were the most successful way of bringing remote farming communities together. At their peak of popularity, there were thousands of such travelling fairs roaming across the American continent. Often times they were the only live entertainment that a remote farming community might see all year. A large carnival was usually made up of ten to fifteen mechanical rides, but also twenty to twenty-five sideshows, what we now usually refer to as freak shows. It might initially sound rather unkind of me to compare camgirls to the human curiosities on display at the circus but some of the most popular sideshow acts were actually "Girl Shows" which ranged from the "Broadway Revue" with fully clothed performers, all the way to full-blown "hootchie-kootchie" strip shows, which is not all that far removed from the modern day camgirl offerings. Alongside the strippers, freak shows were once a staple of American entertainment and gave rise to the likes of PT Barnum, as well as making icons out of many of the performers. Even so, in time, film and TV saw the decline in circus sideshows. Now we have special effects and CGI, not to mention the fact that it is no longer politically correct to gawk at "human oddities," those unfortunate enough to have such physical abnormalities as the public conscience changed. Interest in sideshows declined as television made it easy (and free) to see the world's most exotic attractions. The performers often protested (to no avail) that they had no objection to the sideshow, especially since it provided not only a good income for them, but in many cases it provided their only possible job. The sideshow seemed destined for oblivion, but the tradition is still maintained and even adapted for modern mediums. In the early 1990s, the Jim Rose Circus" featured acts reviving traditional sideshow stunts and carrying some of them to extremes, and "fringe" artists, often exhibiting extreme body modification and performing bizarre or masochistic acts. The show drew audiences at venues unknown to old-time sideshows, like rock clubs and the 1992 Lollapalooza festival. The Jim Rose Circus held its last known performance in 2013 at The London Burlesque Festival. Circus Historian and Ken Harck still runs the Brothers Grim Sideshow, which toured with the OzzFest music festival in the summer of 2006 and 2007. Over in the UK the torch had been taken up by Simon Drake on his late night Secret Cabaret, a Channel Four show that quickly became a cult classic even though it has never been released on DVD due to copyright restrictions. The Montreal Comedy Festival stages a Just For Variety show as an accompaniment to its Just For Laughs festival and the impact of the Jim Rose Circus on pop culture inspired a new wave of performers. It is claimed that there are now more sideshow performers than at any other time in the genre's history. It will be interesting to see if public tastes change again and the current surge in camgirls is later seen as degenerate and exploitative.

In 1991, the very first internet webcam was pointed at the Trojan Room coffee pot in the Cambridge University Computer Science Department and initially operated over a local network rather than the web. The first commercial webcam, the 320x240-pixel resolution black-and-white QuickCam, entered the marketplace in 1994, created by the U.S. computer company Connectix, which later sold its product line to Logitech in 1998. QuickCam became available in August 1994 for the Apple Macintosh, connecting via a serial port, at a cost of $100. Other cameras were mounted overlooking bridges, public squares, and other public places, their output made available on a public web page. Aggregator websites have also been created, providing thousands of live video streams or up-to-date still pictures, allowing users to find live video streams based on location or other criteria.

Long before it was big business, camming was a personal form of expression, kind of like blogging. One of the most widely reported-on early webcam sites was JenniCam, created in 1996, which allowed Internet users to observe the life of its namesake constantly, in the same vein as the reality TV series Big Brother, which was launched four years later. Twenty year-old Jennifer Ringley began broadcasting from her Pennsylvania dorm room. Widely regarded as the first adult cam site, JenniCam offered a glimpse into Jenni's daily life. She was not putting on sex shows, but because she would film her room at all times, viewers would sometimes see her in intimate moments, including her sex life. While she may not have fully anticipated (or welcomed) the resulting notoriety, her personal openness will be forever correlated with sexuality; and credited with ushering in the era of every girl (and guy) being able to broadcast their sex lives worldwide, for both fun and profit. JenniCam rocked the infant internet with the first adult-oriented live cam shows, setting the stage for the growth of today's multi billion dollar camming industry. It quickly became a cultural phenomenon that was quickly embraced by other models and companies, such as iFriends (which is still in operation today), and which may have been the first widely used platform to aggregate individual cam operators into one network, allowing anyone to set up a live webcam, bringing together the technology, traffic and payment processing services performers needed to profit.

The practice was first commercialized in 2004, when MyFreeCams appeared. Users could log in, message with models in an open room, and then take them to an expensive one-on-one "chat" that was often overtly sexual. It essentially dynamited the porn world, and today it is the 344th most visited site on the internet. This was followed by Chaturbate and CAM4 which implemented the system of tokens, and then other players entered the market such as BongaCams, Stripchat, and CamSoda, while Cams and F4F, which despite being private-based cam sites implemented a system similar to tokens. Private show sites are very restrictive, focusing on the client having to join the model in a show that is mostly sexual. In these sites, models cannot share information such as their social networks, which would bring them closer to their clients. Token-based sites aim to be the opposite: They want their models to build strong friendship bonds and become more intimate with their fans through networking. They allow for entertaining, artistic performances that are mainly fuelled by creativity, shows that turn clients into fans who give generous tips in gratitude to the models that make an effort camming, not just for sex. This approach encourages more models and clients to participate more in an entertainment show. A lot has changed since those days, with twenty years being longer than many of today's cam stars have been alive. A new generation of models have always known about home computers and webcams, the internet, and internet porn, something that a surprising number of cammers shy away from. There has been an ongoing evolution in the live cam industry, and there are now multiple business models that have worked and continue to work in the cam space, free chat, paid private chat and cam site social networks.

Having undergone nearly two decades of erotic evolution, today's highly professional live adult webcam industry is big business, and a far cry from its humble beginnings as an exhibitionist's personal project, and the haven of amateur adult website operators. Camming in its latest form has quickly become a lucrative and relatively stable job option in modern pornography and voyeurism. It is ironic that live video over the internet was predicted to shake up the world of business, drastically cutting down on the need for executives to jet across the world for high-powered meetings, and yet telecommuting has most impacted the porn industry. Five years ago, the highest earners of porn were the actresses whose names marqueed big films. Today, they are more likely to be models who will never perform a hardcore sex scene on camera, and whose face will never appear on a DVD cover. Collectively, the webcam industry is estimated to be visited daily by some five percent of the web's global users, with one site (LiveJasmine) reaching over two percent alone, according to Alexa.com. The entire cam girl industry is already valued in billions rather than millions.

Just five years ago, cam girl jobs represented about 5% of the ads on Sexyjobs.com, which caters to more than 80,000 adult job seekers daily. Today they represent 50% of the nearly 2,500 daily job offers advertised on-line and the industry is far more profitable than regular porn. Another thing that differentiates camming from mainstream adult entertainment: people are not only interested in watching young women. Historically, the adult video industry tended to concentrate on the 18-29 age bracket, but the more intimate nature of camming supports a much wider range of ages, as well as fetishes and other interests. A webcam performer only needs to appeal a very small segment of the consumer market and it is still possible to be very successful within that niche. The cam industry is growing because more and more people are finding out anyone can do it. One of the most popular camming sites, LiveJasmin.com was first launched in 2001, and the number of active models runs the gamut, age-wise. There are about 3,000 models who are 18-20 years old; about 13,000 models who are 21-29 years old; and about 5,000 models 30 and up. The oldest performer is 79. If you log on to the ten biggest cam sites on the Internet, and you see the model counts for who is on that day for each of those ten websites, there will probably be 20,000 models on-line at any given time.

More female and male porn stars are doing live webcam streaming in the comfort of their own homes. Male models especially are hurt by moratoriums because their income depends upon shoot volume. Unsurprisingly women are not shelling out tons of money to see guys perform sex cam shows. The majority of people who pay to watch males on webcam tend to be other males. Technology has proven to be the modern porn star's best friend. Live webcam shows, subscription websites, and digital store fronts all bring in extra income. Vivid Entertainment claims that interactive entertainment, a genre that largely includes cam shows, now accounts for around half of the sales in the industry.

Most cam networks all offer more or less the same "service:" The model supplies the body, the network supplies the eyeballs, and then takes a cut of what the viewers pay. Each network will ask its models to fill out a brief bit of biographical information and confirm that they are eighteen or above. Most require some sort of identification proving age, but with standards low, laws international, and documents scanned, forging such a thing is a cinch. In other words, under-age is rarely a problem.

As for the economics of camming, Best Kept Studio Agency, which has more than 2,000 models on more than thirty different cam sites, says that on Myfreecams.com, the top 250 are making on average more than $100,000 a year. Even so, these models are at the very top, while eighty percent of the models make on average $600 per month. Adult Webmaster Empire, which runs LiveJasmine, said the site's top performer made $34,000 a month, by working just four to five nights per week. And that is after both the site and her agent took their cut. Another model, who goes by the name "Miss Kitty," makes $25,000 per month on only two to three weeks of work per month. Ross Love, owner of the Best Kept Secret Talent Agency, said he has one model who makes as much as $2,000 to $3,000 per night - but limits herself to income of $10,000 per month. Some top models, he said, are making between $75,000 and $100,000 per month on the site MyFreeCams.com. Nowadays, the number of studios and models is increasing far faster than the number of paying clients. This results in many models earning less than they could years ago. At the same time the economic environment in Eastern Europe is slowly improving, and combining these trends, camming might not be as appealing as it used to be.

The people getting rich off of this industry are the cam sites, such as MyFreeCams or LiveJasmin, typically taking half of the earnings brought in (models get the other half, often split down to a quarter if a studio is involved). Several of them are generating tens of millions in revenue at this point, and are among the top 500 sites globally in traffic. The cam business is probably already bigger than the traditional porn industry, including the large porn sites, but they guard their numbers very carefully. Tube sites are often just portals that take you to go to a cam site or a dating site. There are fewer also regulations with those sites as opposed to professionally produced pornography.

The most popular sites LiveJasmin, MyFreeCams, Charturbate, Cam4 and Streamate advertise across the mainstream porn tube sites of masturbating ubiquity, sites like PornHub and ClipHunter, There is a good reason why the big guys like LiveJasmin are pulling in such large amounts of money. They have co-ops with some very viral companies that bring in huge amounts of traffic for their webcam girls. Streamate sells its models through a variety of repackaged and re-skinned websites, like PornHubLive using the site's well-known brand as an easy in with porn consumers. Free clip sites, for instance, outrank cam sites. LiveJasmin ranks around 80th in US traffic, while Pornhub ranks 56th. Membership fees and cross-promotions to other adult properties, mainly dating sites are the primary means of monetization. Some of them will have virtual goods and tribute/tip systems as well. Most often (male) users cannot communicate with other members unless they pay for access. And, what is even more scammy, is that if you receive any messages from women, it is highly likely to be a camgirl or female agent from another part of the company. These girls receive commissions for getting non-paying members to convert. Hookup sites are a volume-based business. A common business practice is to whitelabel a successful hookup site; give it a different skin, but share the same database, so it looks populated. Once you are in the database, you will be spammed for any new whitelabeled version that pops up. Worse still, the user population is 95% male, so you have better odds of finding a female hookup at a gay bar.

Trying to find who actually owns a company like Streamate is confusing to say the least. The domain belongs to Flying Crocodile Incorporated aka Accretive Networks, which has a PO box in Seattle. They started out in the late 90s as one of the largest porn site trackers and when that business fell off they started the camming business. Job openings point to a nebulous firm called NaiadDev, also based in Seattle (and hosted by FlyingCroc). But the company's custodian of records is one Rena Erotocritou, employed by "Ariel Secretaries Limited," a shell company based out of Cyprus. The massive LiveJasmin would have you believe it is owned by "Gestao e Investimentos, Lda," a company based in an autonomous region of Portugal, and has a host of fraud complaints lodged against one of its subsidiaries. But a recent tax bust against LiveJasmin's Hungarian CEO György Gattyán, one of the richest men in Hungary, and his corporation, Dolcer Holdings, shows just how muddled the corporate picture is. No doubt deliberately. The owner of LiveJasmin is currently the third wealthiest man of his country. It might not be a big country but he is still worth more than half a billion dollars. MyFreeCams, one of the most popular of the cam portals, has a domain registered to a Leo Radvinsky, and a legal contact in the Netherlands. The founder of MyFreeCams runs a VC business in the US with his cam wealth.

The monetization of cam sites closely mirrors the free-to-play video games industry. Most popular camming websites also encourage visitors to register. This way, viewers can purchase tokens with which to tip performers. The site Cam4 for example usually offers 500 tokens for around $100, 250 tokens for $50 and 100 tokens for $18.99. It is clear that one token is not worth very much, so although though a 20-token tip may seem generous, it is not much really. Tokens are used in the same way that casinos use chips. It takes away the worries about spending actual cash. It is a lot easier to fork over 1000 tokens rather than thinking about the 80 bucks that you just spent in less than five minutes. The more money that customers throw down, the more privileges they are likely to receive, like seeing the shows in full screen, viewing multiple screens at once, private messaging, and private sessions with their favourite performers.

The basic premise of the cam girl game is a simple one: Viewers pay a girl for her time, and in exchange, she will take off her clothes, chat with them, play with herself (and others), or any combination thereof. When the viewer's money runs out so does their time. It is a web-based red light district, and unlike some seedy ghetto side walk, the sex comes to you.

There are a few basic categories of cam performer. To begin with, there is the "friends-only" category, which is PG: no nudity, no kinkiness. In fact, some performers do not even talk about sex with their viewers and not all users are a masturbation-crazed degenerates seeking out pay-for-play sex shows. YouTubers are already showing that you can, to a large extent, sell friendship. It can be a mass market product, or it can be something fairly niche. A history professor with a hobby for collectible card games made a successful transition into a YouTube web series host. There are guys who stream video games on Twitch.tv and regularly pull in 15-25,000 viewers and through ad revenue alone make hundreds of dollars a day. eSports personalities like Day, TotalBiscuit and Neuro address their viewers as friends (with cute nicknames). Twitch is a media empire built entirely around this interaction, but YouTube's success with PewDiePie and Markiplier is essentially the same thing. People are willing to pay to watch friends being friends. When it comes down to it, a lot of the individuals who seek out these kinds of shows are simply lonely, and want to talk to someone. The fact that they have to pay to do so does not seem to deter them.

Moving along the sexual spectrum, shows go all the way from "soft-core" to hardcore. This is where the stereotypes attached to the industry come out and majority of cam performers choose to place themselves. This is where much of the screen is filled with girls (and boys) ramming huge dildozers up their asses. Despite this, webcamming is more than just porn. Camming offers viewers something traditional porn sites can not: a conversation. It is about giving attention and entertaining someone. It is companionship. Apparently, fans see something really appealing about a performer looking directly into the camera to respond to something they typed. People who watch porn just want a mindless orgasm. People who pay for webcam models are usually lonely and want the interaction with a live person. They are looking for some company and some stimulation at the same time. Many camgirls have it down to a science. Usually it is telling guys that they are sweet. The majority of men simply need attention, when they want it, and they will be locked in until the tokens run dry. Regulars will sit in on-line rooms for hours, pouring money away. These are the really lonely ones, the ones who want to hear that they are loved. After you watch your favourite porno a few times, it is boring. Your favourite porno cannot look you in the eye and say Hey Joe. How was your day? Did you get your kids last weekend? At the same time webcammers are not humanitarians, they are professionals and they are there for the money. It might sound mercenary, but these guys are getting exactly what they are paying for and this keeps them coming back. The "girlfriend experience" can turn users into digital sugar daddies. One of model posted an Amazon wish-list full of toys for her son around

Christmas, and fans bought every single one for her. Another made $10,000 by celebrating her birthday on-line with fans.

Most models are able to work from home. And many do this to supplement their income when unemployed or underemployed. But many also choose this route since it does not leave as big a footprint as engaging in a typical porn career. At the top of the webcam food chain are the cam girl "mansions," like an internet version of the Playboy mansion, or perhaps the mansion from The Game. Here multiple cam girls live and work together without a studio "owner." Often they will collaborate on shows, which increases both revenue and exposure. Battle Cams, for example are where two performers appear side by side in a split screen and can compete in a variety of acts: dance-offs, gum chewing contests, squirting contests, whatever they want. Whoever walks away with more tips wins. Then there is the idea of using green screen, where cam performers can literally put themselves in any context they want while never having to leave their bedroom. One of the most famous models in the industry is Sophia Locke, who founded an event series called the Cam Girl Mansion, and who claims that its importance cannot be overstated for model networking and empowerment. The Cam Girl Mansion is an annual event where Locke invites twenty models to a rented Las Vegas mansion to live together, cam together, and attend parties and conventions. Such events are becoming more and more popular. CamCon, is held every June in Miami Beach's Eden Roc Hotel This is an industry event designed to bring eager cammers of all ages together to exchange tips and tricks complete with seminars, meet and greets and vendors. There is still a fair amount of stigma attached to camming and many of the models work pretty much isolated from one another, leaving them prone to the whims of the cam sites they work on. Even though they are forming relationships with the viewers, they do not have co-workers or classmates and this solitude is compounded by the competitive nature of the industry. Most models block other models from their rooms. It is very common for a model to enter another model's room and link to her own site in the chat, or for models to poach each other's high tippers. Physical meet ups encourage individual empowerment in an industry where unionisation might not be the most practical solution.

Then there are those who brave it on their own to avoid paying a commission. They use platforms like Skype and Facebook to host their shows. A lot of people think Skype is safer because it is just them and the client. One on one makes it feel more private. But models can still be recorded on Skype, and there is no one to complain to. If a model is accepting PayPal then her name is exposed, her email is exposed, her identity is so much more out there. But on a cam site, no one knows her real name and they do not have to reveal any personal information. On some sites, performers do not even have to show their faces. There is the performance end of things but then there is the promotional wing, which almost always finds a home on social media. Take for example a randomly selected post from any camgirls's Twitter page, "Getting naked on #cam4 in 15 mins." The message is clear, concise and leaves no room for confusion. Camgirls now tweet their entire life and hashtag the hell out of everything. Some cam performers have gained upwards of 40,000 social media followers. Social media is the ultimate platform for them. There is now a new genre of model similar to the Instagram-famous 400. These Vine and Facebook models are really social media models. This is now evolving into a do-it-yourself kind of business. Others have found additional applications through which they can make money such as charging for Snapchat material. Earlier this year, the release of "Snapcash", a feature added to Snapchat that allows users to send money to contacts, unintentionally opened up a new revenue stream for porn stars and strippers who want to independently profit off their own erotic photos and videos. Although many are now making money by selling pornography through Snapchat, the practice is forbidden in Snapchat's community rules.

The explosive growth of camsites has already created a number of internet sensations with some girls earning upwards of a million dollars a year. A five-year veteran like Ophelia Marcus, a camgirl better known to her throngs of fans as LittleRedBunny, winner of the 2014 AVN Award for "Favourite WebCam Girl" and "Best CamGirl" at The Sex Awards in 2013, creates a 1920s speak-easy feel with mood lighting and sexy pin-up style outfits. Within the past few years, the organizers of the EXXXOTICA Fan Choice Awards decided that Webcam Girl Of The Year deserved its own category. Some people might think it is easy money but in reality it can be both physically and emotionally draining, and despite envy and resentment, it really is a job. There is often a lot of multitasking for a single performer who has to control the music, the dancing, and the lighting, all while handling twenty conversations at once. Private sessions can often last for twelve hours long or even longer. The career of a cam girl is short - they are studying, they get a job, then they peak and drop. A lot of the girls end up getting bladder infections, because they are playing with themselves for hours at a time. Yeast infections are another occupational hazard. Most models claim that they try not to fake it but obviously after four of five private shows, it gets a whole lot harder to orgasm,

Some gain fame through notoriety. Kendra Sunderland, a.k.a. Library Girl, is the 19-year-old arrested for masturbating in the library, while others studied next to her at Oregon State University. Sunderland's fame was largely the result of an hour long video she made of herself at Valley Library in which she stripped and masturbated on camera for a live audience. The performance was recorded by someone who was watching on-line, Sunderland says, who loaded it to a number of porn websites. On just PornHub.com, where Sunderland is now a verified porn star, various iterations of the video have been viewed more than 7 million times. The show earned her a public indecency charge for which she faced a year in jail and a $6,250 fine, she ultimately pleaded guilty and was fined just $1,000, missing jail time, but it also generated headlines around the country and landed her reported deals with Playboy and Penthouse, her own line of sex toys, and a contract with Penthouse parent company FriendFinder Networks purportedly worth six figures. She was "banned from MyFreeCams for violating their guidelines and filming in a public place." along with another model who engaged in similar activity at branches of the Windsor Public Library over a three-month period.

Even before her scandal, her parents found out her secret when she created a Twitter account for camming, entered in her real phone number and then an auto-message was sent to people in her contact list. One of those friends was close to her parents. So far, outside of getting kicked out of school, she sees nothing but up-sides. Office space costs are minimal, and she turned her old room-mate's room into her cam show, complete with a blow-up mattress, pictures of her in magazines on the wall, toys on display and bins filled with costumes and lingerie. She wakes up at eight am every morning and performs booked shows for clients paying between $90 and $120 an hour. That is about sixteen times her state minimum wage, and she does not even have to leave her bedroom. She just pays her bills with a dildo now. She has become something of a celebrity in her hometown of Salem, where she would be stopped for autographs, and guys often asked for pictures.

After applying for and being rejected from a number of waitress and bartending jobs, she looked into camming on the suggestion of her brother's friends. Like thousands of other young women over the past few years, Sunderland found a website and sent it a few photos, a scan of her ID and a short description of herself and almost immediately started performing live webcam shows. Even before her fateful library performance, Sunderland said camming was better than just about any other prospective opportunity she had. The money varies from show to show, but on an uneventful day she earns around $800 for a three-hour performance. Since the excitement has largely died down from Sunderland's library video, she says she has been working as a travelling feature dancer at strip clubs around the country.

Vex Ashley (@vextape on Twitter and Instagram) produces highly-stylized, cinematic pornography out of her studio and artists co-op "Four Chambers" in Leeds, England. She has roughly 6,000 followers who watch her live-cam stream every day, which is more than enough to cover her personal costs. She raises money for her films through crowd funding, which allows her to maintain artistic integrity, work with whoever she wants and experiment. A recent survey by Pornhub and a recent panel discussion on porn for women, established that there is a sizeable portion of the female porn-watching audience looking for rough sex and rape fantasies, but Ashley's viewership shows that there is also a demand for atmospheric, "beautiful" porn. Just looking at her pictures on Twitter, the aesthetic of her photos is like that of an alt hipster craft bazaar: tattoos, piercings, geometric gold jewellery, plant life, multicoloured seashells and sunlight casting artistic shadows on women with dyed hair standing in ateliers beside vintage furniture.

Mila Milan is another camming celebrity, boasting a private resort in Thailand, a Porsche, an industrial design firm, nine cats, eight dogs, an impending book deal, a small child, and one of the biggest tips ever in cam history, 260,000 tokens the equivalent of $13,000. She started in the German porn game at seventeen, and moved on to cam modelling years later in Bangkok. Two years ago she was the number one rated model on MyFreeCams, meaning her link was at the very top of the site's barren layout, bringing in around $37,000 per month. These days, girls in those top slots can earn up to an insane $75,000 per month. The ratings battle is ruthless, as tips beget more tips, ensuring a snowball effect of even more attention and money.

Twenty seven year-old Elisa Death Naked broadcasts from a house in Iceland with glass bricks, a spiral staircase, warm-looking patterned rugs, and a cozy fire crackling in the fireplace. She does not reveal her face, wearing instead, a rubber horse mask with a fedora on top, along with a grey crop top, black sweatpants, and rainbow knee socks. Her primary props are a chair painted with a replica of the Mona Lisa and a strap-on dildo. Although she changes costume into a Halloween mask of a ghost and begins fellating her dildo, she does not interact with her audience, instead exhibiting her free-flowing sexual narrative in a kind of manic trance. Her highlight reel includes clips from even more creative scenarios - her violently ripping apart a stuffed bear, fucking herself with a toy train, and strapping the dildo to a rocking horse and riding it to a soundtrack of industrial metal from Rammstein.

At the other end of the spectrum, is a depressingly familiar template: garish make-up, harsh lighting, dingy rooms, generic techno wafting through the air, and almost certainly some piece of cheap fabric serving as a make-do backdrop. These are the third world cam studios, operations that vary in legitimacy wildly, from large, multinational operations to bleak ex soviet tower blocks. Studios are pervasive throughout poorer countries, where a decent computer and broadband connection are harder to come by. The owners provide the facilities, and, in return, receive a hefty cut of a woman's takings, sometimes more. The studios do not, however, offer performers the option of choosing their own hours, or working remotely, which seem to be two of the biggest perks of the job. These girls are bleakly stripping on-line out of desperation.

West Africa, Thailand and the Czech Republic are host to masses of studios but it is Cali in Colombia, and Bucharest in Romania that are currently vying for the title of cam capital of the planet. Russia is something of a grey area for camgirls. Solo performers are legal, but the country's strict laws against homosexuality and cyber prostitution prohibit any sort of performance with other models. Meanwhile, in the Ukraine, any sort of sexual webcam is strictly illegal but it has not stopped a proliferation of performers.

Much of the time, models who speak next to no English sit staring blankly, with canned text responses typed by someone else, off camera, popping up intermittently. Many appear to be women in catatonic states (possibly drugged?) with a male partner, a "boyfriend", for whom they clearly have no affection, but with whom they are expected to have sex and more on demand. All over Romania's cities you can see large led billboards advertising various studios, but in the sea of Eastern European cam girls, most simply sit around naked all day as a way of attracting attention. This is an option on MyFreeCams, but forbidden on Streamate. Many just remain in a state of near-undress. The sad truth is that rock bottom is not a destination but an expectation for the majority who will sit, naked and unnoticed, waiting for a chance to degrade themselves, while American women demand top dollar to even chat.

A cam studio is often a euphemism for another person's computer (probably a man), in front of which the model must perform on a tight schedule. Instead of only giving MyFreeCams a cut of their take, the studio owner takes a piece as well. Often a large one. If they do not stick to their mandatory hours, they are fired. They will often be living with strangers in conditions beneath the grimiest motel. The boss provides a selection of ghoulish sex toys (along with unwanted advances) and wakes the models at six am each morning in order to hit American Internet prime time. Models are up against tens of thousands of women (and men, to a lesser degree) offering the same product in varying versions. That is a tough way to make a living, even with your clothes on.

Romania is a region with a reputation for sordid conditions and rapacious studio owners. Guys who are in charge of these businesses, rarely respect the girls, because of their job. A girl who does this does not deserve to have respect is the usual mentality. Sometimes the prevalence of studio abuse is a fabrication, a ploy for sympathy and the money that might trickle in with it.

In a like country Romania, whose GDP only stopped shrinking two years ago, with 20-percent of the population living below the poverty line and personal income levels far below Kazakhstan, Iran, and Gabon, these are all too common conditions. Countries in eastern Europe and south-east Asia are known to use camming platforms to exploit already at-risk individuals. MyFreeCams has gone as far as banning all models from the Philippines, where conditions are said to be the most brutal. Moving the exploitation on-line, where girls are under "contract" to stay in a room for days at a time with dubious legal recourse, makes criminal sense. Most sites have their fair share of dead-eyed Romanians and Thai girls. It is still disturbing to see the Filipinos begging for PayPal or Xoom. Looking at their sets, it is obvious that they are in some sort of camming sweat shop, rooms with bright/gaudy wallpaper or big visible curtains that serve as dividers. As yet no NGO that deals with issues of sex trafficking, abuse, prostitution, human rights has yet to catch up with the fast growing cam industry. They could put a stop to this by pushing for the criminalization of payment facilities but as always, Visa, MC, Amex, PayPal and the banks have much bigger fish to fry. If a single conviction for facilitating prostitution or sex trafficking could cost them their license to operate they would soon roll over.

All of this Third World competition is driving everybody's price down. American women can earn a living just by stripping while the desperate bodies of the Third World are locked in a state of mutual ruination. The pretty girls that populate porn pop-up ads are not there to please or have fun. They are there because they have no other options and beauty is the one currency they do have. Even in the US, the Feds are closing down and tightening the control on casino and poker sites, causing criminal elements to move into an operation that takes so little in the way of infrastructure, there is nothing to stop them from proliferating. Cam sites have become ideal for money laundering. The studios are being used to have girls on-line accepting a financed hand that uses 'dirty' money to buy the private time. The studio gets paid for the private session, the girl gets her very small part and so the money comes back clean. Mila Milan claims that most of the Russian and Romanian studios are Mafia owned, a claim she extends to the wider developing world. The picture becomes clearer when you remember how scattered and obfuscated these networks' financial structures are.

Now, the traditional adult entertainment brands like Playboy are hurrying to catch up. Many are getting in on cams as a matter of survival. With declining magazine sales, these companies are most relevant as brand icons. This is your grandpa's porn, and that is a huge hurdle for any company targeting younger audiences to overcome. Penthouse, for instance, purchased Various Inc. for $500 million in 2007. The print magazine paled in comparison to the company's other properties, such as AdultFriendFinder, a cam site and social network that has more than fifty million users. (Today Penthouse Media Group has been rebranded as FriendFinder Networks, which has corporate headquarters in Boca Raton.) Hustler has yet to venture into interactive porn, but some experts say it must innovate or die.

Playboy was a publicly traded company until 2011. Then it split in two: The magazine and traditional properties remained based in L.A., but the camming arm moved to Miami. Converge Media Works, founded in 2007, today manages several cam sites, including Playboy Live, and rents a $2.5 million Surfside mansion, having amassed $65 million in revenue by recruiting 3,200 models. In an attempt to become the new epicentre of camming, Interactive Online Porn has constructed several film sets in a windowless warehouse across from the Haitian Cultural Arts Alliance. One is meant to look like a college library; another, a receptionist's office. A third is modelled after a stereotypical 20-something girly-girl's bedroom, complete with teal walls, a purple comforter, and a yoga mat in the corner. Here in the middle of one of Miami's poorest neighbourhoods, Playboy Live models will speak to men under the illusion that the young women are at home or work, paying anywhere from $3.99 to $10.99 a minute for the privilege. Although other camming sites include hardcore sex acts, Playboy Live has a strict rule of "no pink," meaning there is no "insertion" and no anatomical close-ups and yet locals still complain that the business is a blight on the neighbourhood, Members will log on to order pepperoni pizzas together or watch each other sleep. Some will literally click 'play' on a YouTube video at the same time and watch a whole movie together. This works out to be an expensive movie date as even with the least expensive Playboy Live model. Taking in an hour-and-a-half feature film together would run up a bill of $359. "Say you're a doctor in Kansas," the owner explains. "How else would you ever get the opportunity to meet a Playboy Live model?"

Creating an incentive for young women to humiliate themselves for sport is something that many still find disgusting and demeaning. That being said, there are a lot of places where cam performers can make a very acceptable living. And while they may not necessarily get rich doing so, it does allow them a way to pay their bills and clothe their children, often from the comfort of their own homes. Camming is not big money, but it is all about owning the content that one distributes on-line. Camming represents a paradigm shift in adult entertainment, away from a system that upheld an industry and towards a more sustainable model that focuses on the performer. In many ways, it is the democratization of pornography.

The growth of the live cam market puts it squarely at the forefront of interactive porn, supplanting live phone chat and enjoying its time in the sun. Many industry experts predict that it will be replaced by virtual reality, although I contend that just as TV and changing attitudes sounded the death knell for human freak shows, the vast majority of today's camgirls will soon become redundant thanks to accelerating forms of technology. Once digital avatars are able to match the performance of a typical camgirl, the relatively expensive flesh versions will quickly be put out of business by their computerised counterparts. We have already seen artificial intelligence successfully challenge humans in the arenas of Chess, Go and even Jeopardy. If a computer can achieve dominance in such demanding competitive activities, then they will not have much difficulty in replacing the average Romanian cammer who can barely string together half a dozen sentences of decent English. I will be discussing this development in much greater detail in the last chapter, entitled

Death of the Camgirl.

Selecting a Location

One difference between the traditional adult industry, which is centred around several hubs, including greater Los Angeles, Las Vegas and Miami, with enclaves in Montreal, Barcelona and elsewhere, is that the live cam industry is much more decentralized, seeing significant participation from Romania and Russia, Hungary and beyond, with studios and performers located all around the world. There is also a difference from a model standpoint in different parts of the world. In Eastern Europe and Latin America, the majority of the models work from actual brick-and-mortar studios, because these are necessary to provide fast internet, modern web cams and expertise. In Eastern Europe and Latin America most cam models keep their occupation hidden from friends and family. There it is largely taboo, because of social and religious norms. In the U.S., despite the fact there are studios throughout the country, the majority of the models cam from their own home, work independently and the successful ones turn it into a very lucrative career.

The percentage of cam girls who are based in the U.S. is estimated to be from 15 to 35 percent. Before the recession, the number of U.S. models was actually a lot lower. At that time, Eastern Europe made up the majority of the market, and still has a sizeable stake. As webcams became a bigger part of the adult entertainment landscape, U.S. models began to focus more of their attention there, in part because of the significant earning potential. Top models on MyFreeCams for example earn $10,000 - $20,000 per month but that success comes from working twelve or more hours per day and establishing long lasting relationships with regular fans. Girls in the U.S. Have the added advantage of not having to compete head-to-head with top European models.

Cali in Colombia and Bucharest in Romania have long been vying for the title of webcam capital of the world. There were more than a thousand studios in the metropolitan Bucharest area in back in 2009 and the number has been growing rapidly ever since. The internet has long been filled with people from America and Western Europe looking for advice on setting up a studio in Romania, and plenty of studios were founded with foreign investment. There is nothing particularly glamorous about the business, but the return on investment can be phenomenal. A talented model can generate $10,000 of revenue in a month, which is big money in one of Europe's poorest countries. It is estimated that in Romania alone, more than 40,000 women ages 20-40 are reportedly registered cam models, that is approximately 1.25 percent of females in that age group. If the internet had a designated red light district, it would be Romania. The typical studio building is housed on a Bucharest backstreet in a building that can accommodate up to a dozen "models" at a time, all masturbating in the direction of a webcam for lonesome, horny Americans thousands of miles away.

You might expect such a place to be a disgusting nest of cyberpunk depravity, filled with beautiful tragedy-eyed boys and girls in varying degrees of undress, hoovering up designer drugs off each others bodies to a soundtrack of Prototype Raptor and Bob Sinclair. If so, you will be disappointed. At the same time not all studio managers are weirdo beardos in various states of arrested development, like teenage masturbation addicts recently kicked out of their mothers' basements. Lunchtime in a studio like this is 9pm in the evening, because ninety percent of paying "members" live in North America, meaning that ninety percent of a Romanian studio's clientele are anywhere between seven and twelve hours behind the models. Peak working hours in Bucharest are between one and 7am or midnight to 8am, UK time. Different sites get traffic from different regions of the world. When the football is on, some sites' traffic tanks while others boom, because they are mostly European customers who could not care less about the NFL. The typical customer is a male, aged 25-34, from the U.S. or other English-speaking country.

Officially, the Romanian government is not a fan of adult entertainment. The law requires that anyone starting a porn site in the country must password protect it, and multiple laws have been proposed over the course of the last decade to allow for the blocking of adult websites. Unofficially, a lot of work has gone into the country's telecommunication infrastructure, with the result that Romania now has a faster download speed than any G20 nation. One of the reasons why Romania has one of the fastest broadband connection speeds is due to the very dense population (think 10-20 floor cheap residential towers from the times of socialism). The other is because of the large number of independent ISPs. As far back as 2008, there were 1338 registered internet service providers, meaning that there was a great deal of competition. Large numbers of aggressive ISPs were wiring up neighbourhoods with LAN cables for 5-10 EUR/month at "all our router can handle" speeds. In many cases only international traffic is metered. Domestic traffic - where all of the torrent trackers and other torrent users are - is virtually at wire speed. Similar situations also now exist in other ex-Eastern Bloc countries such as Bulgaria. The fact that most studio owners or individual performers do not declare their income and pay their taxes, as in the CAEN code (Clasificarea Activitatilor din Economia Nationala) is most certainly illegal. Most studios register as 'internet consultants' offering non-adult services and then bribe any authorities that are sent to check on them. This often means no working papers for employees, and no medical insurance even though the owners take an additional 10% which they say goes to taxes. Still, when the minimum wage in Romania is 114 Euros, things are unlikely to change any time soon. Many girls claim that the Romanian and Russian studios are 99% Mafia owned. Some also double as sex clubs. So the story that all Romanian girls are also hookers gets around, and is of course a generalization and not true. Even so, Romanian cam studios are used for white washing stolen credit cards, laundering drug money and related businesses. It is said that in Iasi there seems to be a large number of studios exploiting models who cannot afford their own apartment and/or an high-speed connection or even a proper PC and a HD cam. A number of studios in Cluj had similar reputations with the bosses demanding free sex all the time and then absconding with all the wages just before pay day.

While there are a few big brand, nationwide studios, that offer work contracts, training and a clean, safe environment to work in, but there are also plenty of "no name studios that have three computers in the same room and a predatory boss. Romania also boasts professional cam studios that support this fast growing industry, studios such as the popular Studio 20. The problem is that most Romanian girls do no speak English, do not know how to create an account, or have any privacy or equipment. One reason why many Romanian models do not go independent is because some of them have already had their request for a new MFC account application denied (it is claimed that some studios have enough connections to put in a good word" to make this happen). All over the world there are girls who are simply poor, uneducated and do not know how to do any of this stuff. Many of these girls have never used a computer and do not even know what a "cam" is. For them, studios provide a ready opportunity to start making some money and if they are smart, they will eventually set out on their own. We might think that $200/month working all day is lousy, but wages and living conditions are not the same in those countries. For a poor country girl in the Philippines, camming for $200/month is a lot better than working all day in the rice paddies for $50/month (or more likely for free if they are with a family). Unfortunately, this means that many of the girls that work in Filipino sweatshops are treated like slaves. Pinay girls are working 12 hour days 7 days a week (with their baby 'one sheet' away)for $100-150 a month and the rest is for the studio. The bosses in these studios are nothing better than modern day slave traders. And then you hear the premiums in the lounge bragging about how they had a Pinay girl do really extreme things for just five or ten tokens.

Consider carefully before selecting an overseas location to set up your new studio operation. As an expat you will find that living in third world Africa or China is actually more expensive that being in the US. For everybody except the super rich, international travel requiring residence in other countries is actually becoming more difficult. Visas are more troublesome and more expensive than ever before. While most industries are replacing their staff with robots on a wholesale basis, immigration and visa application offices are endlessly expanding, to cope with the ever growing mountains of paperwork that are being requested. Living abroad is in many ways far more complicated than it ever used to be and the concepts of individual sovereignty and perpetual travel are inconvenient loopholes being sewn up with a mass of complex bureaucracy. Despite these facts, there are a number of factors to take into consideration when selecting a business operation. First of all, hi speed internet is a must. There are probably thousands of super sexy Nubian stunners in places like Somalia, South Sudan and Puntland. No matter how many Naomi Campbell and Grace Jones lookalikes you might find in places like Addis and Khartoum, you will have more chance of finding the Ark of the Covenant up here than a good reliable fibre connection. Consider carefully the reliability of the local electricity. The Philippines is notorious for its rolling brownouts and the expense of having a 24-hour generator running at your studio is going to add a big chunk to your overheads.

Having said that, there are always plenty of new locations worth scouting. My personal preference is for South East Asia but as I have just stated, power and connectivity can still be very limited outside metropolitan areas. Muslim countries are probably best avoided, as are those with very strict anti porn laws. This might rule out the likes of China, Malaysia and Indonesia, but there are still plenty of other options including Thailand, Taiwan and perhaps now Myanmar.

There also needs to be a good steady supply of girls willing to do the dirty on camera, preferably girls that western men with plenty of disposable cash find attractive. So this probably rules out aboriginal Australia and much of India, despite their many other potential advantages. A lot of white guys especially are very conservative in their tastes. While they might deny being racist, they much prefer white to African, Asian or other races. Unfortunately this is a global trend that many developing countries are now catching up on. In much of Asia for example, white skin is very highly prized, even though most of the locals are darker than ground gourmet coffee.

Finally, there is little or no point in setting up a business in a location where you cannot speak the local language. If you have some good local connections and can speak the language, then I would recommend using these advantages to your full advantage. Opening shop in South America is probably not such a good idea if you speak neither a word of Spanish or Portuguese. Starting up in Russia might not be a great plan if you can manage little more than 'dobray dien' and 'dosvidanya.' Paradoxically, while you will be wanting to hire girls that speak good English, you will most definitely need local language skills in order to manage the business properly. Of course, you can always hire a local to take care of day to day activities, but this gives them the opportunity to takeover the business whenever you are not around. This is most dangerous in Asian countries (try reading China Cuckoo by Mark Kitto) but can happen just about anywhere in today's toxic business climate.

Try to keep a low profile when it comes to the local government, especially if you are not a citizen. None of them want foreigners launching sex businesses, but as long as you keep your head down you should be able to avoid most problems. Apart from keeping your head down, it is always good to be humble. There will always be the temptation to live life as some kind of imaginary Tony Soprano/Pablo Escobar fantasy when down in Latin America, but it is never a good idea to pretend to be some badass gangster in a country that is full of real badass gangsters.

A good example of what not to do, was the owner of the Expat Chronicles website that did most of its business through the many pay-4-play forums. He ran brothel tours to a number of Latin American capitals and high tourism destinations including Lima, Buenos Aires and Santiago. Being a typical loud mouth New Yorker, he upset a lot of people, both natives and foreigners. One really awful piece of advice that he gave out was to always try to put assets in a local partner's name. As far as I am concerned, this poor advice anywhere, especially if you are not a citizen. First he was deported from Venezuela. He then became a regular in Costa Rica, but burned too many bridges there as well, and so eventually made his way down to Barranquilla and Medellin. Here he was murdered in broad daylight at a popular downtown restaurant by a professional hit man.

Setting up a studio in a developed country can sometimes be difficult to make the numbers work. Overheads can be extortionately high in a city like Los Angeles or London. In addition, local girls in English-speaking countries are far more likely to already be independently camming. It might sound exploitative, but lower GDP nations with equally low standards of education. I personally am very interested in looking beyond the traditional Eastern European countries to places like Moldova and Transnistria, or even further across to

the Caucuses in places such as Georgia, Armenia and Azerbaijan.
Setting up almost anywhere in the Middle East would take nerves of steel,
although having said that I am currently discussing this option with a friend
based in one of the more working class suburbs of Tel Aviv. Opening a studio
elsewhere in the region is likely to get you stoned to death if discovered.
Perhaps better options might be the Baltic states of Latvia, Estonia and
Lithuania. Maybe even Finland would be an option now that the Russian
connection is dragging down their economy. Being so close to Sweden there must
be plenty of Abba type Agnetha and Anni-Frid lookalikes around to recruit.
Russia is something of a grey area for camgirls. Solo performers are legal, but
the country's strict laws against homosexuality and cyber prostitution prohibit
any sort of performance with other models. Meanwhile, in the Ukraine, any sort of
sexual webcam performance is illegal, though that does not seem to prevent
girls from doing so. Some countries have archaic laws dealing with this subject
matter. Italy, for instance, makes it a criminal offense to cam. It is for this
reason that sites like CAM4 do not work with studios in France, Italy or Spain.

With rising unemployment rates across Europe, camming represents a viable
means employment. It is a shame that governments seek to impose oppressive,
outdated laws that restrict the opportunity of Europeans to pursue this exciting and
rewarding industry. As live cams continue to grow and prosper, not only are
there live cam sites that target the entire world, such as LiveJasmin,
Chaturbate and ImLive, but there are other localized sites that only target
local markets, such as Germany, Russia, the Netherlands and others.
Germany is one of the worldwide top markets when it comes to traffic and profits
in the adult industry. The most profitable services these days are webcams and
dating. Germany does not have a porn star scene. For whatever reason, German
consumers do not like the high-glossy porn star. In reality amateurs
dominate the German scene. Amateurs are producing their own contents,
uploading them to different amateur sites and working in front of webcams. A lot
of them are producing content with their fans. The fan has the option to meet his
favourite performer, have sex with her and the only thing he needs to do is sign
an agreement that the performer is allowed to use the video material.

The worldwide sites although they have translated versions for all major
languages, they tend to focus on the English-speaking market. While most users
are predominately from the U.S., Canada, Europe and South America, India and
the Middle-East are rapidly emerging markets. The level of exposure to cams in
the general eligible population is so low, around five or six percent, unlike
tubes, for example. The one thing that these millennials all have in common is
that they love playing video games. They have all the free porn they want, but
still pay for cams because something about real person-to-person interaction is
more suitable for webcam users. Countries with a higher GDP tend to provide
more customers, however, the number of models from those countries are usually
low. Cultural and language related differences may occur because of this, and
might dampen the user's experience.

Considering China's infamous gender gap, the excess of single men should
logically make for the largest camgirl market in the world. In reality, the
Communist Party's constant meddling in the private lives of individuals means
that the industry is being driven underground and in some very unusual

directions. The government incessantly plays the role of interfering busybody, banning gay-themed TV shows and warning female viewers not to fall in love with Korean actors like Song Joong-ki. The government recently banned all any Korean produced content whatsoever in a political tiff regarding America supplying Seoul with hi tech weaponry. Of course, the general population were kept entirely in the dark about the political machinations. Every Chinese person I spoke to knew about the ban but not a single one had thought to question the reasoning behind it. The country's regulator has now even banned the live steaming of Chinese women seductively eating bananas, in an attempt to clamp down on erotic and improper content on-line. Other specially created laws forbid nudity or even behaviours that generate sexual fantasies. To enforce the order, Chinese firms providing live-streaming services are now required to track all their output 24 hours a day, seven days a week. In April 2016, China's Ministry of Culture said that the five major video platforms, Huya, Zhangqi TV, YY, Panda.tv and Douyu, were are all under investigation for hosting content considered too sexual, violent or vulgar. Many internet users protested by posting videos of themselves licking a popsicle, which when melted, would drip slowly into the cleavage and present an even more suggestive image. Authorities are now grappling with how to regulate the rapidly growing sector saying that live-streaming programs should not contain unlawful material and should consciously resist vulgar content, including money worship which now seems to be China's national religion. Some industry insiders are predicting that the regulations would prompt consolidation in the industry because smaller competitors would be unable to meet capital and other requirements for licensing.

In China, camgirls are known as on-line hostesses, and despite a strictly non-porn policy, many earn good money, between 10,000 and 100,000 RMB (USD 1500 - 15,000) a month by enticing and teasing their viewers into purchasing virtual gifts, like roses, chocolates and designer bags, and then splitting the revenue with the streaming companies. Bobo.com, is one of many live-broadcasting web platforms where more than 10,000 hostesses record themselves singing, playing the piano, dancing or just chatting. The hostesses are predominantly singers, playing to an audience that is ninety percent male, and mostly between the ages of 20 and 35. Acting cute is okay. Anything explicitly sexual is not. They put on little dance mime routines one minute, and then seductively eat strawberries the next. Many specialise in acting 'sa-jiao' - a very Chinese type of flirting characterized by the woman acting in a cutesy, childlike manner and speaking in a whiny voice, like that of a spoiled child. Most westerners find this behaviour incredibly annoying. This is one reason why I like my Chinese girls that same way I like my coffee, securely tied up in a burlap sack.

China had nearly 200 live streaming platforms with a total of 200 million users in 2015. It is estimated that the market has now grown to 15 billion RMB (USD 2.1 billion) this year, bigger than the country's film industry. By comparison, Twitter's live streaming platform Periscope claims only around 10 million users worldwide, while the top five Chinese live stream apps have more than 85 million active users. The platforms typically take between fifty and seventy per cent of the money donated by users. Guangzhou-based YY.com.cn for example, began as an on-line community dedicated to World of Warcraft but now claims nearly half-billion registered users, with a hundred million active users spending an average of more than sixty hours a month on more than a million channels. These figures have caused its shares to soar 500 percent since the company's public offering on the Nasdaq stock market in late 2012. In August, Douyu said it had raised $226 million in a funding round led by Chinese internet company. Tencent Holdings Ltd. Alibaba Group Holding Ltd.'s Youku Tudou video arm launched a live-streaming site in 2014 and last year invested in Huomao TV, a game-focused live-streaming site. Smartphone maker Xiaomi Corp. set up its own live-streaming platform, Mi Live, earlier this year. Ingkee leads the crowded market with nearly seven million unique, active daily users, according to research company Quest Mobile.

Even so, with this being China, one has to wonder how accurate such figures really are. In one suspiciously well-publicised incident Wang Sicong, a son of China's richest man, Wang Jianlin, and a board member of his father's entertainment giant, Dalian Wanda Group Co., spent thousands of RMB on one hostess called Yanghanna who was dancing on Panda TV. One user sent several "fotiaoqiang," a virtual gift costing 1,000 RMB (USD150), when Wang junior joined the "room" and engaged in a "gift war." At one point the first user sent a gift worth 140,000 RMB (USD 20,000), after which Wang sent one worth 400,000 RMB (USD 60,000). Wang himself is a founder of Panda TV, the website in question, and so this was clearly a poorly contrived stunt meant to encourage more high roller type of behaviour.

Given the government restrictions on all manner of media, consumers in China seem more willing to go on-line for movies, music and even role-playing fantasy games. State-run television, with its steady diet of propaganda, game shows and stale dramas, is boring beyond belief and just does not offer the same variety. Being a largely homogeneous culture, Chinese media lacks a diverse and sophisticated palette for entertainment. Media and technology companies across the globe have tried for years to attract viewers en masse to live Internet broadcasts, with X-rated websites being the only real success stories. On the surface, China, appears to have cracked the code. Millions are now tuning in every night to watch karaoke performances, comedy skits and talk shows. The reality is that viewers tend to be single men in smaller locales with fewer entertainment options. The two main reasons for the popularity of live streaming are boredom and loneliness. Many Chinese men are wealthy enough to spend significant sums of money, paying for poor quality entertainment mainly because they have money and simply cannot think of a better way to spend it in their undeveloped, backwater home towns. Very often in second and third-tier cities and rural areas, their only places for entertainment are Internet bars which offer web access for a fee, plus drinks and snacks. On larger apps such as Ingkee, Douyu and Qiqi, fans shower the top stream queens with virtual gifts during shows that resemble mass on-line dates. Five roses for example represents a gift of 13.4 RMB, or $2. Typically, the platform takes half the income. Hosts and their agents divide the rest. On Qiqi, fans are labelled based on how much they give, with $7.50 conferring the title Rich Man. The labels progress all the way up to Divine Emperor, at $750,000. There are around 70,000 hostesses on Qiqi alone.

Many punters will splash out more than a thousand dollars simply for the V.I.P. privilege of driving a virtual Lamborghini Aventador LP 700-4 Roadster to and from the virtual concert halls during performances. In the upper left corner of a Chinese webcam screen is a running count of how many viewers are in the virtual concert hall. Digital cars, representing the V.I.P.s who spend large sums, speed in and out of the imaginary hall all the time. The average hostess takes home between 5,000 (USD 750)and 10,000 RMB (USD 1,500) a month by hosting a radio show, a live video broadcast, and playing multi player on-line games with fans.

At least one college is offering internet fame as a career track. This fall, Yiwu Industrial and Commercial College in Zhejiang enrolled 25 of its 3,000 freshmen into its live streaming training program. The school said some students in the year-old program have already drawn more than 10,000 fans. Classes include etiquette, dancing and physical exercises. For a final exam, students are asked to strike poses in quick succession for a thirty-second streaming segment. Yiwu is well-known for its vast wholesale markets that sell the cheapest possible Chinese tack that is headed for Africa and the Indian sub-continent. It looks like this low end mentality is now spreading beyond its manufactured products and into its education sector.

The talent pool of young women in China is far greater than any westerner could probably imagine. In tier-one cities such as Being, Shanghai and Guangzhou, local estate agents target provincial officials and businessmen looking to put their money into Beijing's property bubble, and the men fill up the apartments, bought as investments, with their women. Half of the apartments are empty and the other half are full of girls, locally known as 'ernai' or second wives. Many could easily free themselves from their sponsors, although the vast numbers of sexually frustrated, bitter young men mean that 'slut-shaming' is a regular habit on the Chinese internet: women exposed by angry ex-boyfriends or lovers' wives have found themselves the target of a vast wave of abuse, including messages sent to their workplace or their parents. This alone keeps many away from the temptation of doing anything sexual on-line.

Rivals from South Korea have now joined the battlefield and are quickly decimating the local competition. Chinese hosts are pretty, and some can dance, but generally they lack variety. For Chinese men, the opportunity to sit down for an intimate chat with a gorgeous South Korean beauty, where even a simple and cheap gift will cause her to blush with praise is a dream come true. In Chinese culture, where so many girls would rather 'be crying in a BMW than laughing on a bicycle,' there are literally millions of men who cannot even get a peasant girl to look at them. The pressure on domestic hosts from their new Korean rivals is real, and many Chinese hostesses were literally crying on air as they saw their viewer numbers drop dramatically. At the time of writing, the highest-ranking host in China was a South Korean hostess who had more than double the number of concurrent viewers of her domestic counterpart. More than 1.5 million users flooded into South Korean hostess Heo Yun-mi's live streaming chat room. The chat window on screen was just a blur due to the sheer amount of messages being posted by viewers. Before bringing her channel to China, she was a hit hostess on South Korean live streaming platforms. At her peak back then she could have maybe 12,000 concurrent viewers, yet in China she gets almost 125 times as many viewers. Like many Koreans, she is a product of the country's highly organised talent agencies. These South Korean entertainment companies have the resources to carry out market research to better understand customer preferences, train their hosts and provide support in the form of costumes, interpreters or schooling so they may learn Chinese. How long will it be before Hollywood is going to have to chase after this captive market?

Back in South Korea, there is a bizarre new trend is known as gastronomic voyeurism, where live-streams of meals can attract viewers of thousands night after night. Western observers have dubbed it 'food porn,' but in its home country it is known as meok-bang: 'broadcast eating' (meok is a shortened form of the verb meokda, meaning to eat and bang is short for bangsong or on air). Despite Korea being the world's most connected nation, a quarter of households are occupied by just one individual, many of home do not want to eat alone. A single broadcast can earn hosts as much a million won ($830), while most have an average monthly income of around £5,600, although a sizeable amount of that money goes on food. These evening meals are not simple cheese-on-toast affairs, but feasts that can go on for hours. One hostess spends almost $3000 each month, on top quality ingredients and in a single sitting can eat as much as 12 hamburgers, 12 fried eggs, and three bowls of kimchi stew. Anybody expecting to experience a sophisticated webcam kisaeng is going to be mightily disappointed.

Afreeca TV, the peer-to-peer video network that offers both recorded videos and live-streaming content, has become the home of meok-bang, utilises a virtual currency called Star Balloons that can be converted later into Korean won. Looking at fan-made YouTube compilation of the 'greatest hits' of actor Jung Woo Ha, this seems to entail cramming your mouth full of food and making exaggerated facial expressions as you scoff it down. Given western audiences' love for cookery shows and personality chefs, it will not be surprising if meok-bang or something similar finds its way to the UK some time in the future.

Another bizarre aspect of Asian cam culture is the amount of internet voyeurs in china are getting off to girls doing meth on camera. In the past few years, the Chinese North-East was flooded with meth from the North Koreans, who are desperate for hard currency. In the nineties, the rogue nation cultivated huge swathes of opium to supply China's vast numbers of heroin addicts. Of course, the ruling Kim dynasty is under the protection of the communist elite, so there was never an Opium War declared, as there was with East India Company a hundred years before. During the nineties famines, the opium crops also failed and so meth production quickly took its place. After all meth is so easy to produce, all you need are a few precursor chemicals and a bathtub. This valuable export has since been replaced by domestic batches, as the Chinese themselves have developed cheap methods of mass production. Inspired by Breaking Bad, makeshift labs have sprung up all over the vast rural areas of China and there is now a national meth epidemic. Visit any karaoke bar in China and you might be offered an ice-skating package. Most clubs are fronts for brothels, and since users insist that meth heightens their sexual arousal and strengthens their stamina, it is no surprise that the drug has made its way into the escort and entertainment industries. Managers make extra cash by charging Johns for narcotic voyeurism. Apparently, some men get off by watching young girls do meth. Karaoke hostesses are typically paid 350 RMB (less than $60) for ice skating with clients. Drug education in China is almost non-existent and few have any idea what meth will do to their bodies because they never learned about it from their parents or teachers. Questions about drugs are met with responses like, Don't ask about bad things. The unfortunate hostesses are eventually fired for not looking pretty enough. Even though their bosses are the culprits who introduced them to meth, the girls themselves are blamed her for losing weight and not keeping up their appearances. Addicts in China are not offered any kind of rehabilitation or therapy. The Chinese treat addicts as the worst of criminals, so the punishment for users who are caught can be disproportionately severe. On paper, China recently abolished its reform through labour programs, but the reality is that the labour camps were converted into forced drug rehab centres, where inmates perform unpaid factory work and can be incarcerated for years without trial.

In some ways, the Chinese head-in-the sand attitude toward drugs mirrors the hypocrisy surrounding porn. Although pornography is completely banned in China, Japanese porn stars such as Aoi Sora enjoy huge celebrity status, even being referred to as Cang Laoshi (Teacher Cang). In the west, Aoi became widely known among porn fans as one of the few Japanese porn-stars that did not sound like she was being stabbed to death during sex. Because there is no sex education in schools, Chinese youngsters receive their entire sex education through porn, specifically, Japanese AVs, as porn production of any kind is also illegal in China. It is for this reason that Aoi Sora and other AV idols are referred to as teachers The use of the respectful title also demonstrates the general attitude of ordinary people towards political officials. It is not unusual to read sex scandals about corrupt government officials, such as the disgraced Minister of Railways, Liu Zhijun who was said to have slept with every single actress of an entire TV show. The fact that Aoi Sora's account at Weibo (Twitter's counterpart in China) had nearly 15 million followers says that many Chinese would rather respect a Japanese porn star (the authorities constantly reinforce a national hatred of Japan) than their so-called leaders. Many Chinese feel that although porn stars have a dirty job, they put forth an air of honesty and integrity, as opposed to those government officials who have the most sought after positions, but are mostly dirty hypocrites. The respect shown to an AV star was therefore actually a symbol of defiance.

Starved of outside information, young Chinese are very easily influenced by mass marketing. It is no coincidence that as Aoi approached her late twenties, and her fame was waning in her home country, she was keen to make the transition toward more mainstream lines of work, such as fully clothed singing and acting. She was easily able to convince impressionable young Chinese by professing a love of Chinese culture and even practicing Chinese calligraphy. She raised 100,000 RMB (USD 15,000) in 2010 when Sichuan was devastated by a massive earthquake. While Japan as a whole is still portrayed by the official media as baby raping monsters, it was relatively easy for her to gain sympathy from young Chinese netizens. Lei Jun, often referred to as the Steve Jobs of China, is the founder and CEO of Xiaomi, which now sells more than ten million smartphones annually, invited Aoi Sora as a special guest to a company event. Due to her popularity among employees and consumers, Chinese companies were quick to capitalize on this. In the past, one of these events could reportedly earn Aoi one million renminbi (USD 150,000). At another event, fellow porn star Annri Okita showed up to promote NetEase. Even so, not all porn actresses are greeted with such warmth. At last year's China International Adult and Reproduction Exhibition in Dalian, protesters (most likely Government agent provocateurs) hurled eggs and plastic bottles onto the stage at two Japanese starlets while yelling at them to "Get out of China." A host was injured by the barrage and government officials have reportedly been using the incident to block other Japanese porn stars from appearing at events. Aoi has since been barred from making live appearances at fan events by the State Administration of Press Publication, Radio, Film and Television (SAPPRFT). Their puritanical indignation has now become a symbol of widespread mockery. In yet another example of official heavy handedness, strict guidelines were issued for showgirls hired for cosplay events. Documents leaked on-line detail fines for sartorial transgressions, such as showing more than two centimetres of cleavage (5,000 RMB - USD 750) and wearing pants less than two centimetres below the waist (5,000 RMB -USD 750), while engaging in vulgar poses or obscene performances could set models back 10,000 RMB (USD 1,500.)

It is interesting to note that while China is cracking down hard on webcam girls, business is booming in the equally authoritarian Singapore. Under Section 29 of the Films Act, the production, reproduction, importation, distribution and possession of "obscene films" is illegal in Singapore, with penalties involving heavy fines and/or jail terms. "Obscene publications" are criminalised by Section 11 of the Undesirable Publications Act although, Section 202 of the Penal Code has a religious exemption, presumably for Indian lingams and yonis. One camgirl who goes by the moniker of Miss Lim, arranged for 200 litres of baby oil to be delivered to her apartment, which she used it to fill an inflatable pool. The resulting show was downloaded over 30 million times by Singaporean internet users. Although she previously worked as a low paid accountant, her 2015 salary from performing as a cam girl was over US$800,000. Twenty seven-year-old Rebecca Ong had the usual problem of family disapproval but was eventually able to repair the relationship, giving her father free passes to the site to share with his friends. Maybe Dad is now proud that his darling daughter earned an impressive US$1.2 million in 2015. 24-year old model Satin Kitty was working as a retail assistant, earning around SG$2,000 (USD1,500) per month. After quitting her job mid-2015, she put on a record-breaking show, performing on a street bench in the suburb of Hougang. Normally models prefer to perform in the privacy of their own house, but Satin Kitty's public exposure earned her millions of views. Her 2015 salary came in at an amazing US$2.2 million. Singapore's highest-paid cam girl for 2015 was actually two women, identical twins, Veronica and Jennifer. The 22-year old twins only started camming in October 2015, but they proved so popular that their income in the last three months of 2015 totalled US$5 million. Being a duo, the sisters are able to charge their viewers a premium far higher than that of solo performers. To watch five minutes of their show will cost you US$250, but that is a price that thousands of fans in Singapore and across the world are more than happy to pay.

The rest of Asia has a growing number of studios but in most places, the ladies' English is so bad that it can be difficult to succeed. There is also the Far Eastern approach to management that has to be considered. Now there are arguments over the girls taking breaks, and managers are strictly enforcing the ten sessions in two weeks rule or models do not get paid. This is on top of the minimum must be made before they get paid. Models are pretty much banned from making friends or talking to friends. All models chat logs are reviewed to make sure that they are not speaking to friends and warnings are issued if they are. Most Asian studios are little more than sweatshops with the girls treated like objects that are only there to line the pockets of the bosses. Ironically this kind of inefficient business practice leaves an opportunity for entrepreneurs who understand the benefits of cooperative working. At the same time the risk of coming up against criminal elements is much higher. Pattaya in Thailand for example it is reported that out of a census population figure of 107,406, a whopping 27,000 are working as hookers. Of course, in a country where prostitution is technically illegal the authorities deny everything. In a farcical recent statement Pattaya's police chief Apichai Kroppetch stated that tourists come to the resort for its natural wonders. Even though Pattaya is well-known as the sex capital of the world with one in five of its female population being sex workers (not to mention Asia's largest gay scene based around Boyztown, the Jomtien Complex, and Sunee Plaza), it has also taken over from the Costa Del Crime, being a haven for international fugitives and criminals. Cost of living is cheap but the local police are so corrupt and inept (as can be seen from the ridiculous statement above) that the cons probably outweigh the pros. What is worse, Burundi is the only country in the world that is more likely to undergo a coup in 2017 according to recent studies. Thailand has been under martial law, with strong restrictions on civil liberties, since the 2014 coup. The country approved a new constitution in 2016 and scheduled elections for 2017, but, as some researchers point out, elections often increase the risk of further coup attempts. Probably not the best place to set up a new business.

Cambodia next door has long been run by gangsters under the guise of government but is at least more stable that its neighbour. The southern beach resorts such as Kom Pong Som (Sihanoukville) tend to attract a crowd that is too cheap even for Pattaya but could still be an interesting location for a studio. Unfortunately, Khmers tend to be very dark skinned which is not something that is in great demand on the webcam scene. I have always been quite partial to cities like Kandy and Colombo in Sri Lanka but unfortunately the locals are even darker, which is an unfortunate disadvantage in a world where cosmetics corporations have such sway on public sentiment.

Whatever location you choose, it is important to make sure that the numbers work will for you. I considered setting up a webcam studio in the U.S., but no matter how I worked the numbers I could not figure out how to get the profit margin to a level where it was worth doing. You may also find that once you have started the business, the headaches of managing the business and the girls are just not worth it for you. Assuming that you have found a suitable location, the next chapter examines the nuts and bolts of actually setting up a webcam studio.

Pre-Broadcast Set Up

Once you have selected a suitable location, starting a web cam studio is as simple as creating an account with one of the sites listed above. Most sites will let you register as an individual with only your SSN. You might consider filing for a limited liability company for your studio as well. Once registered and verified, your studio will immediately be able to sign up models, meaning that will be paid directly for all the models earnings and you are responsible for the payments to the models.

Much of the pre broadcast phase will involve setting up the studio infrastructure such as the LAN and the hardware, as well as teaching the models basic English, if that is necessary. Begin with standard Windows machines. Keep the set-ups simple and then hopefully, you should be able to deal with most breakdowns and repairs in house. Second hand machines or refurbs are fine and are available for the fraction of the price of new models. Do not be tempted to invest everything you have in a bunch of Macbook Pros. The customers will not be able to tell the difference and they will probably start going missing quite quickly. Many camgirls use laptops but in my experience a desktop set up is far more suited to a studio. Laptops tend to have much shorter lifespans and are often more difficult to repair or upgrade. Some such as the Dell Studio for example look flash but are very badly designed. Some idiot decided to put the on/off switch exactly on the joint where the screen opens. Needless to say, this particular model needs to be replaced quite quickly. Look for reliability when selecting your hardware.

Whatever you can save on PCs, try to re-invest in good quality web cams. You will not last long if your viewers can barely make out your girls' faces, because you are using a cheap web cam, or worse yet, a built-in laptop web cam. There are some nice remote-controlled cams with tilt/pan and zoom functionality but they often turn out to be too noisy - at least the cheap ones. A better alternative is to run a software layer on top of a wide angled web cam that tracks the position of the girl.

If you are looking for a budget option cam then you could do a lot worse than the Logitech web cam C270, which is small and light, but a huge step from a built-in web cam. It even has auto light correction and a built-in noise-cancelling mic which makes video calls look and sound great, but I would say it is the very minimum for a studio set up. A much better option is the Logitech 920 which has full HD 1080p video capabilities and yet is still under $100. It is hard to believe that it has Carl Zeiss optics with a 20-step auto-focus for that price. Logitech have a special 'Fluid Crystal' technology which is a step above most manufacturers, delivering smoother video, sharper pictures, richer colours and clearer sound. Always choose higher light sensitivity over higher resolution. It is preferable that customers see your girls, even in low light, but not every single pore, pimple and freckle.

Most ordinary customers are now buying notebooks that come with a webcam built in. This means that the market for webcams has been cannibalized by laptops and all-in-ones. Consumers are notoriously "good enough" buyers and when it comes to quality, price is far more important. The margins on cams are razor thin which leaves little room for a high end or innovative market. At the moment it still very difficult for anybody to make a USB 3.0 webcam at a popular price point and make a profit on it.

The desktop PC market is declining because people are finding mobile devices to be handier, cheaper and "good enough" for most tasks. This has led to a certain amount of stagnation in the web cam market as consumer demand has waned. Apple's displays for example already include built-in cameras. They also include a 3 USB ports, a Firewire 800 port, Thunderbolt port, and an Ethernet port but with its $1,000 price tag I would it expect that and a whole lot more. Google Trends seems to confirm that webcam related searches are falling (except for "hd webcam" which plateaued in early 2011.) Since Microsoft bought Skype, FireWire-based pro cameras no longer work with current versions of Skype. To be fair, you should probably direct your ire at Apple for locking pro gear to a proprietary interface (FireWire) rather than at Microsoft for buying out a proprietary VoIP network protocol. FireWire is pretty much a dead standard to PCs. (If it was popular, support would be on motherboards, not as a dedicated card by 2nd tier companies.) Skype was never a professional medium and for Microsoft to drop support for a feature that ordinary consumers can not even use is hardly hateful.

Performers looking for a step-up solution should check out the Sony EVID70 remote controlled cam (pro.sony.com/bbsc/ssr/product-EVID70/) and its sister units, which although considerably more expensive than the static C920 and its brethren, enables viewers to control pan, tilt and zoom functions, as long as your service provider offers compatible software. Always check with your program's support staff for specific recommendations of pan/tilt/zoom camera set-ups proven to work with their system. If possible, invest in high resolution smart web cams, calibrating contrast and colour whether it is day or night, connected simultaneously to the phone, TV, tablet and/or computer, and updating constantly where the model is. Ultimately, a high-end or professional three-chip video camera and external microphone set-up will deliver the highest audio and video quality, although at a much higher price and often at the expense of incompatibility with viewer-initiated controls.

Some Logitech cams have face-tracking, and can even be used in a video-conferencing capacity, where there are multiple people sat around a desk. The Polycom CX5000 for example has both amazing audio and video quality, but it also automatically turns and puts focus on whoever is talking. It is slightly more pricey than other models but it is also much quieter as well.

Another consideration is the computer attached to the web cam. For example, Microsoft Windows users will need at least a 2.4 GHz Intel Core 2 Duo processor with 2 GB of RAM or more, in order to enjoy 1080p HD video recording. Monitor size is also important, with larger, higher resolution displays being a preferable choice, since software controls and chat panels must be shown, in addition to cam previews and the cam-to-cam windows used by many operators seeking to enhance their private shows. Consider if can you really push 1080p upstream? With upload speeds typically capped in the single digits, the bandwidth provided to you by your ISP is by far the biggest limiting factor. Of course, if money is no object, get a Matrox frame grabber and their SDK. Or maybe grab a PS3-EYE camera.

Lighting

Some girls do not want anyone in their house to see a bunch of professional looking lighting equipment. Therefore, studios provide a safe environment for them. At home, they can hide smaller things or use regular lamps, since they are seen in the house anyway but big three-point umbrella set-ups are going to look very suspicious.

One of the biggest factors in overall image quality (and as a result, revenues), is your lighting quality, since no one wants to pay to see dark, grainy video streams. Great lighting can make decent cams better and better cams produce excellent results, but it takes more than a bright light, control over your light sources is necessary to maximize image quality. This means a separation of sources, with adequate modelling to provide depth and texture, which is something that is not possible with simple on-camera light sources. Harsh lighting is also an issue, with diffusion being vital to softer, more sensual, skin tones.

Keep in mind that traditional quartz video lights generate a tremendous amount of heat, which can make prolonged sessions extremely uncomfortable, while incandescent lighting can cause off-colour casts. With this in mind, inexpensive quartz shop lights are a poor choice, but attractive to budget-conscious shooters who would be much better off investigating the latest generation of fluorescent lighting kits.

Good lighting is essential when using web cams to obtain that natural sunlight effect, especially when opening the curtains up wide will probably not be a viable option. The best option is to use two or three bright lamps. For models working from home, lamps from around the house will do the job fine but a studio needs to be a little more professional. Ideally there should be three light sources, the most important one being directly behind camera. Whenever you see a girl who is 'glowing,' looking beautiful and clear, it is most likely that she is using special studio lights. Work on a three point lighting set-up that utilises two specialty umbrella lights (key light and fill light) as well as the room's overhead light. This will give you a great advantage over someone without extra equipment.

There are lighting kits on Amazon for under $100, and plenty of tutorials on YouTube on how to set them up. One of the better options is the LimoStudio-Photography Photo Portrait Studio 600W Day Light Umbrella Continuous Lighting Kit. These umbrella lights will showcase the best features of your models, and all the shadows that make them look old, dull and not as attractive will disappear. It is the one investment that will give you the most return for the money. If you wish to try something different and give your models a warm, sunny glow, try a gold umbrella. A model such as the CowboyStudio 43in Black & Gold Photo Studio Umbrella can be interchanged with the white ones from the lighting kit to can create your perfect lighting set up. I would recommend a kit which includes two white umbrellas and a gold one for maximum versatility, so you can try out different options to see what works for you.

ePhoto (www.ephotoinc.com) offers a variety of slightly more expensive solutions, including a decent three-light fluorescent kit for less than $300. A big step-up in budget buys higher quality, more flexibility and greater longevity, with lighting kits from Lowel (www.lowel.com) fitting the bill. As a side benefit, using a decent video camera and three-light kit allows performers to produce more than simple web cam shows, including generating enough usable content to produce a solo site. You can use the same lights for photo sets as the cam lighting. Many studios regularly take a set of promo pictures once a week for their girls.

Cam models need to stay fresh and exciting, so try playing with wardrobe and backgrounds. A room and the decor can be a deal breaker sometimes, messiness never cuts it in a romantic setting. Once you have figured out what lighting kits to get for your basic cam room lighting, you can move on to some fun lights to set the right mood and atmosphere for the room. Lights are movable and customizable, so if you do not like a particular look, you can easily change it around. Fairy lights are so soft and girly that they give your models that sought after girl-next-door look. Back lighting on the other hand is sultry and mysterious. Dimmed lights and coloured LED light strips are easy to install and give off that ultra exclusive club vibe. Disco balls instantly liven up a room and will put the model in a great state of mind to entertain. Do not underestimate the power that lighting has on creating a fun and sexy vibe, which will in turn increase tips. Soft lighting in a room makes it look more expensive, so even just a strip of Christmas lights can improve the overall effect The most popular external microphones used by cam models are the Blue Yeti and the Blue Snowball. Having excellent audio capability is increasingly necessary in order to remain competitive and key to keeping hands free for performances.

In this arena, shock mounted and windscreen equipped studio microphones minimize noise from fans or air conditioners; noise-inducing vibrations caused by bed-flopping or other movements; and generally contribute to cleaner audio. The Dealpeak Multipurpose Professional Condenser Microphone is a cheaper option but the difference in quality will be especially noticeable if your models play music/sing on cam.

In terms of Internet infrastructure, you will need a location with a broadband internet connection, and set up computers with webcams in every bedroom. Sometimes studios put up a cheap partition in the bedroom and cram two or three girls in each room. The studio need not be in an apartment complex, you could also consider renting office space, preferably in a semi-empty building. Finding something spacious and modern can be a challenge in some countries, but to get you started you should be able to find a two bedroom flat with everything you need, that would be considered luxury by locals. How good is the broadband internet? What is the maximum number of girls that you can have on-line and still transmit a quality signal? Go for the best internet connection that you can find. The more bandwidth you have at your fingertips the easier it will be to meet customer requests for HD and 4K. Cam sites actually factor in the quality of video stream when they are presenting the models on their sites. Those with the higher quality are usually presented before lower quality feeds, similar to a Google search result. The higher you rank the more eyeballs that see you. The websites are spending money in bandwidth for every model that is actively broadcasting, so they need to make the best possible stream available to their customers. This is one reason why so many of them prefer to work with studios in the first place. Video quality, lighting, set design and other technical factors are usually far more professional with the studios than the solo models broadcasting from their bedroom. These days, some of the bigger studios will even have a variety of rooms catering to all sorts of themes (including bedrooms, showers and dungeons).

HD streams can usually charge more per minute as well. If possible look for at least a T-1 connection. T2 and T3 circuit channels carry multiple T1 channels multiplexed, with a T3 line comprises 28 T1 lines. It is also possible to get a fractional T3 line, meaning a T3 line with some of the 28 lines turned off, resulting in a slower transfer rate but typically at reduced cost. Your Internet connection is often an item that needs upgrading, since many service plans focus on the user's download speed, rather than the upload speed, which needs to be a minimum of 300k to support a web cam. A much higher 1 Mbps upload for 720p, or 2 Mbps upload for 1080p (rates not available on many home packages) may require an upgrade to business-class service. Consider also that multi-site chatting and cam-to-cam sessions effectively dilute your bandwidth by splitting it up among multiple users.

Perhaps the easiest issue to address is that of software. AWE, Pussy-Cash and Video Secrets are good options while solo-operators still make use of Skype or other instant messaging tools. Small multi-performer cam studios have other options available including ManyCam and EvoCam, which can provide a number of value-added features. If your ambitions range higher, then 2much.net will provide you with a robust and feature-packed platform. Many factors will affect your choice here, such as the software your marketing partners require you to use and the level of traffic they can provide; the better the hardware and faster the Internet connection you have, the higher your profit potential will be. ManyCam allows live cam performers to deliver their content to multiple web cam networks, including Skype, MSN, and YouTube, simultaneously. It can add thousands of amazing web cam effects and custom graphics inside any web cam application, as well as many additional features, including approximately 8,000 special effects plug-ins, which provides a wide range of audio and video effects, such as an underwater background (perfect for marketing the naughty mermaid fantasy), various holiday themes, and artistic overlays that allow performers to appear as pencil sketches and more. An underused resource for adult web cam performers, these creative add-ons could provide deep niche marketing opportunities, when properly marketed. Upgrading to the Pro version adds the ability to switch between audio and video sources using the software's live video studio switcher and unlocks the company's Pro series effects.

If you would prefer an open source screen casting software, Open Broadcaster Software (also known as OBS) is a free and open source streaming and recording program that is available in 41 languages. Written in C and C++, OBS provides real-time source and device capture, scene composition, encoding, recording and broadcasting. Transmission of data is done via the Real Time Messaging Protocol and can be sent to any RTMP supporting destination (e.g. YouTube) including many presets for streaming websites such as Twitch.tv and DailyMotion. There are also a variety of plug-ins to extend its functionality.

Think also about equipment costs. You will often find that electronics are generally two to three as expensive in third world countries as they are in the US. Are you going to buy locally or import from the U.S.? Or are you going to try and save even more money by buying at source. Once you have all of these computers, you will definitely need tech support. If you are a techie, you can maintain, troubleshoot, and repair your own systems. If not, then you will need to find someone local.

Any business that involves working primarily with young women is going to give you seismic level headaches. There is a very old joke in Thailand which says that if you want to make a small fortune, the easiest way to do so is to invest a big fortune in a go-go bar. Anybody that has had any experience supervising 15-21 year old girls in a busy retail environment knows that it is not an easy experience. They are incredibly moody, and you repeatedly need to snap them out of whatever drama that they came into work with today. Apart from the girls themselves, you will also have to deal with jealous boyfriends, pimps and other assorted lowlife. As a studio owner, you will need to adopt a pimp like mentality, because that is effectively what you are. Girls are flaky, fickle and often mentally unstable. In fact, there definitely seems to be proportionately more screwed up head-cases among good-looking girls than there is among the rest
of the population. In countries where education is limited you will always find insanely hot girls, although many of them will appear rather stupid. This is especially true in autocratic nations where it is most definitely not in the interest of the ruling dictators to have a population of intellectuals capable of critical thinking. As I was writing this, the news was filled with obituaries for Carrie Fisher. I do not mean to be disrespectful, but here is a perfect example. On screen, she played the assertive leader of an Intergalactic Republic. Off-screen, she was a bipolar coke-head. This is about par for the course and something that you will have to learn to deal with.
This is partly why you find that so many brothel/massage parlour/strip-club owners are older guys. They are now at an age where it takes an awful lot more than a cute young thing shaking her booty to break their concentration. Younger guys still think with alternative parts of their anatomy and girls will certainly take advantage of this biologically inbred weakness. Most of these girls will be incredibly flaky. Part of the reason girls get into this line of work is because it is "easy money." How will you handle a performer just not showing up for work for two weeks, then coming back like nothing has happened? If you recruit girls that are not experienced prostitutes, then these problems will be even worse. In the eastern European cam studios it is very common to find that girls have been raised by a single parent, been borderline alcoholics since they were thirteen and have been sexually abused by a selection of their male friends or relatives. To the casual observer they look like smoking-hot porn stars, but in reality that are just confused girls wanting to make some extra cash. They are not doing it because they like sex, they are only doing this because they need the money. Expect their untrained performances to be incredibly awkward.

While a studio atmosphere is generally fun, you will have to deal with occasional issues. Most of the time the girls will be ordering pizza for lunch, while laughing and joking about the weird things that their customers get up to. Even so, you must be ready for the occasional breakdown which could happen at any time. It might be a girl locking herself in the shower for three hours, after a client paying premium per minute kindly asked her to stick an incredibly oversized dildo up her ass. Another guy paid extra for the girl to get a laptop and take it to the bathroom/shower. Initially he asked her to just take a shower. Then it got to golden shower stuff. Once it got to copro, the girl snapped.

Not all pornography is degrading to women. Even so, a large portion of it does seem to include those themes since domination/submission is a huge part of the human psyche and regardless of how it is executed (e.g. a macho Mills & Boon man sweeps a lass off her feet and his strong arms overpower her little arms vs a guy forcing his cock down a girl's throat). It also depends on what you define as 'degradation'. A person who is very open, sexually might consider gag porn or light BDSM as dirty but consensual. This might not be the case in other cultures but that does not automatically make it exploitation. There are lots of female porn stars out there who are intelligent, conscious of what they are doing and dictate the terms of their employment. Bobbi Starr, Kimberly Kane and Stoya, to name a few. Ironically porn is pretty much the only section of the media that actually glorifies women. Certainly not like the mainstream print media that constantly belittles and mocks women. And as for women's magazines, readers can kiss their self-esteem goodbye. Plus it is one of the few industries where women are consistently paid more than their male counterparts.

Not every female performer is sacrificing their soul. Some girls might not actually like the job, but let's be honest who does? Are these girls committing suicide? Do studios have to install nets around their building like they do at Foxconn in China to prevent workers jumping to their deaths because they hate their lives and jobs so much that they cannot stand it anymore? No! These girls rake in hundreds of dollars a day to sit on a bed and masturbate. They do not even have to go to the strip club, let alone a dark street corner or some john's house. They can feed their kids, stay warm in the winter, and never ever have to worry about their physical safety. Many girls do this because they enjoy it. It is not always enjoyable, but then, what job is? When it is good, it is great, and when it is bad, it is blow your brains out depressing. Some models worry that being paid to perform sex acts and strip over a web camera will impact their personal lives but considering the stigma now attached the long-term unemployed, most are not sure that could be much worse.

Reports of big spenders are not exaggerated. Take for example the guy who spent $780k in just one year on a single girl. That is almost a million US dollars. She was charging him at an insane rate too, because they had some sort of deep connection where they would eat together in front of cams and then have webcam sex. You would not believe the amount of money some guys spend on webcams. While not every guy drops a ton of money every month, you will occasionally get a "whale" that will blow huge sums in a single month, or sometimes every month for several months. I have seen guys rack up several thousand dollars in cam fees on one or two girls in a single month. I have seen more than one guy drop $1,000+ on a girl every month for 3-5 months. I know of multiple instances where some lonely guy spent two hours+ talking to a girl in a single night. Keep in mind, this was at $2-$4 per minute. These whales are the exception, but there are enough of them out there for someone to make a good living.

As a guideline, $2000 per month is the minimum you should expect from the average model. Do not buy into all the hype you will find on the various websites that talk about $500 per day or $10,000 a month. 15% of the time the model is in private chat. Multiply that by three bucks per minute private and you get an idea (but do not forget that the website is going to take about half of that). If you can average $2,000 gross per model per month then it is all about numbers, i.e. how many models can you get working in your studios. In exchange for the workspace, the studios take a percentage of the model's pay from the website (which, in general, takes a 50 percent cut of what viewers donate).

Are you prepared to deal with a girl whose boyfriend comes in several times a day to talk to her while she is supposed to be working, a common situation in retail environments, such as department store perfume counters for example. You can warn them a couple of times and even tell the boyfriend to take a hike, but they will likely just ignore you at first. Are you willing to call his boss to tell him that his employee is slacking on the job and adversely affecting your business to have him fired? Expect the girl to blame you for getting him fired and throw a hissy fit, but rest assured that she will soon get over it. In fact, it probably will not take long for here to get over it completely, dump the boyfriend, forgive you and go back to being a good worker, as long as you have the balls to deal with the situation promptly and firmly. Although you will find that 90% of the girls who work for you will have boyfriends, there will rarely be any confrontations. good-lookings girls like these usually have an entire orrery of orbiters that extends all the way out to the Ort Cloud and so boyfriends are careful not to ask too many questions in case they are quickly 86-ed. He knows that there is always a queue of guys waiting to take his place. Death threats from enraged fathers, brothers and other family members are another thing completely. Especially in countries that are very religious or face orientated.

How do you deal with two cliques of bitchy girls who are meant to be working together but often will not even speak to each other? When they do deign to acknowledge each other's presence often times it will only be so that they can hurl torrents of verbal abuse at each other. It is you that will have to break the ice and make them work together. It is important that you can be strong and ignore all of the immature nonsense. They certainly will not respect you if you try to be everybody's friend. You will need to come down hard and fast whenever it is necessary.

Sometimes during start-ups for example they earn fixed fees per hours. For every $10, the studio will earn about $7 from the site. Out of that, about half goes to the girl, so $3.50 which is over 30%. Bear in mind that a smart girl can sign up herself on the cam site and get 60% of the total herself. Anytime you push content through a traffic generator, they will take a cut. Sometimes you score from the volume of traffic they bring, but if you start building up a large enough group of women, then it may be better just to start offering affiliate programs of your own and gradually building up your own site. So do both, use the existing services, but gradually build up a site of your own, this way maximising their chance to earn. Gradually, as your own site starts growing, you take a cut off that.

My recommendation is that you recruit models for sites that get the girls on-line and working fast. This should be same day, no messing around with "we don't like her profile pic, we need 10 forms of ID etc." The site should allow you to choose your own percentage of the girls pay and pay them directly for you if possible. You do not want the burden of starting an LLC just to pay girls that may or may not stick around long term. You will receive payments from the webcam studio. You can be incorporated in the country and have legal agreements with the girls where you pay them as "single person corporations" where they are responsible for their own taxes. This way, you do not have to pay any taxes for them and they are responsible for paying it themselves.

Always try to simplify, even when it looks more expensive on the surface. Do not try to save pennies that may cost you pounds in the long run. If it requires a little investment in a girl that will eventually earn, give her a few days free. If she sticks around, charge her more the first few weeks so she can pay it off (not too much, just a little) and before you know it she is going and you are collecting. Give it to her free just to get her going.

You will improve productivity by incentive. If the girls are making a lot of money, they are going to be bringing down friends and cousins in no time too. Treat them well, let them make their money, and if you need to help them out a little to get them started, then do it. Once they are hooked with what they can earn, you are not going to have to worry about managing them at all. Some will waste your time, but the ones that do not will pay you back ten-fold. It is better to charge them less or nothing to get them going then it is to take a cut of pay until they are on their feet. It is all about time management, but also making sure they produce more from day one. You want them to feel like they are getting a good deal and that they cant not do better elsewhere. Enable people to be self-sufficient. Do not be tempted to micro-manage them because you are worried you may lose out. Always think of their pocket, and you will take a little knock here and there, but it will work out well and you will more than make up for it over the long term.

Managing employees is always a hassle and this particularly employee demographic is by its very nature lazy and flaky. Paying them a salary or commission is therefore probably not the best option. Managing any contractor is always a pain, no matter what industry, but something like this is going to be particularly frustrating. You will need to oversee their productivity, their attendance, and what they are willing to do. This is a waste of time and it will slow you down substantially. Even if it is just for a little while or even just a few of them, it is a waste of time and would be a waste of money as a result. Simplify things and treat them like contractors/salespeople/strippers. If they do not have the money to pay the fees for the day, offer the newer girls discounts for the first few weeks if you have to. Make it policy to never take a cut of their pay/tips. You make them pay weekly in advance, and if they do not pitch up on specific days without adequate notice, that is their problem, and you still get paid for it. You will see a lot less flaking this way and your earnings will also be more consistent. Do not even consider paying salaries or taking a percentage of what they earn. Instead, I would urge you to consider the stripper model, which is them paying you a set fee per day regardless of how much money they make in your studio. Consider the way that strip clubs handle their dancers and base your model on that. Alternatively think about how a successful love motel operates. You provide the facilities and the customers. What they do after that is completely up to them. This way they will need to work off their day's cost before they begin to earn anything. This is a much better way to do things for your books too, because a large part of it can be cash. It will be a lot less to manage and the less time you spend managing the girls, the more time you can spend growing your business. Charge for the room by the hour, or in blocks of hours. This way, what she does in there is her business, all you are doing is providing an internet connection and webcam. Just like strippers, they will come back when they realise how much money they can make, and just like strippers, they are going to know they have to work or they will not cover the cost of what they are paying to work there. You keep your earnings consistent, and focus solely on keeping the rooms full. After that, it is up to the women in there to do their thing, but you are still getting paid no matter what else happens. Renting them space in this fashion does away with many of the managerial issues and makes the whole operation much, much easier.

Your next step, once your rooms are full is to make them sign agreements, but it is an agreement between you both and it is more informal. While you may not be able to enforce them in a court, it is more a case of them understanding that they need to turn up consistently but that you are also looking after them too. So the agreement is for them to pitch up for a specific amount of hours on specific days. You guarantee them their room for those times and those days. It is their space for that time, and you can review the agreement at any time. What this allows you to do is forecast your earnings better before you jump into setting up the next studio in a new location or adding more rooms. You will be able to track your income in advance with some accuracy and it will help with your planning.

Just as you probably scavenged off the competition to populate your studio, once established, you too will have to deal with girls being poached by other studios and/or making private deals with clients to cut you out of the action. The best way to deal with this is to have the girls sign NDAs, where it made clear that if the NDA is broken, the content will be released up to the local region (in the normal set-up customers cannot view the girl on the cam site from the region in which they are located). Fortunately most good-looking girls will not have a clue how to do anything other than what you tell her to do i.e. take off her panties and touch herself. There is good reason that there are so many dumb blonde jokes out there. You will find that even the best looking girls in this game are unable to resist the temptation to coast through their educations and end up not being the sharpest knives in the block. To most girls, this will all seem completely new and revolutionary, and so they will not even think of cutting you out or searching for other studios. Even if they do manage to get a direct non-studio account, they will probably fail to set-up the software without your invaluable guidance.

There are always a number of issues that are very common for anyone opening a business in a third world country. Here are some of the things that you will inevitably have to consider/prepare for:

Is such a business legal in the country/city you are operating in? Do you have a lawyer that you can trust? This is actually more difficult than you would think, as some of the biggest crooks around are the attorneys, and many will not hesitate to screw over foreign client if they can make money from it. Even in developed countries, lawyers are regularly tempted across to the dark side. Two Minnesota lawyers -- Paul R. Hansmeier and John L. Steele -- used the copyright system to extort roughly $6 million out of porn downloaders over the course of three years. The lawyers uploaded their own pornographic videos to torrent services -- including the embattled Pirate Bay -- then aggressively targeted users who downloaded the content, discovering names through the standard copyright violation process and then threatening pirates with damages up to $150,000 unless they agreed to a settlement. The typical cost of a settlement was $4,000, far less than the cost of challenging the order in open court. Throughout the process the corrupt lawyers concealed their role in uploading the videos, and obtaining copyright to the videos through shell companies, although in some cases, they actually filmed and produced their own pornography as part of the scheme. Lawyers being what lawyers are, they were able to do this for a long time before the hammer came down on them. Bear in mind that schools have been graduating lawyers in record numbers in recent years. Law degrees are highly desirable to schools. They are cheap for the school but expensive as hell for the student which means that we now have a glut of fully certified sharks. Thousands of highly educated people that have been taught to have no scruples so they can focus on their clients interests, and now they have no job prospects. At the same time, having access to a good lawyer is absolutely critical. That said, does the Rule of Law even operate in the country in which you are proposing to set up your studio? In most developing countries the law is something that looks great on paper but has precious little relevance to daily life. The legality of being a webcam model varies from country to country. Even if webcam services are fully legal in the country of your intended incorporation and operation, it is still important that upon registration, the models agree in writing to indemnify you from their activities. In addition, all models must supply government photo identification proving their date of birth. Does your budget include paying an in house team to monitor the output at all times to ensure no illegal activities occur, and to ensure no minors ever appear on camera?

Are there specific labour laws (e.g. employment taxes, rules regarding hiring and firing them, etc.) that dictate how you handle your models? Is the political climate such that the government will try to shut you down with mickey mouse complaints (zoning issues, department of health citations, etc.). In third world countries you will need to expect extortion from local authorities. Often this can be overcome with some carefully placed bribes, even if you are doing everything by the book. This usually involves simply asking how much they want and for how long will they leave you alone. Even so, offering bribes to a government official in a foreign country might actually constitute a crime for which your own country can press charges, and so this is an area in which you should proceed extremely carefully.

As far as discussing the legal aspect of this business, many studio owners operate on a catch me if you can basis. Webcamming basically consists of a woman (usually) in some semi-private place playing with herself while people pay to watch. There is no sex involved, so it is not prostitution (which is legal in many countries anyway). Masturbation is not prohibited by law and activities that are not prohibited and are conducted on private premises are afforded constitutional protection. So, according to the law, the actual business activity is permitted. Of course, our concept regarding the rule of law simply does not exist in many countries. In totalitarian countries such as China for example, the police force is the simply attack dog of the elites and there is certainly no illusion of having to 'Protect and Serve' the ordinary citizen. Paramilitaries serve to protect the rights of the wealthy rather than the average man. In such situations, mafias, black societies and other criminal organizations spring up to fill the void of law enforcement. Visit any brothel and you are likely to see the local police and local mafia all there drinking together. After all, they probably went to school together.

In contrast, the US is largely a country ruled by law. Yes, there are unfortunately many examples of kleptocratic and frankly criminal behaviours among large companies but it does not rise to anywhere near the level you see in countries like China. Beijing can make lots of rules, but the military owned companies and local governments are free to ignore them with little risk to themselves. Very occasionally, some Chinese corporate head is offered to the masses with a lead lined hole through the cranium, not necessarily as a deterrent for the 'bad things' he did, but as a warning to not be left holding the bag. Even organisations such as the Ministry of Environmental Protection are empty gestures and the concerns of the environment come second the economic concerns. They are laws designed to disadvantage people the government does not like, for example someone running a competitor to a state owned business. They are subject to enforcement while the state run operation is not. It is about picking winners and losers and more generally cronyism, not environmentalism. Poorly/Selectively/Arbitrarily enforced laws are the worst kinds of laws. The west is moving closer towards this model every year, although some might argue that the US is no long ruled by law but by law-yers, which is some cases is even worse.

A city business license may be required depending on how you want to play it. Some operators try without and see. Other try obtaining a license as a call centre. Zoning is not so much of an issue as it is in first world countries. What is usually more important is to have some good local contacts and have a good understanding of how the local baksheesh system operates. Try to hire the best 'protection' that you can find before some undesirables begin insisting that you use their services.

When it comes to taxes, most websites pay their studios with an on-line payment processor, like Payoneer, with models being classed as independent contractors. In other countries there are financial taxes on transactions on money that stops moving within the country. If there is no income that is actually made domestically, then there should also be no corporate income tax. Of course, American citizens are subject to US taxes no matter wherever they are in the world. Renouncing your citizenship is a very serious step to take and I would definitely recommend consulting with an accountant' before burning any bridges. As a studio operator, you will probably be called upon to provide some degree of guidance for your adult live webcam models in connection with many of these issues. One reason that many studios and camsites set up outside the US is that they do not require the complex record keeping obligations for adult media that the U.S. Requires, such as the 18 U.S.C §2257 compliance. American law requires every producer and/or publisher of adult content to keep "2257" records to ensure that the performers are of legal age. A record must be created for each performer that appears in each depiction. These rules also apply to live cam performances. In fact, numerous special rules apply to 2257 compliance where live material is involved, such as the need to capture and preserve a representative video sample of each 2257-triggering production, the need to record the date of the production, and the need to maintain a full copy of any archived shows with the 2257 records. These requirements exceed the standard 2257 obligations, such as recording and cross-indexing the performer's legal name and all stage names, the date of birth, a copy of a valid ID (which can vary depending on the location of the performance), and the maintenance of a full list of URLs associated with the performer's material. Selling adult clips, videos, movies, toys, photos, used panties etc. will also require a 2257 stating that the model is over 18. Failure to comply with these rules may result in fines and/or imprisonment.

The records you keep must supply the following information:

The legal name and date of birth of the performer;

A legible copy the performer's identification document;

A copy of the depiction;

The depiction's original production date;

The depiction's title or unique identifying number;

Any URL associated with the depiction. If no URL is associated with the depiction, the records must include another uniquely identifying reference associated with the location of the depiction on the Internet;

Any name, other than the performer's legal name, ever used by the performer, including a maiden name, alias, nickname, stage name, or professional name. This ensures that no model in your adult publication is or was under-age at the time of filming. Each performer must be indexed by the title or identifying number of the depiction. Records must be retrievable by both the performer's name (real or assumed) and the title or number of the depiction

The name of the person responsible for maintaining the records must be published along with the street address where those records may be inspected. All of these requirements are detailed on the www.2257.info web site.

XXXLAW.com and EFF.org are two websites that have more information on these subjects. Walters Law Group provides legal guidance to webcam operators, performers, and service providers throughout the world. Lawrence G. Walters can be reached at larry@firstamendment.com or www.FirstAmendment.com.

Intellectual property issues can arise in the context of live webcam performances as well. Something as simple as displaying a copyrighted picture or painting in the background of the performance, using copyrighted music during the performance, or displaying a trademarked name or logo on clothing or other objects appearing in the performance area, can result in an expensive infringement action by trolling lawyers and other lowlife. Unfortunately many of the current laws relating to copyright, and trademark have been written by lobbyists, which has resulted in massive overreach, where big companies now have enormous unfair advantages over small businesses. Corporations like Disney have bribed successive governments to extend copyright durations to lengths that were undreamed of when these protections were first made into law. The rigged copyright system that big business has bribed the lawmakers to put in place is a minefield for individuals and small companies. Corporations have been incessantly molding government policy, persuading corrupt politicians in every part of the world to contract out as much of the apparatus of State as possible, including the laws themselves, for the sole benefit of big business. The UK in particular, is according to many, regressing to Victorian times. Changes to UK copyright law for example will soon mean that you may need to take out a license to photograph classic designer objects, even if you own them. This is the result of the Enterprise and Regulatory Reform Act 2013, which extends the copyright of artistic objects like designer chairs from 25 years after they were first marketed, to 70 years after the creator's death. In most cases, that will be well over a hundred years after the object was designed. During that period, taking a photo of the item will often require a license from the copyright owner, regardless of who owns the particular object in question. Bear this in mind when you are furnishing your studio. The result of such ridiculous regulations mean that smaller businesses are often at the mercy of their larger counterparts, and are forced to operate well under the radar, utilising guerrilla tactics to find a niche in the market.

In most cases, treating infringement as legally actionable benefits lawyers, but not the artists they represent. Several years ago, for example, an artist saw one of her paintings hanging on the set of a television show. One of the television show's actors happened to be an art collector. One way that he expressed his support for the arts and for the artists in his collection was to hang their art on the sets of his shows. He did not show their art to make money or to save the costs of having to use prop-art instead. He showed it to honour the artists, pay them tribute, and encourage people to buy art; he certainly did not show it for personal gain. Instead of taking legal action, the artist might have accepted this showing of her art as an honour and a compliment, and proudly added that fact to her resume. After all, how many artists can say that their art was seen on national TV by millions of people? The exposure certainly did more for her reputation than it did for either the lead actor's reputation or the show's ratings. Perhaps she should have paid them for the exposure. Instead, she filed suit against the show's producers based on the fact that she had not given them permission to use her art. She won the suit, but in doing so, she made life more difficult rather than easier for her fellow artists. The detrimental ripple effect for artists here is that when people are not exposed to original art, they are less inclined to buy it.

It is only fair to mention that legally speaking, cosplay can still be considered a derivative work of the original copyrighted material. Simply producing and wearing a costume for home use may not be an infringement, at conventions though this may be a different story altogether. Wearing a costume on cam is like sending a personal message to all the scum ball lawyers that make money in this field. This is worryingly similar to the Disney Corporation's prohibition on dressing as Disney characters. Saban Entertainment DiC have previously filed copyright infringement actions to manufacturers of unlicensed Power Rangers and Sailor Moon Halloween costumes, and the analysis for this infringement could be almost identical if they were to sue a cosplayer.

Cosplayers do not own the rights to the original character for which they based their costume and if it remains too similar to the original work then it can be considered a derivative work and an infringement. This is important as cosplay becomes an ever larger part of the web camming industry.

Basically, the profits of music companies and movie studios are more important, in the eyes of the law, than the lives of average people. What a perverse set of priorities in a thoroughly obscene legal system.

Here are some average jail times for crimes in the UK to put this into perspective:

Administering drugs to obtain intercourse Sexual Offences Act 1956 s4 - 2 years

Abuse of trust: sexual activity with a child Sexual Offences Act 2003 s16 - 5 years

Distributing copyrighted material proposed new act 2016 - 10 years

In a criminal context, it would seem difficult to impose liability upon a live webcam portal operator for the content of communications, such as the obscenity laws for example. This would be like attempting to impose liability upon the telephone company for a conversation discussing illegal activity, in the absence of any advanced knowledge of the nature of the conversation by the phone company. Even so, there have been many cases of torrent tracker sites being persecuted for hosting illegal material, so expect the unexpected if you are targeted by a legal team keen on improving their Christmas bonuses. As with all evolving business models, it will take some time for the courts to clarify the legal rules that will be used to impose liability on the various actors responsible for civil or criminal violations in the webcam arena. We are moving towards a situation where an individual can be hounded and sued into oblivion for providing a platform which others use to distribute copies of music and videos. This is particularly ironic when gun makers and sellers are considered harmless, and continue to profit, while the products they sell result in illegal deaths on a more-than-hourly basis.

Under-age content is the largest content-related concern. The possibility for use of fake, forged, or another person's ID to get access to webcam broadcasting is always a problem. Obviously, liability for use of a fake ID could be imposed on the model, but if that performer is a minor, law enforcement will likely view the under-age model as the victim, and turn its attention to other responsible parties. If ever you are suspected to have any under-age persons involved in your adult work, the FBI can at any time inspect your records and content and they can do it without notice. The FBI also use this an excuse to target activists and free speech advocates, and anybody else that has the courage to stand up against them. A good example is the FBI campaign against Mark Edge and Ian Freeman of Free Talk Live Radio (FLT is a libertarian talk show that has promoted the Free State Project which is a migration of liberty minded activists to New Hampshire for the purpose of pursuing liberty and freedom.) The government has been targeting Ian Freeman's reputation for some time and slandering/libelling his name by making claims that he is a paedophile. The FBI used this as a basis to seize computers and other equipment utilising warrants that did not name a person, place, location, or even specific items to be seized. The courts literally rubber stamp these types of warrants and higher courts have ensured this continues.

In 2014, we saw Operation Choke Point being brought out in full force by the U.S. government. This had some serious negative consequences for adult companies and individual adult performers. Many U.S.-based adult businesses discovered it was harder to conduct business internationally due to closer scrutiny from banks and federal agencies. Adult performers experienced sudden bank account closures purely due to the nature of their business. The FDIC issued a letter effectively ending Operation Choke Point at the end of January 2015, but the aftermath of these actions is still being felt by those affected in the adult industry.

An escrow transfer service can be very useful for cam studio owners who may not wish to deposit all cam performer payments to their own account. As a result cam studio owners can enjoy clearer money management, which is particularly handy for tax calculation and compliance purposes. Of course, there are different billing scenarios, depending on country. One company that operates in just three main markets is offering 15-plus different billing methods because users have their own preferences.

In the E.U. market, there are many different alternative billing solutions, as in most E.U. Countries, the credit card usage percentage is much lower than in the North American markets. Some consumers do not even have a credit card, but they want to pay. And believe me, the credit card penetration is way beyond that compared to the penetration in the U.S. Such users have a lot of alternative options to pay. If they can not or do not want to use credit card, then offer direct debit. If they do not want direct debit they can use pay safe card or even dial a 0900 premium number, where they pay a certain amount per minute. Having said that, we all love to collect user data. Once you have their email, you can send them interesting information about your product. But a lot of people prefer to remain anonymous. They do not like to provide their email address or any billing information. Consider offering consumers the option to chat with hosts via a 0900 premium number. They simply call that number and get a computer-generated code which they have to enter on the website and as long as they do not hang up, they can chat with all the performers they want. The use of credit cards for adult purchases is very expensive to the merchant - in most cases, 12-15% of sales is paid as merchant fees. Some models prefer to get paid for their messaging app conversations through Google Wallet or Amazon gift cards because they get to keep 100% of their earnings. Neither platform takes a cut like adult content sites do.

Every website in the adult space has to deal with charge-backs. Adult-related merchant accounts such as CCBill, charging 12-15%, exist and are used by the adult industry successfully, including cam sites. Their large discount rate reflects the risk (or so they say). Bitcoin transactions are of course a long term focus, as the charge back rate for that is, well, zero, and the discount rate is also effectively zero. The use of Bitcoin in adult markets is certainly increasing, with some companies now offering clients additional credits for purchases made by Bitcoin. Some have pegged estimates as high as 15% of sales. Cams are the best kind of adult site for use with Bitcoin. It is not subscription based, and does not depend on re-billing.

Some sites pay as high as 75% and some as low as 50%. From what I have seen, the less popular sites tend to pay more, especially fetish related sites. There are dozens of reputable sites out there. They all have their pros and cons, but it is really just a matter of figuring out what works for you. As a webcam studio, you will sign up with one or more of the big webcam companies. When you have models in your studio on-line, these webcam companies will display your models as being available for cam chat. If a customer likes the look of your model, they will do a private chat with her. Whatever money the customer pays is split between you and the webcam company. The webcam company might then also have to split their share with the affiliate who brought the customer to their site. Chaturbate is a good one for new models. Viewers can tip their favourite performers with tokens, Chaturbate's official currency. Chaturbate takes a 50 percent cut, such that each token costs 10 cents for the person who bought it and is worth five cents for the person who earned it. I would also recommend Streamate. Both sites are newbie friendly, have good traffic, and they are very different from one another (private based vs. token based) which can help narrow down what style of camming works best for you. Unfortunately Chaturbate just does not have the same amount of high paying traffic as Streamate and Myfreecams.

Do you want to be like Walmart and get reliable regular business or the boutique shop which can sometimes be really busy but often thumb twiddling and waiting. One person's nightmare is another person's gold mine. Streamate in particular gets a bad rap sometimes for having a lower percentage cut than MFC and CB, but the earning potential for your average model is much higher there. They use white labels (which are actually easy to get yourself if you want some of that affiliate money), which skews their Alexa rating.

Fetish models do not work as well in a tip-based, free chat heavy site because the subjects of the models' shows are much more niche and there is a smaller crowd to draw from. Also, because it is niche, and sometimes a little controversial, that makes it a sort of 'specialty' and models can, and should, charge more for it. Vanilla shows, however, seem to work fine in a tip-based format, and many models prefer it. For example in private or gold-showbased sites (such as play sessions on MyFetishLive), a model's room count is considerably lower, but there seems to be fewer beggars and free loaders overall. Generally speaking, the quality of traffic goes up significantly when you raise your rates. I personally would rather wait a little longer for a higher quality customer rather than deal with dozens of cheap, entitled jerks while I get paid pennies. This is more of an issue on private sites than on token sites, since your per-minute rate is what sets the tone there. Initially you can go through the usual routine of feeding content to large cam sites, but later on you might want to make an exclusive deal with a start up cam site.

How you handle the physical security of your site will be critical. It is simply not enough to keep your fingers crossed and hope that no one finds out about your operation or hope that you have located a crime-free neighbourhood. How will you deal with the fact that you have a dozen or more hot, webcam models coming and going at all times of the day and night? This is itself will quickly draw unwanted attention, not to mention the fact that they are might also be popping in and out during the day to get takeaway food. You will essentially have thousands of dollars worth of computer equipment in a house/building located in a third world country. Do not let your girls roam the yard and outside doing shows, drawing bad attention to the studio from police and neighbours. Do not let them do things other than camming on your computers during working hours. A cam studio is - a shared space with everything set-up so models do not have to do any set-up. It is a place of work, not to hang out and relax. It is a working space, not a living space. Keep in mind that the girls you are employing are going to be from some distinctly dodgy neighbourhoods, and almost all of them will be acquainted, and sometimes even related to some seriously hardcore thugs. It is quite possible that one may mention to her gangster cousin about all the computers you have in the house and he and his home-boys then come to pay you a visit. What kind of security will you employ? Do you have any extra financial resources stashed away to replace equipment in the event of theft? Webcam operators are obvious targets for hackers/gangsters.

While money laundering is obviously an issue, transparency in business operations is a liability for them too. I can name half a dozen adult oriented websites, some well-known names, that routinely get shaken down (or at least attempted to) by non-criminals. For a worst case scenario, try watching Lock, Stock and Two Smoking Barrels. The quote from Winston is particularly relevant here.

Winston: Just make sure if you do need to buy sodding fertilizer you could be a bit more subtle.
Willie: What do you mean?
Winston: We grow copious amounts of ganja, yah? And you're carrying a wasted girl and a bag of fertilizer. You don't look like your average horti-fucking-culturalist! That's what I mean Willie.

Of course, it is important not to go to the other extreme. When I first lived in Cambodia in '94, much of the country was still under the control of the remnants of the Khmer Rouge, who with Chinese funding had been responsible for the slaughter of two million innocent civilians, nearly a quarter of the country's then population. Even the capital Phnom Penh was a hairy place to be. The UNTAC peacekeepers had mostly left and the streets echoed with gunfire every single night. There was only one train a week down to the beach town of Kom Pong Som and the week after we rode on it, Khmer Rouge bandits ambushed the locomotive and kidnapped three Europeans along with thirteen Cambodians. Following the hijacking, rebels held the three foreigners for two months and demanded a $150,000 ransom. But the money, released and handled by the Cambodian government, went missing before it reached the captors. And to this day, it is unclear where it went. While negotiating for the men's release, the government repeatedly shelled the Phnom Voar region where they were being held, despite appeals from the diplomatic community, and the hostages themselves, not to do so. The three foreigners were forced to dig their own graves and were then executed. Khmer Rouge fighters have since been granted amnesty to encourage them to defect to the government. We had been down to visit a French couple who had started up a dive shop. By the time that we returned three months later, both had been murdered in their home. Back in Phnom Penh, a Belgian friend had rented a five bedroom villa on the outskirts of the city for just a hundred US dollars a month. For security, he paid a visit to the Russian Market where at the time, all kinds of surplus weapons and military ordinance were openly on sale. He bought a couple of dozen land-mines at five bucks a piece and buried them all the way around his new rental property. That evening the monsoon arrived and washed every single one away into the night.

Do you speak the local language? Unless you speak reasonably good Spanish (or Portuguese) operating in South America is going to be vastly more difficult and leave you much more vulnerable to exploitation. If you do not speak any of the language of the country you are doing business in, and have to work with a local translator then your chances of being ripped off are exponentially higher than would other-wise be the case.

Do not expect any of the girls to speak a word of English. In most countries, there are very few opportunities for girls that have mastered the English language. After all, there is only a very limited demand for full time translators and interpreters. Most girls that study English do so in order that they can emigrate to an English-speaking country. You will inevitably find that most girls with any get up and go have already got up and gone. Unless you can communicate with them in their own language, things are going to be a lot more complicated than you ever anticipated.

As an aside, studying a foreign language overseas is a great way to make lots of overseas contacts. I studied Mandarin at a number of Chinese universities and was always amazed at the general make up of the classes. The ruling elites of other countries will often pack their offspring off to distant lands in the hope that their fluency will eventually land them a job as a diplomat or some such other cushy civil service job. Family businesses will often send their scion off to become their import/export representatives and the more entrepreneurial types will spend far more time in local factories and wholesale markets than in the classroom. In China especially, where teaching methodologies are still appallingly Confucian, many students find that they improve much more quickly by practicing out in the real world, rather than in a classroom that focuses on exams that they will never sit. Just as the wealthy send their children to Oxbridge or Ivy League schools so that they can network with other elites, you to can gain similar benefits by studying a foreign language overseas. For example, the class drug dealers at my first university were all Venezuelan teenagers that had been packed of by their families for a four-year stint in Southern China. A few of these guys became my good friends and I know that I will always have a willing business partner in Caracas if I ever need one. By far the richest guys in my class were the students from Equatorial Guinea. To be honest, I had never even heard of the place and was gob-smacked when I found out that their country's GDP was higher than both the UK and Germany. I am still in touch with a number of Bangkok Hi-Sos (members of the Thai-Chinese high society) and still receive invites to go and work in Seoul with some of my ex Korean classmates. Unless you expect to join the Skull and Bones or the Bullingdon Club, forking out for a university education in your own country is largely worthless these days, and so I would instead recommend mastering at least one foreign language for your efforts.

As with any business, you have to understand you upfront costs, your fixed monthly expenses, your variable monthly expenses, and your monthly revenue. The whole process is an exercise in continuously working to maximize your returns relative to the time and capital you have invested.

One final word of advice before I continue. If you do open your own studio, make sure that you run it like a business, not like your personal brothel. I know of guys that do this in both Colombia and in Costa Rica. In both cases, some of the girls were happy to sleep with the boss on the side. My advice is to never get high on your own supply.

Recruiting

Attracting and retaining quality performers will be the deciding factor in your operational success. Finding girls will be the easy part. Keeping them will be a different matter and will be discussed more in the following chapter. Where to find them will depend entirely upon your geographical location. In South America where prostitution is already legal, it is simply a case of hitting the brothels, massage places, hooker bars, and strip clubs. Compared to the work that they are doing at the moment, most girls will just jump at the opportunity to work in a webcam studio. The key thing is not to be a complete dick about it.

There are so many places to find girls that there is simply no need to screw up someone else's business for your business to be successful. Bear in mind that the aforementioned types of business are not generally run by charities and friendly societies, so do not go into and try to poach a whole bunch of girls at once. In a place like Thailand, there are inevitably instances where a huge number of massage girls will quit within a week of each other to work at a new massage place. This has often resulted in a lot more than hard feelings, and you do want to find yourself on the wrong side of a turf war in your very first week of business.

In Eastern Europe, prostitution rings are run by the mafia, who will not think twice about sending Igor and Sergey to break a bone or twenty. Latin America is notorious for drug cartels, kidnappings, and muggings but because prostitution is legal in multiple countries, there are not so many pimps. I recently heard about two studio recruiters who were constantly plucking girls from one particular massage parlour. The worst that happened to them was that they were told not to come back. In most South American nations there is an abundance of pretty young girls willing to sell their bodies for a little extra some cash. These girls come and go, so the owners are used to a really high turnover. The nature of the business means that this is true all over the world, but even so I would think twice about poaching girls from operations in Thailand, Cambodia or Indonesia, which are obviously run by the Chinese black societies or the Chinese ruling class. This is not the kind of business where you can look towards the local police for protection. Out there, the boys in blue are far too busy cracking down on political dissidents to become involved in legal disagreements. Enforcement is therefore carried out triads and other home-grown mafia type organisations.

Avoid targeting the superstar at the local massage parlour/brothel. This is a foolish move for two different reasons. Firstly, the owner will certainly be more than a little annoyed if you stroll in and try to "steal" his best earner. Secondly, superstars make so much money from all of their regular customers that they are less likely to be hungry enough to make a good employee. Even in the big fish bowl parlours in Bangkok, it is quite common to see guys line up and wait their turn for a superstar, while literally hundreds of other girls might be sat around waiting for a customer. Try instead to find girls that are attractive but not in very high demand, as well as the girls trying to get out of "the life". For many of these girls, their only option besides whoring is unemployment or backbreaking labour as a housekeeper or similar for $1-$2 per hour.

Once you spot a potential candidate, book her for a session at her work place and then ask her if she will come to see you at your hotel or your apartment. This is a common enough customer request, and it will give you an idea of whether she is interested in working outside of the brothel. Somewhat surprisingly, there will be girls that say no to this, but they will usually be the minority. Once the girl is at your location, enjoy your private session and then discuss the opportunity of her working for you, but not the other way around.

As an example of how easy this can be, I would like to share the experience of a fellow studio owner own that found a smoking hot Colombiana in a down town Medellin strip club. Without question, this girl would be a 9.5 in any first world country and yet she was earning the equivalent of just US$10 for every guy she slept with at the club (Short time fees were typically $20 or 40,000 pesos, with the girl getting half). If she could not attract any customers, she simply did not get paid. When she was offered a flat fee of US$5 per hour to do cam shows in a studio, she jumped at the idea of earning consistent money without spending her days pinned down underneath a continuous stream of old fat guys. Of course, the $5/hour model will not work everywhere. In Europe salaries would need to be significantly higher.

For example, webcam modelling is now very popular in the Czech Republic, with a lot of university girls doing it to make extra cash. Over there, most are paid by the minute, with studios splitting the money so that models are making at least $1 per minute. They might not be busy all time either, but it still works out at quite a bit more than $5/hour. This is certainly not the case in parts of South East Asia. The key is to look at the hourly wage a girl could get in a "normal" job, and the hourly wage she could get in other sex-work jobs. For instance, in Medellin, the mid range massage places are basically $15-$20 per half hour (the girl only gets half of that), and the girl has to actually sleep with the guy. Also, since these places are so close together, it is not uncommon for a girl to be at work all day and not get one customer. Maybe three or four customers a day for an 8-10 hour shift is more common for a cute girl. Now, if you take a girl who is only making $25-$40 per day sleeping with three or four fat, old smelly guys per day (with no guarantee that she will make anything that day) and offer her a consistent $5 per hour ($40 per day) where she does not have to touch anyone, and there is less of a chance of her friends/family finding out, she usually jump at the opportunity.

Once you hire your first girl, offer her a little commission to recruit other girls for you, especially those that are not working at the same brothel where you found her. You will soon discover that every single one of these massage girls knows at least two or three other hotties that desperately need the money, but simply cannot deal with the social stigma of being a prostitute. They might envy their hooker friends, but they can not do it themselves. Offer a girl a flat fee of $10-$20 to find another recruit for you and you will never have to worry about finding girls again. Most of the time, they will be ecstatic because they no longer have to sleep with fat, sweaty johns, plus their friends and family will not find out what they are doing. Most webcam companies have a feature that allows a studio to block viewers from a particular zip code, state, or even country. So if you were based in Colombia for example, you would block the entire country from accessing your webcam. This will make very little difference to your bottom line, since the vast majority of the paying customers will be accessing the camsite from Western Europe, USA, Canada, and a handful of Asian countries.

If you are doing it right, girls will be finding you. If you are offering your current girls recruitment fees you will soon have more girls now who want to work than you have studio capacity. You will find that the word gets out really fast, especially when you are paying models more than three times the national minimum wage, and there will soon be plenty of applicants.

In places where prostitution is less open, girls can be hired through classifieds ads disguised as something else, i.e. modelling jobs, etc., i.e. "Looking for models, good pay, must be comfortable working with a camera." Just make sure that tell the girls that the job is involves "naked modelling" or "erotic modelling" during the e-mail conversation or telephone call, otherwise a good number of them will freak out and cause you a lot of wasted time.

Superficially this might seem to be unprofessional and misleading. Some might see it as exploitation of economically disadvantaged women but it is not as if they came in under the assumption that they were doing a "modelling job", and were immediately handcuffed to a metal bed frame and forced to perform endless degrading sex acts without any pay. Certainly it is taking advantage of human psychology but bear in mind that a good studio is a big step up for many of these girls. Would you rather they be working in the streets becoming STD incubators? If it makes you feel any better, this is exactly how many reality television shows operate. The main "cast" have very little idea what they are getting themselves into, and the "supporting cast" of friends, relatives, neighbours, customers are blatantly lied to. This ensures that there is a good level of spontaneity on the show.

There are so many misconceptions about webcamming, such as how all the girls are sex slaves being whipped by a pimp telling them to make more money. There is a dark side to every industry and every job, but our industry gets the bad publicity for it from media. And even if you are not even doing sex things in this industry you are still 'immoral' because you associate with people that like sex.

As for which models will make you the most money, go for what sells, no matter your own personal preferences. It is important to learn early in your adult industry career to base decisions on statistics and not personal opinions or taste. The perfect cam model is approximately sixty percent charming personality and forty percent physical attributes. This is a relationship service, so charming and creative personalities are a must. Everything else is secondary. Your customer should fall in love with the performer and want to keep coming back for more. Many studios pay bonuses to performers depending on a combination of several factors, including time per-chat session and user rating after the chat. The ideal candidate will have the largest natural breasts possible and the patient demeanour of a kindergarten teacher. In all honesty, regardless of whether they are fat or old, large breasts always make money.

Consider also going into niche markets. This is the one of the main advantages of working with cam sites. There are always opportunities for every kind of body type and sexual fetish. Older girls, fat girls, transsexuals, pregnant girls (especially pregnant girls), they all make good money. Best of all, these girls will be happy making less money than the catwalk super model. Superstar stunners will demand more money and be more flaky while a girl in her forties with extremely large breasts will be happy with less and will always show up to work on time. You might even make more money with the big breasted older girls simply because there are less of them on the cam sites. This is not to say that you should avoid the hotties, it just means that should be open to other models if they can make you money.

A simpler way to maximize return on investment than spending a ton on marketing and/or investing in a spectacular girl is to invest in a niche performers. You can try to promote the hottest girls but the problem is that everyone is promoting those hot girls (often times the exact same girls as you). One affiliate marketer explained that he had promoted some truly beautiful girls, but by far his biggest moneymaker was a 300lb+ woman in her 40s with gigantic breasts and a super feminine looking Thai shemale. For guys that were into that stuff, there are so few models that fit the bill, any model that does will make money. In the case of the 300lb model, she could be marketed in three separate niches, huge (natural) breasts, BBW/Fat, and mature/older. This is one of the areas where the businessmen are separated from the hobbyists. The hobbyist only goes for models he thinks are hot, while the businessman goes for models he thinks will make him the most money. The key is to find a niche that works for you. Think about doing business in some Latin American countries before African or Asian countries. There is a greater level of physical diversity in these countries.

There is no longer any such thing as the most popular type of girl. Asian, white, Latin, black, athletic, glasses, Eskimos, all have their own niche segment. The real skill here is to find something original that could go viral. I have yet to find a cam site that allows menstruation, nor a good reason why there is such a discrimination against this fetish, which just so happens to be a normal bodily function of most cam girls of reproductive age. Perhaps it is these kinds of unmet needs that you should be trying to fill.

My own first experience in this business began by helping out a friend set up a cam studio in South East Asia. At first, I was only helping him by sourcing supplies for his studio set up. He was planning to open up a fifteen stage operation in a part of the world where it was cheap to operate but where it was difficult to find quality products at a good price. This was where I came in. He remembered that I spoke Chinese and that I knew Guangzhou like the back of my hand (Guangzhou is known as the Workshop of the World, and has more vast wholesale markets than anywhere else on the planet), so I worked with him to put together a shopping list and we made an estimate of how much money he would save. Even after covering my flights and accommodation, it was still less than a third of what he had originally budgeted to spend. So, we agreed a small fee for me, and off I went. At the time, I knew the computer markets in Ganding intimately but I was also able to pick up some refurbed equipment at Dashatou, including some very nice professional quality webcams. Over at Hong Yun Photo City, I stocked up on pro lighting at wholesale prices and even splashed out on a bunch of wall-sized backdrops for photo shoots. As well as some really nice soft furnishing items from the places that kit out high-end karaoke clubs, I knew quite a few cosplay specialists, so I picked up a few stunningly sexy outfits from them too. Finally, it was over the lingerie wholesale market for a big box of assorted play-wear, and then last but not least the sex toy market for a selection of the latest in teledildonics. Most of the stuff I shipped by freight forwarder but the dildos and stuff I stashed in my luggage, praying to god that I would not get stopped at customs. I knew all of the locations really well, and so I had the whole trip wrapped up in just three short days. This meant I had the weekend to myself and this was where some strange synchronicity began to play its part. By coincidence, I bumped into a Chinese girl that I had known from nearly a decade before. At the time, she had been the main squeeze of this nasty mafia type that hated me, because I was with a gorgeous girl that had repeatedly turned him down. He managed a bar in Tian He but was really little more than a petty drug dealer, running a line of mules from Hong Kong into Guangzhou, Dongguan and Shenzhen. It really was hate at first sight for him. He had this broad cockney drawl and swaggered about like he was Reggie Cray. I, on the other hand, had an educated accent and I could tell that this really grated him. Anyway, he had a wife and family in Hong Kong that provided his local ID card but his Guangzhou girlfriend was this huge-breasted hooker called Ivy. She was definitely a case of 'you can look but you better not touch,' not because I was afraid of the wide-boy wannabe boyfriend, but that I would, as the song said, I would need an 'ocean of calamine lotion.' Guangzhou night-life is a real filthy scene and I was willing to bet that in those days, she was incubating all kinds of nasty infections that I would probably need a cabinet full of antibiotics to get rid of. I have no idea how she recognised me after all this time but there was no way that I could have mistaken her. She still had the most enormous fake breasts that her boyfriend had insisted upon when they were together, and in a country like China where most girls are about as shapely as an eight-year-old boy, she stood out a mile. She told me that she rarely if ever went out to bars any more and that she was working part-time, teaching the Chinese zither. Although she looked a little down on her luck compared to the last time that I had seen her, she was still had something about her. I do not know what possessed me but found myself asking her if she wanted to jump on a flight with me to come and work as a cam girl. The fact was that I could not have found anybody better qualified if I had tried. She had worked for many years as a hostess and so knew how keep guys talking, she had had a British boyfriend and although a little rusty, was streets ahead of any of her compatriots in terms of English. Best of all she had the most enormous breasts. Not my cup of tea at all, but a physical trait that goes down great guns on all the cam sites.

So, apart from heading back with a fully ticked off shopping list, I also went back with my first recruit in tow. Initially, my friend was not best pleased to say the least, but Ivy quickly turned out to be one of his most popular performers, and I was duly sent back to China to see if I could find some more of the same. By then, it was already 2010 and China had already well past its peak, at least in most of the coastal cities, where work was becoming scarce and costs of living creeping up. This was long before YY and all the other singing cams sprang up. Basically, I hit the gweillo bars and foreign language universities and within a couple of months, I had uncovered more than a dozen young hopefuls. This was how I got my first-hand experience of a cam studio, not as an operator but as a supplier. I was able to see the inner workings in fine detail and watched first-hand as my friend made plenty of mistakes along with suitcases full of cash. Some of those experiences I would now like to share with you.

I personally would advise not to hire models who want to try camming just to test it out and see what they think. Girls that cam part-time have a tendency to blow their money on expensive clothes or drugs. They might make good money today but they are becoming accustomed to a lifestyle that they will not be able to sustain. When a girl starts camming, you want her to go all in and do her very best from the start, as this is one of the primary factors of a successful cam model.

Models are more than a mere commodity to be used for separating clients from cash, they also have value as corporate assets, especially those who have a head for business as well as for flirtation. Models need to be confident in this business. If they do not believe in themselves, it will immediately show up on cam. Models must be prepared to put up with plenty of extremely rude people. It is definitely not for the thin-skinned. Models need to have a great deal of mental strength and if they are unhappy they will simply crack under pressure and someone else will replace them because the business is so competitive. When most girls start camming, they think that they just have to sit in front of the camera and touch themselves to make money. Camming is ridiculously more than that. It is entertainment, and it is whatever you want it to be. People do not 'just' want a female figure encountering orgasm, they want a woman with thoughts, who is sexy to them. Having a nice body and a pretty face are really not essential for becoming a successful cam model. Patience, naturalness and spontaneity are indeed undeniable qualities for such a job, and of course, a very rich imagination adapted to each member. For many girls camming can be an empowering experience, helping them to feel more comfortable in their own skin. And this confidence often carries over into their real lives, making them more outgoing and sassy. Girls who are extroverted and a little quirky are ideal for camming, even if they introverted in their personal lives. Camming can actually help a lot of girls embrace their quirks.

Staff Training

From both a model's and studio's perspective, today's cam industry is becoming ever more competitive. Models need to come up with new types of shows and experiences to offer their members. This requires them to be more professional and invest more time and money to stay ahead of the competition. Models will often need a little help getting viewers into their rooms when they first start broadcasting. Camming is not easy in the slightest. You try keeping 2000 horny, multi-gendered people happy. It is both a physically and emotionally draining job and despite what some people have in their heads, it is still a job.

Camgirls have to be creative, entertaining, funny, witty, smart and come up with things to do that keep members returning to their room instead of moving on. Camming is a sales job. Some sites, like Streamate, allow actual sex to the point of orgy, while others limit acts to a solo show. Your models are up against tens of thousands of women (and men, to a lesser degree) offering the same product in varying versions. That is a tough stab at making a living, even with your clothes on. This means that the more training and support that you offer your models, the more money that everybody will make.

Start by installing a message board in the studio that gets updated daily with each models favourites, paid percentage, their weekly goal and their actual money. Nothing better than a little competition to get your models working harder. The best studio managers use training methods that are based on direct daily contact with their roster of models, providing them with some very valuable insights. The resulting training programs are designed to help beginners learn on how to perform on-line include body language tips, make up lessons, hairdresser training and language courses.

Here are a few basic points to get you started

Whenever possible models should speak directly to the cam and chat through voice. Members will mostly be English speakers and find themselves to be more interested in girl who can talk and flirt in free chat. Typing the whole time quickly becomes boring for the viewer. Models should be "vocal" in private chat as it is seductive language and flirtatiousness that will earn them five star ratings. As studio manager, you can role-play with your models to ensure that they are up to scratch before they go live.

Encourage your models to cam in order to have fun. Convince them not worry about making money as the most successful cam models get excited every time they go live. They love what they do instead of dreading the hour they have to appear on cam. It is something they will think about constantly when they are not working. The best models will think about how to better their performance, what outfits to buy and new ways to improve their shows. If that is not the case for any of your models, then cam modelling is probably not for them.

Always ensure that models have props, toys, etc. close by. Fans might want to see a model change their outfit or see a few toys to chose from before they take them private. The more time that is spent off cam to go fetch accessories, the more valuable earning time that is wasted. Keep toys, lube, and some commonly requested sexy outfits within easy reach. It may be a perfectly innocent mistake, but if a model does not have what she needs during a show and tells a paying customer you she will be right back, she will probably lose the customer as he will think she is stalling to squeeze him for more money. Even if he waits, he is more likely to give a model a lower rating or an unfavourable review after the show.

Always make sure models let their clients always know when they will be back on line, whether it is hours from now, or tomorrow, but be sure to give them a time and date. You will be amazed at how many return at exactly the time they are told. Never tell them a time and then be late. Maintaining a consistent schedule, four hours every morning, four hours every night, six days a week might sound incredibly regimented, but in many ways it is far easier than changing schedules all the time. The model knows when she will be on-line and more importantly, so do their customers. Consistency is a key ingredient to success here.

Help your models to build a following. Make sure that they follow a schedule and stick to it. Help them out making social media pages and post teaser photos using hash-tags. The more active they are the farther they will go. Start out by making a stage name and creating a Twitter account with that name. Follow up with an email and Instagram account that is not connected to any of their day accounts or their real phone number. Textnow and Sideline are both free downloads and will link everything up to one number which means that there will be cross contamination of phone contacts that social media will inevitably try to "help" connect with a model's everyday accounts. This is all very important to maintain a model's personal privacy.

Somewhat surprisingly, girls that have all nude pictures in their profile gallery, tend to make less money. Something always needs to be left to the imagination. Every model can show off her best body parts without being nude. Lingerie is great and do not underestimate the power of a head shot. Psychology teaches us that human faces attract people's attention more easily than body parts do. Many marketing tests that track people's eye movements on-line have also backed this up. Head shots also tend to attract better quality traffic, guys who will stay in model's room longer and have good manners.
Models need to be careful with outside promotions, because many members that try to take models off the site are looking for ways to get something for free. It would be nice if members had to request to take models private but on most sites this is not the case. She could have a room filled with people tipping and getting ready to take her exclusive and then a member takes her private but only stays in for thirty seconds. This will clear the room and then suddenly she is back to no one in her room.

Always ensure that models use a customer's on-screen nickname. If a model wants to abbreviate it down to something easier if it is too long, just make sure the customer understands and approves. This is a simple as asking a Christopher if it is OK if a model calls them Chris. Make sure that models learn the real names of their customers, to memorize or write them down, and use them often so that when a customer returns, they will be impressed that they have been remembered. Encourage models to get to know their regulars and keep notes on them. Customers love it when models when a model remembers little details. Knowing a member's dog's name or their favourite sports team is something that will always keep them coming back.

Encourage models the change outfits and lingerie frequently. Have a variety of bra and panty sets, skirts, themed outfits, etc. and always wear more colourful clothes because they will look better on cam than plain flesh coloured garments, or even black and white. Make sure you models are dressed well whether they are doing yoga routines in bike shorts or lip-synching to pop hits. Focus on the importance of music and body language as details that make a difference. Make sure that everything a model does is perfectly combined with their outfit, their environment, background music, and so on. Make sure that models know to regularly switch positions in when in private chat. Clients love to see different angles and imagine that they are really there with the model.

Girls that use toys should also use lube to keep from getting sore genitals. Encourage models to change the hand with which they use their mouse every few days, to avoid carpal tunnel. Have them take mini breaks to stand and walk in place often when they are camming for more than a few hours; to keep from developing blood clots and other problems. Make sure that they give their eyes a break from staring at the computer and focus on something in the distance for a few seconds every 10 or 15 minutes.

Once broadcasting, a model will be able to see two chat boxes. One is for paid members while the other is for free chat. Even when a model is taken private, often times people will wait around in the free chat area for them to come back. Once a model is in private chat, she will no longer be able to hear or see the customers in free chat, but that does not mean that they will automatically stop typing in the free chat window. Even when performing in private, models can try and convince members waiting in free chat to come join the show. They might type something in the free chat window like, "I'm Naked! You're missing out. ;-)". Many times a customer will decide right there and then to join in on the fun. If that does not work, then a model can let free chat viewers know exactly what act they are performing at that moment. If a model types something like "I'm doing anal" into the free chat window, do not be surprised if another half a dozen guys suddenly join the private chat.

Remember that this is called webcam modelling so you always want your models to be presentable and beautiful when on cam. Any girl that goes on air with wet hair or no make-up needs to be 86-ed. Foundation make-up is essential for high-definition cameras so that your models do not get that cake look. Find a girl that can become your resident make up trainer and pay her well to train your newcomers. I openly admit to recruiting a couple of Mary Kay girls for this reason alone. Many of the these girls are barely scraping by on a very high pressure MLM program and yet are very well suited to webcam modelling. The same goes for perfume counter and make up girls in big department stores. Most are on lousy commissions and will jump at the chance to make some serious money.

While you want your models to be seen clearly, very few will have the same confidence in their appearance that you do. Most will consider themselves far less than perfect and would rather not be so clear that every flaw can be seen. Some for example bruise very easily and at any given time will have several marks on their body that they will want to conceal. Many will have experimented with make-up, only to wind up with a splotch of oddly coloured flesh. This is where your in-house make-up trainer will prove invaluable. There are plenty of YouTube videos that cover the best long-lasting make-up to use for camming as well as written posts on sites such as camgirltoolbox.com.

Encourage your models to be themselves, because that is the easiest way to be original. Models should be themselves, do and talk about things they enjoy. Rest assured that there is an audience, smaller or bigger, for everybody. Being original allows models create their own niche and audience. When a model types 'I'm so glad to see you again,' but nothing in her facial expression or body language is confirming that, the customer will immediately know that she is faking it. Regular users can easily detect the difference between acting and real personalty, and it is this that is the difference between earning $1,000 and $10,000 per week. Authenticity in a show is everything and facial expressions tell so very much about how real it is. It does not have to be over the top. This is one of the main things that regular customers will be looking for. Tip-based sites especially are extremely conversation oriented and require that models who are active and high-energy. A large chat room experience should be engaging and fun. It even encourages members to develop friendships with each other. The sex component of camming is becoming ever less important over time. Instead, models need to engage members by sparking new areas of interest and interaction, for example coming up with games or musical and theatrical performances, etc.

The standard way of sitting in chat hoping someone finds you attractive, has evolved into fun, lucrative games. Broadcasters benefit by fans paying to participate in games such as Spin the Wheel, Hangman, and Token Keno, etc. Try doing trivia games! Stay in free chat and have them tip on Gold for a guess and give them a deal on how much Gold for how many guesses. Offer the winner of the game a 10 minute, 99c exclusive.

Some girls have lots of fun on cam. They just love to dance around, tell jokes and basically have a good time. If a girl does not like what she is doing, it obviously shows. Customers are always looking for models who are able to really connect intimately and be themselves on-line. Models should strive to increase the fun element in their rooms, offering more games and interactive toys to get the customers as engaged as possible.

Simple porn is turning into a real social relationship between the model and the visitor. People do feel more comfortable meeting entertaining cam models, and develop a daily routine with their presence. Being attentive to viewers and talking a lot helps.

Remember that camming is a luxury service. Most models make more money and have a better overall experience by keeping their rates high, or at least competitive. Higher rates equal better customers and longer shows. It may seem counter-intuitive, but starting out with decent rates will attract better customers and give them a better image (basically the same concept as luxury product pricing - products with a higher price tag automatically seem higher value). Avoid starting out with cheap rates. There is no need to go crazy with astronomical rates, but making your new models slog through the hell that is cheap customers will result in a massive rate of attrition.

Playing music is fine as long as it is appropriate or something that everyone can appreciate. Some girls find that doing close-ups and body shots gets viewers higher faster too. Sometimes they need to let go of preconceived notions of what they typically think that men will find sexy. Much of it is simply about telling people that they are sweet. All a man really needs is attention, when he wants it, and then he will happily stay on-line until the tokens run dry. Regulars will sit in a room for hours, pouring money away. These are the lonely ones who want to hear that they are loved...that they are sweet...that they are kind. This is what will keep them coming back. It might sound mercenary, but these guys are getting exactly what they are paying for. Only a man in the deepest bog of delusion truly believes that cam love is real. If he is spending hundreds of dollars for a companion on his computer monitor, he has to be willing to suspend disbelief. Plenty of men are willing to buy into the act and pay for the privilege of jerking off to something interactive. Some even say that American egos need to be stroked more fiercely than the rest, but that is debatable.

There will always be husbands whose wives are not giving it up or no longer look good, that want to have hot chicks taking to them. Webcamming is not just porn, it is about giving attention and entertaining someone. It is companionship. People who watch porn just want a mindless orgasm. People who pay for webcam models are usually very lonely and want the interaction with a live person. Train your models to use lots of eye contact. Ideally they should be looking directly into the camera, making each user feel as though they are the only person in the room.

Cam models need to develop the skill of deciphering what men want sexually. More often than not, most will beat around the bush by mentioning just the opposite of what they were actually into. For example: "Hey, I bet you like guys with really big dicks right?" Naturally, in the beginning, a model will say no for the sake of winning the popular vote, but then she learns what they really want is for her to talk about how much you love big dicks, and hate small dicks, because they are S.M.P (small penis humiliation) fetishists. They want their "little dicks" to be exposed, degraded, and mocked. Another example, of the more extreme variety: "Wouldn't it be gross if you saw a guy suck his own dick??" The correct answer is of course, "I would love it if you sucked your dick for me, it would really turn me on." It can often end up being pretty entertaining, especially when the model makes them swallow.

Contrary to the popular belief, order to make the big bucks in webcamming, models do not have to do very extreme sexual hardcore things. Some of the more artistic models have found the industry to be quite the opposite. One of the most popular shows of an English burlesque model are live body paint nights where she paints herself live on cam. With porn now being free for all, nudity and sex is everywhere. In order for a model make an impression she has to offer something different and some who are suitably creative, focus on trying to entertain people with art instead.

Inexperienced models trying to play a role, no matter what that role is, in most cases will not bring any kind of results. Horny men behind computer screens are surprisingly perceptive and a model's mood always has a major impact on how the customers talk to them, no matter how hard they try to fake it. As they become more familiar with camming, they can be anyone they choose on cam. They can be themselves, an inflated version of themselves, anything they like. They get to explore new situations and learn something new every day, all of these things help with self discovery and are a huge confidence booster

Camming is at its most basic level a sales job, so why not suggest a few books on successful selling techniques that models can read on their downtime. Business is business, and learning good sales techniques and how to close the deal is important. The basics of business, sales, on-line marketing, SEO, and branding are the same no matter what industry you are in.

One key skill that cam models need to develop is the ability to deal with trolls in open chat. The best advice is to just ignore them. These are people who get their kicks from making models feel bad, so when they are ignored they often get bored and move along. If your models are native speakers, then another strategy is being witty with them. You will be amazed how many trolls will react positively and change their attitude. Find what turns them on or what they like and the obnoxious man will become the most friendly one. For girls that are just beginning, trolls can ruin a girl's entire whole day, but they have to stay positive. A skilled cam girl can turn any troll into a fan if they are smart enough.

Guys will say things like, show me a nipple and I'll go private, but in reality the members who go private never ask for a free show first. If a model accepts their requests, they will either keep asking for more things or they will leave the room. Do not allow your girls to respond to begging. Just have them say with a smile, "Mmmm... sounds like fun, let's go private so I can do that for you." Many new and naive broadcasters fall for deception whereby people are promised tokens or other remuneration only after they do something.

Do not allow girls to beg for tips, stalk premium members or use deceit and trickery to win sympathy. Instead, they should always be happy and polite, with a big smile on their face and a good word for everyone. Do not let your girls complain about their lives in free chat. If your girls were taking calls in a high-tech call centre and they started whingeing about how bad their day was and how every other customer been getting on their nerves, they would soon be fired. The job here is to be a fantasy model. The customers can go to their girlfriends or wives if they want to hear complaints.

Make sure that a model knows her limits. If she puts that she loves love anal on her profile/bio, she had better be prepared to do a lot of anal penetration shows. That does not mean that she is going to get those requests all of the time, but some days she will, so she better know what she is are willing to do a lot of. If a girl promotes deep throat on her profiles, then some days she might get only toy sucking requests for hours in a row. Every model does not have to do everything under the sun. Adjust profile texts to suit individual models and you will avoid excessive model burn out. Some tippers can be very demanding, and promise big tips, for really niche fetishes. Models get asked to do everything from poop in a glass and eat it, to getting 'fucked in the ass with a vacuum cleaner.' If a girl is happy with anal, cam2cam, BDSM, fetishes, feet flashing, pee/poop etc. then make sure that it is advertised it in her bio and/or title and watch the money roll in. Ensure that they understand that they are in total control of their room and can choose to decline anything they wish. If you find that a model is refusing to perform some of the more profitable acts, then you can simply replace her with somebody more extrovert and exhibitionist.

Fetish models stand out from the crowd due to their willingness to cater to some bizarre, and rather esoteric, fetishes. ABDL (Adult Baby/Diaper Lover) and clown fetish for example are both very niche and the audience for them is considerably smaller than, say, people who are into anal, but they are also things that very few models are into. So the fetishists themselves are often just excited to find people that are interested in the same things as them. If your model logs in dressed in a frilly pink outfit with a pacifier, it will immediately draw a lot of attention. So think carefully about outfits and the effects will be immediate. Costumes can range from a big red clown nose and bra that squeaks when she squeezes her boobs to being covered in glow-in-the-dark paint under a black light. If viewers never know what they are going to find when they log into a model's room, that is often what keeps people coming back. When it comes to cosplay, make sure that both you and your models are well versed in at least some of the more popular characters. This is an area that is really taking off and you may have to do some homework to make sure that you are up to speed.

Any model can broaden her base by capitalizing on an interest in cosplay, and dressing up in sexy outfits. This will give her access to many more mainstream websites that might otherwise frown on adult content. She need not state that she is an adult webcam model star, but viewers will soon make the connection. Good old fashioned shock tactics are still the best way to make a big splash. In 2015 for example, MyFreeCams.com model, Sunny Olivia made an amazing $30,000 in tips just by wearing a Nazi uniform before the webcam site shut down the show. Olivia, a favourite model on the website, was named Miss MyFreeCams for June 2015. The stunt may have infuriated viewers, but it raked in a small fortune in tips, when she live streamed her bizarre burlesque show, appearing in an SS officer's uniform in front of a Nazi flag. Wearing a Nazi jacket with no shirt underneath, she stood in front of a podium, tipped her military cap and wrapped herself in the red, white and black flag. Social media users slammed the 34-year-old model for the controversial performance, using the hashtag #SuspendOlivia on Twitter. This is not performance art. This is offensive, one user tweeted.

The mistake that Olivia made was doing nothing to separate herself from the genuine Nazi party. If she had been smart she would have linked her performance to one of the many anime or Hollywood depictions of Nazis. This is why I say that you need to do your cosplay homework.

Space Nazis have long been a staple of science fiction. In "Patterns of Force", an episode of Star Trek: The Original Series: The Ekosian civilization copied the Nazi Regime to the point of having similar ideologies, clothing, symbols, etc., in an attempt to emulate Germany's rapid economic recovery during the 1930s. In the Star Trek: Enterprise episodes "Storm Front", parts I and II, a species called the Na'kuhl time-travels to World War II and helps the Nazis conquer America. In the movie Iron Sky (2012) Nazis escaped the fall of Germany in 1945, travelled to the Moon's dark side and established a base. In 2018 they return to Earth to establish the Fourth Reich. You may not know all of this movie trivia but I can assure that the kind of guy who spends money of webcam site probably will.

The first-person shooter game Wolfenstein: The New Order (2014) stated that the Nazis had successfully landed on the moon after their victory in World War II, and they built a base on it. The protagonist B.J. Blazkowicz infiltrates the Nazi lunar base in order to steal a nuclear weapon activation code for the resistance.

There are many more examples of Japanese anime and manga about fighting Nazis, that can be utilised as a form of cosplay. A phenomenon called "Nazi chic" is rampant in Asia. People over there wear Hitler shirts like folks in the West wear Che Guevara shirts. This is because teachings of the Holocaust are not as prevalent amongst the curriculum in Asian schools. There is a coffee shop in Indonesia called Soldatenkaffee, where all the waiters are dressed in SS uniforms. A touch of xenophobia with your daily latte and doughnut, served by a dude dressed as Himmler.

In the anime AKB0048, idols fight the space Nazis who terrorize the galaxy with an entertainment ban. Hellsing Ultimate is the anime equivalent to Indiana Jones, the best known fictional Nazi fighter. The Hellsing Organization's battles against the Millenium's Nazi vampire cyborgs and assorted crazy enemies. Adolf Hitler himself appears as a minor villain in the 12th Dragon Ball Z movie, rising from Hell with an army, before being swiftly defeated by Gotenks. This is after the former Japanese prime Minister allies himself with the pope, while George Bushes Senior and Junior and Putin take out Bishie Sparkle Super Saiya- I mean Super Aryan Hitler on his Nazi moon base by playing Go. The Black Lagoon crew fights off a more realistic group of modern neo-Nazis in one of the anime early story arcs. Johan, the main villain in Monster, was bred in a eugenics program, taken in by a Neo-Nazi group as a child and trained to become a supersoldier. Mazinger Z features giant super-robots fighting a decapitated Nazi. Lupin has fought Nazis many times throughout his franchise's long history, from the 1977 episode "To Be or Nazi Be" to the 1995 special The Pursuit of Harimao's Treasure to even fighting a Nazi version of himself in the 2008 Red Vs. Green OVA.

If you still need convincing that Nazi inspired cosplay could be a big earner, take a look at the softcore Nazi anime porn card game called Barbarossa which debuted on Kickstarter in 2014. The game is "set in a fictional Second World War setting in which cute German military girls rush against Moscow to defeat the evil magician Stalin." Basically, it is a re-imagining of World War II, as if everyone involved was an absurdly sexualized anime girl. Barbarossa achieved its funding goal of $10,000 within three hours of being posted. Not even children's cancer research can match that pace. The highest allowable donation level of $200 was totally maxxed out. Barbarossa literally received so many $200 donations that the creators had to tell people to stop. Barbarossa was actually released in Japan a few years ago, but is now out of print. The Kickstarter campaign was to merely translate the game into English and bring it to the States. Personally, any world where Hitler and his cronies are being reduced from genocidal maniacs to schoolgirl anime spank-wank is OK with me. To be fair, there are far more shameful masturbatory aids out there. A Nazi anime card game is pretty high on the list, but as something of an Internet porn frontiersman I can assure you there are far, far darker corners of the imagination that contain unfathomably disturbing, terrible things. Especially when the average CEO is wallowing in prostitutes on overseas business trips.

Do not let free chat guests wind a model up so much that she starts to yell or show anger. Imagine walking into a department store and finding the sales clerk yelling at another customer, telling them to get the hell out and that they suck. Models only get one chance to make a first impression. The VIP customer with $300 in his account who left the room after seeing a model's bad side may never return to see how sexy and sweet she usually is. Never let customers see a model angry unless they specifically ask for it in a show. Anger is actually a fetish for a lot of guys and they may try to get models angry just to get a free domination show.

If guys are consistently rude, have a model put on sweetest smile and say, I'm sorry you're having a bad day, but it's all about fun in my chat room so I'm going to have to ban you now. Then they should immediately say hello to someone else, to show that they have moved on. Why bother to say something nice? Because it wows the guys who are in the free room. They saw what the jerk wrote and they are probably used to seeing girls lose their cool in that situation.

Responding in such a way makes a model stand out and it impresses them. Some camgirls will ban members for not tipping. MFC has large numbers of girls (especially Romanians) who will write something like "too shy for tip?" and then simply ban the user a few minutes later. This only discourages users from ever coming back again and tipping, and is pointless because even banned user can return immediately as a guest. This is idiotic and disrespectful. After all this is a platform that relies on tips. A waiter would not throw people out for not tipping them at a restaurant. Buskers do not insult a crowd that is not tipping. If someone is disrupting a room and not tipping, then that is a different matter altogether

Some companies give members the title of VIP if they spend a certain amount of money on the site. Encourage models to keep their own system of determining which customers are VIPs. If a customer stays in a model's room for longer than 20-30 minutes at a time, he should probably be considered a VIP. The trick is then to find out his name and remember what his kinks and turn-ons are. He should be made to feel special being greeted by being greeted by name the next time he is in the room. This will keep him coming back. Keep a pad and pencil near all work areas. As soon as the show ends, a model should write his member name down with short notes on what he likes. On some sites this can be inputted directly into the system and accessed with the click of a button whenever the customer returns to a room. Streamate gives models a note option, but if the member is on a different platform the model can not access their notes.

Model Retention

The reality is that most girls do not work for at studios for long. Some move on to use Skype/Messenger for shows and are paid via PayPal or Western Union. More and more indie cam sites are opening up, offering niche-specific content, and many models are moving away from big box sites to smaller sites where it is easier to be a big fish in a smaller pond, and can really narrow down to a specific niche that they want to work within. The smart ones will eventually figure out a way to open their own accounts and therefore it is up to you as the studio owner to ensure that your models are happy and want to stick around. It is for this reason that more and more studios are beginning to realise that they need to offer more than just monetary benefits for their models. Top models are able to earn bonus cash for being the highest earners on the site, but especially in the case of big box sites, if these models are making enough to be in the top ten percent an extra $500 at the end of the month is basically a drop in the bucket. We are now starting to see both networks and studios treating their models like valued employees. New trends include offering stipends for healthcare, or 401K programs for models who make above a certain amount every month. There is plenty of money to go around, and if you want your studio to be successful, then the best way to achieve this goal is to make sure that your performers feel valued and well rewarded. There are many innovative ways to make sure that you keep the models that you have spent so much effort recruiting. Many of these are solely financial reward systems allowing models to earn more. These include video contests, earning-based prizes as incentives for the model, increased commission, and referral percentages for signing up new hosts and new members.

Many of the studios in Las Vegas are owned by Streamate or other larger companies. Their largest studio is Sin City Studio run by Sage Montana and in the face of such serious competition, the independent studios are most definitely having to up their game. Sin City Vixens for example is not a Streamate studio, although Streamate is certainly their preferred platform. Not only are all of their computers hard-lined rather than the cheaper Wi-Fi option, but the studio provides everything an imaginative cam girl could ever need. This includes bedding, lingerie, clothing, shoes, make-up, wigs, toys, toy cleaners, condoms, baby wipes, lube and pretty much every prop that could possibly be requested for a show. If they do not have it, they figure out how to make it on the spot. They even have a shower that models can use for both shower shows and for personal use. If they make their weekly goal, they get an extra ten percent bonus. The owner runs regular studio contests for a cash bonus that they receive the same week, instead of having to wait for the following week for the money. When all the Pokemon GO madness started, competitions for PokeCoins were a huge hit.

The real success of camming has been its ability to move beyond the borders of Internet sex chat rooms and into the everyday social lives of camming's customers, or fans as they are known in the trade. Many fans communicate with cam models via text, Twitter, Instagram, Snapchat or Kik on a daily basis, often multiple times a day. Cam models are even on Periscope and Meerkat, performing live shows for their followers or simply checking in to say hello. Maintaining this kind of personal connection can be extremely time consuming. They are getting Twitter messages all day long, literally constant interaction, twenty four hours a day. In the morning, they are talking to East Coast U.S. people; as the hours progress, the career models are chatting all day, Instagramming, direct messaging, and it never stops. Any successful model will tell you, that this is a real money maker, but they will also they will also tell you they never stop working. It just does not stop. The most successful models make their fans really feel like they are actively involved in their day-to-day lives. The very best are able to give the illusion that every fan is their on-line boyfriend.

Consider offering some sort of support for performers who are facing a crisis because of the work they do as cam performers, whether it is because a fan is harassing them, their family members are unsupportive of their work, or their home cam set-up is threatened by discrimination from a landlord. There is more to supporting performers than just maximizing cash flow.

There will always be cases of model burn out. The endless traffic of faceless males became monotonous. After a while men checking models out no longer feels like a confidence boost for them and their vanity is destroyed from seeing themselves day after day on the screen. At this point, you will need to recognise that the model should be replaced, although sometimes a touch of variety can create a temporary cure.

Creating an employee suggestion scheme can be extremely successful in a cam studio environment. Generally speaking, good-looking girls are typically treated like air-heads and bimbos. Anybody that is used to dealing with such girls knows that they respond very well to anybody who treats them as an intellectual rather than a focusing simply on the physical attributes, as most guys tend to. According to HR Magazine, 6 in 10 employees said they would already be coming up with more creative suggestions if they were rewarded for them. You will find that this number rises even higher with girls that want to get past the common perception that they are little more than porcelain vases, beautiful to look at but with nothing inside. Employees are always an extremely valuable tool in idea generation, as they often see possible improvements from the front line that managers perhaps cannot. Involving employees in improving company processes is an excellent way to make them feel engaged and loyal. They will want your studio to do well, and will feel that they are contributing to its success. One problem that faces suggestion schemes in traditional industry is that they have to get factory workers, who were not regular PC users, to use computers. This will not be an issue for camgirls who are quite used to spending all day in front of a computer.

Staff in all industries can be cynical about engagement programmes, hardly a surprise when the mindset of employers, has, for years or even generations, has been "keep your mouths shut, lay low and just follow orders." Good suggestion schemes can produce high levels of employee participation and real commercial results. Toyota for example, is famous for its successfully implemented staff suggestion schemes which have improved product quality, reduced costs, and enhanced employee morale. The company receives more than two million suggestions a year from their 300,000 workers and the large majority of ideas are implemented. Sometimes even the smallest ideas make a significant difference. In

2011, British Airways launched a Staff Suggestion Scheme, hoping that the creativity of its staff could help. Right from the off, suggestions and ideas flooded into the suggestion scheme and by January 2012, overall savings resulting from the scheme totalled over £20 million, equivalent to the fuel cost of 550 flights from London to New York. Thanks to just one suggestion alone, British Airways is saving £600,000 a year in fuel costs simply by descaling the toilet pipes on planes, thus making them lighter. Other clever suggestions included replacing glass wine bottles with plastic bottles, washing/cleaning the engines more regularly, switching to lighter catering trolleys and cargo containers and the introduction of lighter cutlery. Sainsbury's operates a Tell Justin ideas scheme, which has been running since 2004 and has so far generated around 57,000 ideas. An Energy company in the UK received a suggestion from an employee that all the printers should be set to print double sided not single sided. The idea was implemented and saved $400,000 in the first year. A telecoms company received a suggestion that it should auction off its old and redundant stock to staff. It did this with an internal auction that raised $100,000 but it led to savings in storage and insurance costs of over $1 million in the next three years.

To fully harness the power of your in-house creative ideas, you must develop a culture that actively solicits input from every level of your staff. Markets today demand greater innovation. Changes are coming faster than ever before. Your competitors are ever more nimble. Customers have rising expectations. You need new ideas, better processes, more innovative products and services, and more effective ways to build strong futures with those customers. Employee suggestion schemes can be a powerful engine for new product growth, for cost savings and for improvements in all areas of the company. Often, what drives the success of suggestion schemes is quite simple. Staff who are distributed around the business and interacting directly with customers can often see things that managers can not. Your staff can see all sorts of ways that things could be made better for the customer and the company. They have plenty of ideas for process improvements, product enhancements and thrifty savings. So why not put all that creativity to work? Listening to your employees and encouraging them to submit useful ideas will help your company thrive.

The most common business benefits include the following:
Improve staff morale
Increase job satisfaction
Create a feeling of ownership and engagement
Build team spirit
Reduce costs and increase profitability
Increase revenue
Improve customer satisfaction

Here are some tips on how to ensure your scheme will be a glittering success. An internal promotion plan is essential to your scheme's success. Staff suggestion schemes are bound to fail if you do not take the time to promote and drive them. Invest time in launching and promoting your suggestion scheme. Many schemes start with a fanfare of publicity, a burst of initial ideas and then they lose momentum and energy. The best way to overcome this problem is with a rolling set of campaigns throughout the year. One month you ask for ideas for recruiting staff. The next you ask for cost savings; the next for ways to delight customers and so on. Each campaign is supported with posters and messages emphasizing the importance of the request for ideas. The communication should be ongoing, and should make sure employees are aware of how the scheme works and how to make a suggestion. Give your suggestion scheme a name.

Develop a launch plan to create initial buzz and encourage staff to submit ideas. Create an ongoing training plan to ensure staff understand the type of ideas you are looking for. Consider how to maintain momentum and celebrate successes. Agree on how to respond to accepted and rejected ideas. Consider communication channels from emails to old-fashioned paper newsletters

Set up a cross-functional suggestion review team. The review of ideas is best done as an interdisciplinary effort. All key departments need to be represented to ensure ideas can be properly evaluated and implemented. Make sure each committee member understands the time commitment required to review and evaluate ideas. Make sure that your performers, your programmers, your PR and even your cleaning staff are represented. Try making an evaluator's position a reward in itself.

Bear in mind that if you under-resource the evaluation side of the process with too few evaluators, then people have to wait a long time for a response to their suggestion and this kills motivation. One successful company makes every line manager an initial idea evaluator and they have to respond to a new idea they receive within four working days. Long feedback cycles may demotivate staff, so ensure committee members can get together on a regular basis. Staff across disciplines will need to make time to participate in and contribute to the scheme. Another thing to watch out for is evaluator overload, you have to give time and recognition to those who assess the suggestions. A common mistake is to set up an idea committee which meets once a month and reviews all suggestions. They argue over a few ideas and never get through the backlog that simply sits in an in-tray for weeks. You need a much slicker approach with individual evaluators empowered to make fast decisions, especially on smaller value suggestions.

You need to show your commitment to the scheme by backing it with resources, both money and people. A nominal financial reward for all accepted ideas, not just the good ones, is imperative. Recognition and fast responses are better than big rewards and slow responses. The best schemes give a small award to any idea that gets initial approval whether it reaches final implementation or not. Give an award, prize or monetary incentive for best suggestions, and give it right away. Small rewards and recognition on acceptance are a better incentive than larger rewards delayed until implementation. Many suggestion schemes invoke a multi-step process for evaluation and eventual granting of an award. First, the suggestion boxes are emptied (sometimes only once a month). Second, a Committee sifts and sorts for "realistic" submissions. Third, a management committee appraises the freshness, viability, cost savings or increased revenue from each suggestion. Fourth, someone in "senior management" decides upon the amount of reward to be given to the appropriate staff members. And finally, an actual awarding of the "prize" is conducted.

Try this approach: Dedicate $1200 to the project. Give the money away in $100 increments every month for one year. Each month, give $50 to the best idea, $20 for the second best idea, and $10 each to the 3rd, 4th and 5th best suggestions. In the first months, few may believe that you will give out the money in a timely manner, and possibly only a handful of staff will participate. But no matter how small or meagre the suggestions, give out the money anyway. As soon as staff realize you are serious, the boxes will be filled with suggestions. Establish categories for regular awards. Categories can help staff focus and generate new ideas. Here are examples of categories that you can use: Ideas that can be implemented immediately, ideas for getting closer to our customers, suggestions for cost savings or increasing revenue, new ideas focusing on a chosen theme for the month, ideas that most dramatically challenge the current paradigm of our thinking, recommendations for the future direction of our business.

Make a big event out of awarding your suggestion scheme prizes. Some companies use lunches, staff teas or monthly meetings to award prizes. One company makes up large, special "dollar bills" for each winning suggestion. In the centre is the face of the staff member who contributed. In the corners is the amount of money his or her suggestion earned. And surrounding the portrait is a description of the suggestion itself. These "dollar bills" line the wall of the staff lounge and company cafeteria. The result is popular group recognition for winners and a "culture building" impact that keeps the suggestion scheme going strong.

At the end of the year, give recognition to the volume of suggestions received, the winners who have been rewarded, and the changes enacted as a result. Then, pose a challenge to everyone to double the volume of suggestions in the coming year. And, if the quality of ideas warrant, double your cash prizes, too. Four winners a month last year? Increase it to eight winners per month next year. Most of all, implement. Act upon what your staff suggests. Nothing demonstrates your commitment to this approach better than a staff suggestion recognized, rewarded and immediately put to work.

Respond to all written staff suggestions immediately (within one week) and in writing. Be candid. If the answer is no, say so. If the answer is yes, state when staff will see implementation. If the answer is maybe, explain the issues involved and give a date for further reply. And stick to it. Nothing builds trust and credibility faster than making new promises... and keeping them. Respond to suggestions publicly, for all to see. Usually, when one staff member writes, she states what is on the mind of many. Reply openly on a designated bulletin board, in a weekly printed update, or by electronic mail. Thank the writer(s) for their query or contribution. Include staff names on suggestions to be implemented. One exception: do not reply to obscene or abusive suggestions. A strong company culture has no place for such destructive "input". Your best response is not to reply.

Some suggestions do not work, but you should always respond, reply and explain why you have not taken them up on the idea. The key thing is you have to listen. The worst thing you can do is ask for suggestions, but not listen. That actively disengages people. Communicating the status of an idea to staff is key. It maintains momentum in the scheme and reassures staff that their idea has not disappeared into a black hole: What you are trying to do is encourage behaviours, so do not be afraid to say no to an idea. You are trying to encourage innovation, so it is important to say 'you have taken time out to provide this idea, here is the feedback, and here is a model of a good idea'.

Remember also that public recognition of ideas that have worked well can also go much further than a financial reward. It is pointless having an ideas scheme unless you celebrate success. It is important that the best ideas are implemented and their success broadcast across the company. People believe actions not words and they need to see ideas turning into real innovations. If the idea is implemented, ensure this positive news is communicated across the company, this will ultimately encourage staff to make further suggestions. Staff see another person receiving recognition for an idea and want to emulate that. Create a buzz. Celebrate your successes. Be passionate and believe in your suggestion scheme because your enthusiasm is contagious.

Any suggestion scheme will require guidelines to ensure its success. The focus must be on quality over quantity, you do not want to end up with hundreds of suggestions which are all completely infeasible. If you do not have clear goals and just ask for ideas you will get a lot of 'Would it not be nice to have a summer picnic' type suggestions. Tell staff their idea has to be authentic, measurable and that there has to be a reason for its implementation. You have to clearly articulate would a good idea looks like e.g. it will increase customer satisfaction, reduce process times or save costs. Be specific about what you want and people will respond. Set guidelines around specific aspects of the company where suggestions will be welcome; cost saving ideas and process improvements for example. This will help ensure that the suggestions received are sensible and well thought out.

Which ideas are useful? And how much information is required for each idea submission? A staff suggestion scheme can easily end up as a channel for employees to vent their frustrations or suggest merely self-serving benefits. To prevent this from happening, ideas need to be backed up with solid information such as:
What prompted the suggestion?
How will the suggestion benefit the company?
How will the suggestion benefit the employees?

However, avoid making your suggestion form too complicated, as this will dramatically reduce the quantity of suggestions. It is better to err on the side of keeping the form as simple as possible. Asking for too many details such as a brief implementation plan and the associated costs will only discourage employees who are not so strong on financials. If a young girl with little formal education has to try to assess the costs of developing some new product idea she has, she might be worried about embarrassing herself by being way off with her cost estimate and just keep the idea to herself.
There are many great software packages to help with idea collection and evaluation. Many systems allow both staff and management to track and update the status of an idea. There are also self-help groups around the world where you can get help and advice from companies large and small, public and private, who are running suggestions scheme. Try IdeasWorldWide.Net

Large companies like Siemens and Sainsbury's manage their schemes on-line and track how many staff participate, although staff can still submit suggestions via postcards or paper forms from the shop floor. This is a time honoured process of wooden boxes and pre-printed forms, for staff to write out their ideas and submit them for management consideration. Even so, an increasing number of organisations in the both private and public sectors are finding that they can drive innovation and reduce cost by moving their suggestion box from the office wall to the intranet. This can help streamline submission, evaluation, and implementation of ideas. It can also support your internal promotion plan and keep employees (who have submitted ideas) updated on the process. Staff suggestion software ranges from free, simple software suitable for small organizations to feature-packed software for large enterprises. Vetter for example helps you evaluate and generate more ideas. It enables managers to track participation, which means it is possible to demonstrate tangible evidence of how involved staff are with the business, proving the scheme goes beyond a mere show of being interested in what staff think. There is a growing trend is for greater collaboration on suggestions. This may be a system where staff put in ideas, and other staff can vote, comment or expand on them. Staff can log in and submit suggestions, which are then given star ratings by their peers. If the suggestion averages two stars or more, it means it has been vetted (hence the name) and is passed on to a manager. The initial submission is anonymous, so staff can be unbiased about the idea, and the suggester is credited once the idea has been approved.

Another interesting possibility is to publish league tables of ideas implemented by department with awards for the most successful departments. Not only will managers be incentivised to accept and implement ideas but you will find that your models will be highly motivated to come up with more and better ideas that their egg-head techie counterparts.

Marketing and Branding

The current trend is for new cam models to do a little bit of everything: affiliate, content producer, social media expert, webmaster. The model who spends time and energy on developing her on-line (when live on cam) and off-line portfolio, and knowledge about the internet and adult business in general, will make the most money. Every independent model knows how much "off cam work" is needed in terms of social media, personal site, etc. Just getting naked and shaking her ass simply does not cut it anymore.

It is therefore more and more common for a studio to have dedicated PR staff that are in charge of all the social media for a set number of models, and this really underscores the value of studio partnerships. PR staff will need to pester models for content, from videos to photos to blog posts, so that they can make her look good outside the cam. These people work so hard in the background that Raquelle Diva, winner of last year's LaLExpo 'Social Media Star' award, openly admitted that she did not even know what her Facebook page contained.

There is no such thing as too much social media. In fact, a cam model needs to promote herself on as many platforms as possible. It is sometimes difficult to keep up with them all, but a studio PR can help out with routine tasks such as daily postings on sites like Twitter, Instagram, Tumblr, Facebook, Snapchat and all other available social media outlets. Cam sites do provide traffic, but they are not solely responsible for getting people into a model's room. The best and most successful performers in the cam world, are those who have invested time in creating their own unique image and persona that they can sell to clients. Preparing chat systems and profiles for sharing social media is paramount. Denying the access and exchange of this information is putting a stranglehold on both models and clients who are living in other times. To not do it is to be stuck in the past, and sooner or later, these models will perish. These additional projects are not always about doubling down on income. In some cases, they might result in significantly less income than actual camming but they do help build awareness in the long term. This is why an in house PR is such an invaluable resource. Managing thousands of potential fans, and creating endless content is a full time job in itself and needs to be treated as such.

Models are now focusing more on their own branding and persona beyond just being sexy and enjoying private shows. More and more models are self-branding, and developing brand recognition among their fans. This in itself is going to have a huge effect on how users will consume the cam product. The webcamming business is becoming more and more brand-oriented, and that those types of companies will see the most success. Cam models need to continually cross promote themselves through multiple avenues, in order to maintain their competitive edge.

Not all sites promote all categories equally. Sometimes a large amount of advertisement is given to transsexuals and girls alone, so couples are not promoted very much. There is also a lack of watermarking provided on the video feed by some sites, while Flash-based cam sites often crash or cause issues if both parties' software is not up to date. Many sites are still relying on Adobe Flash to provide video, and that does not mix well with mobile traffic. Models know this and are very displeased with the level that these sites run on, 35 percent payouts with decreased traffic and constant issues are a very hard sell these days. Also, model placement on these sites is extremely ambiguous and it is most certainly not based on money earned or self promotion.

An ambitious model begins her promotional activities as soon as she wakes up. This might initially be signing into Google Hangouts, where she says good morning to her followers. Then, she sends snaps to her fan club members as she is getting ready to shower, and then maybe again when she is in the shower. Some models juggle so many different platforms that they have to set alarms on their phones to remind them to Tweet, snap, stream, or chat. This is why in studio promotion can be so valuable. With Snapchat, Kik, Facebook's WhatsApp, Viber, and Microsoft's Skype there are plenty of apps to choose from. Smart girls will even develop a presence on up-and-coming platforms such as Vine and Wechat. Most charge each client a monthly subscription fee to chat with her through the apps: $10 for Kik, $15 for Snapchat, and $20 for both, for example. (A spokesman for Kik said the messaging app bans the selling of photos and videos. Charging people money to chat is also prohibited.) Sometimes men ask for specific photos or videos. A set of ten pictures can sell for anywhere from $5 to $50 (in addition to the monthly fee).

Keep your eyes open for new platforms that can be monetised by your models. For example Amazon recently announced Chime, its new Skype competitor. Even though they seem to have overlooked Linux in their list of compatible OS's, it is well worth a look to see if it can improve existing apps, such as GoToMeeting, JoinMe etc. No Linux or Java option, in the day of Raspberry Pi's everywhere and an increase of Linux powered devices, including those from Amazon, the fact that they did not bother with a Linux version was certainly a mistake. Still, it certainly cannot be any worse than GTM, where every version remains fully intact on your machine until you find and manually delete it. And they have a release schedule that makes Chrome look good.

As an alternative WebRTC is a free, open project that provides browsers and mobile applications with Real-Time Communications (RTC) capabilities via simple APIs. You can even host it yourself, internally, inside of your firewall if you are that security paranoid. There are also solutions hosted by other people if you do not want to deal with that: Appear.in, Opentokrtc.com, Talky.io and jitsi.org, although screen sharing is still quite buggy on the last one.

At the time of writing it looks like Chima costs $15 per user per month for any plan that allows calls with more than two participants. For comparison, I believe Google Suite is $5 per user, and includes email, calendar and an office suite apart from the conferencing software. Or if you want just video calls, I think hangouts is free for up to five participants. Hangouts and Skype are not anywhere near perfect, but most of the time they are good enough.

If you want killer features for a conference calling app consider investigating Webex which allows you to

1 - Highlight on your screen all the people who are currently talking.

2 - Automatic transcription of calls with the individuals talking labelled.

3 - Ability to pass along a 'talking now' and 'request talking' tokens so that someone can "raise their hand" while someone else is talking. Also the ability to cede the talking now token to one of the other people talking (for when a lot of people are on a conference call)

There is also a very worthwhile free alternative in Ring.cx. This is a video chat app that puts user privacy and freedom as a priority. By design, there is no big brother, no middleman, no trust problem. Ring leverages the same architecture as bit-torrent (DHT), a decentralized network to connect peers. From there, all communication is encrypted peer-to-peer. Best of all, it is free software, backed up by the Free Software Foundation: https://ring.cx/ [ring.cx].

Did you know that social media accounts for less than 2% of all Charturbate traffic, while over 21% is from referrals? Social media is important to maintain the regulars, but the real money is made by getting to that top line of the page sorted by viewers (on Charturbate) or cam-score (Myfreecams). Do you know which types of ads convert the best or which sites are best to advertise on? Or, where to go to get internet traffic and legitimate advertising that will not cost a mint? Or, how to get specifically scheduled advertising? Or, how to advertise specifically within a certain niche to optimize conversions/cost? Or, how to advertise to the best region of the world depending on which hours you are camming (First world countries so you actually get tokens)? For example, a new model might cam at odd hours to avoid getting buried on page four....but, if she sets advertising for UK/Germany/France at their peak internet time then she gets the best of both worlds by being ranked higher more easily while getting customers who actually pay. Google and bit.ly make it really easy to track internet traffic...but, it is what you do with that data that makes a difference, and each model is different. Continue to receive reports on what is working and what is not in terms of $/min. Do you know how to combine all of these methods with the affiliate programs so that you make extra money from customers who go to your page through the advertisements, whether they buy tokens to pay you or another model? That is income you would get without even doing anything. Do you know how to drive traffic to video/gallery sales too, such as those on Manyvids?

Those models who you see raking in a ton of money month to month are doing so by being good performers and having studio promotion and support. The best way to approach this is to find a web marketing specialist that can help you out. Sometimes they will advertise on related sites, otherwise you will need to seek them out for yourself. I personally like Fiverr.com for smaller individual tasks, but you might also be able to find a camgirl promotion specialist that you can add to your team. Reddit occasionally has ads for this kind of specialist but my best choice would be a private torrent tracker called Thevault.bz. Difficult to access but well worth the effort. Look for a split where the studio gets to keep 80%, with a 5% referral bonus.

By providing good quality content (e.g. sample photos, and videos) to affiliate/internet marketers, a studio owner can quickly double their revenue. The biggest challenge promoting webcams is how little model content is out there. With extra content a marketer can send a huge amount of guys to the webcam company's website where the customers would be looking specifically for this cam studio's models by name, not just any model that tickles their fancy. The beauty of a cam studio marketing their own girls is that not only do they get the webcam studio portion of the sale when a guy finds them on the cam site, they also get the affiliate portion of the sale, as well. For example, at

Webcams.com a model studio gets 37% of every dollar a customer spends watching their cam shows. If the customer was referred to the website by an affiliate, the affiliate gets 25%. This means that if the studio is also the affiliate that referred the customer, they receive 62% of all the money the customer spends with the girl. Plus since the studio is the affiliate they still get 25% of what the customer spends on other girls on the website.

In terms of model promotion, you need to treat the model herself as a brand and get creative. Connect with other models and cross promote. The future is creating a site that is a one stop shop for her fans. This can include Skype shows, clips, phone sex, Snapchat subscriptions, tangible items, and more. Once a model has her own site, I would highly recommend installing a suite of analytics tools to gather qualitative data such as heatmaps, funnel tracking, user polls, surveys etc. As a marketer, you focus a lot of time making sure your users are engaging with your content. Anything from opting in for an offer, to purchasing something, to leaving a comment on a blog. Sometimes it is tough to know exactly what actions your visitors are taking on your site. This kind of technology is not new e.g. UserTesting.com for finding participants for research, Clicktale for mouse and click tracking, Crazyegg or Abtoanalytics for heatmaps, Qualaroo for surveys and so on. I personally like HotJar because everything is now all in one place. The script is as easy to install as Google Analytics and it automatically categorizes heatmaps into desktop, tablet and mobile users. As you click through each one of those, the preview adjusts so you can see exactly what those device types are seeing. Mobile traffic is consistently increasing, so sites with responsive layouts that leverage HTML 5 will be those that reap the most rewards. It lets you record the entire visit. So you can literally watch a movie of how your visitor is moving through your site. The screen recordings alone makes it worth the cost. And I imagine models would love to be able to find out from someone if people are looking at their top row of videos, or scrolling down to other rows, or which video pages have the highest abandonment rates, etc. By seeing your visitor's clicks, taps and mouse movements you can identify usability issues on the fly and issues they encounter. Funnel Tracking means that you can track your sales funnels and see step by step what the drop-off is. Great for finding those leaky points. Find the biggest opportunities for improvement and testing by identifying on which page and at which step most visitors are leaving your site. These tools offer great insight into page interaction, highlight content that could be distracting or confusing visitors, and show the effectiveness of call to actions.

One trend in cams is that models tend to have more real relations with their customers, and they are playing an increasingly important role in the business of camming. Think also about real world promotions as well as those that take place in the digital environment. Consider organising an event where your girls talk shop other camgirls. To anyone else, just talking about dildos and masturbation can be awkward and even intimidating. This will give your models chance to get a lot off their chests and make some useful contacts for future cross promotion. If you do not want to host such an event yourself, you could always organise a field trip and send your models to a webcam convention.

I would also recommend that you consider adding an option for premiums to attend a party event at the studio. The guys on camsites are not creepy Craigslist killers, who will rape and murder any girl they meet the party. Obviously that is ridiculous, and they are a very successful (and safe) way for the girls to meet their fans. Most guys will in fact be extremely intimidated when they are around so many girls at once, and will probably have nightmares about ending up in some situation where the girls make them their bitch in front of everyone. There again, this might also be their ultimate fantasy. This is one way that Hugh Hefner was able to popularise the Playboy brand before he descended into drug addled senility and began sabotaging his own creation from within. The magazine might be staring into the abyss but the Playboy Mansion is still a very valuable piece of PR equity and can just as easily be applied to a web cam studio. And if you do not want to host it in the studio for security reasons, then this is the perfect excuse to hire a yacht and throw that sexy model bash that every red-blooded male has been fantasising about since he was a teenager. Unfortunately, in some locations, meeting customers who viewed performances is a recipe for disaster, given the allegations that could be made by law enforcement (investigating a solicitation charge) that the webcam performance was a demonstration of the type of activity that could occur on a date, particularly if any element of commercial activity is involved in the real-world meeting. Use your common sense based on the culture of your geographical location. Sex related events can quickly get out of hand. Last year's Guangzhou Sex Festival had to be cancelled because the underwear show almost caused a riot. If your location is similarly puritanical, then maybe it is a good time to think about moving.

You will also need to ask yourself whether you are you willing to go on camera as well as be the mastermind behind the scenes. While it is great to have a control panel where can see all of the outgoing video streams, sometimes you will also need to take on the role of stunt cock. Research has shown the male subconscious wants to see a cock and a girl, not the other way around. Often times these sessions can be taped and used as for promos of the girls. A web cam performer known as SophieX recently retold the following story that might give you some inspiration.

"One day, I was at home working when all of a sudden my internet unexpectedly dropped. I was in the middle of a show, and by this point, I lived a half-turned-on/half brain-dead existence. A young and attractive cable/internet boy arrived at my door. He was in one room of my apartment fixing the router, and I was in the trying to log into the wireless. Once I was able to, I told my viewers that there was a hot internet guy in the other room and hit the "Gold Show" button. A Gold Show occurs when you list something (anything) that you are willing to do for a certain amount of money. You then get bidders willing to pay up to see it. I titled the show Should I Seduce The Cable Guy? and set the amount for $500 bucks. Almost instantly, I got a bidder for $600.
The Gold Show started and the Internet boy came in to my room to tell me he was finished. My heart was racing with so much extreme adrenaline I could have orgasmed right there. I told him, "You know, I actually do webcam and would love to fuck around with you while streaming, would you be down?" He stared at me, then crept over to me like some kind of slow-motion porn. I began to blow him, then he fingered me until I came, and I collected my $600."

It is quite easy to roleplay this scenario as most guys are familiar with the scenario as a regular staple of traditional porn. You can take on any number of roles from pizza delivery to an engineer who has come to fix the air conditioning. Make sure to keep a record of which girls you perform with or the more perceptive viewers will soon catch onto your deceit. This is a great way to give a girl a thousand dollar boost every week or so.

In addition to not allowing men in the same room, MFC actually does have a rule against cam "operators" (people typing for the model), but clearly enforcement is sporadic at best. I have gotten messages in first person ("what can I do for you?" "want a private with me?") from a model when both her hands are clearly ... ahem ... busy ... which is really unsettling. I would also add that reporting it to MFC will almost certainly just result in her account being warned or closed, so that is something to keep in mind. Even if there is not an operator, I know that the bosses at some studios have access to PMs and public chat, though how much monitoring happens surely varies by the individual studio or boss. I suspect that most of what gets said is really just noise to them. Reading what happens in chat, often on multiple sites, must become pretty tedious and boring.

Offline Profits

Members crave more and more material from models, and this is having an effect on how models are using non-adult apps such as Snapchat and Periscope, etc. to maintain engagement with members. In the future, we will see more companies creating tools that are able to capitalize on the model being able to engage members while not on camera.

For many reasons, cam models are not making the same amount of money they used to make a few years ago, so everybody is trying to monetize other resources, such as their social media traffic, building personal sites using tools such as ModelCentro or selling content on platforms such Clips4Sale. Others sell subscriptions to their Kik or Snapchat and they sell content through their own clip stores in a variety of locations. These days, the more revenue streams the more money a model can make, but is also another means of promoting herself. Once a model starts a clips store, she will soon notice her traffic, and overall earnings, increased on cam thanks to this upselling and cross selling.

While webcam shows pay well, they are not the only part of a cam model's potential revenue stream. Supplementary cammer content refers to content that customers can purchase when a model is not on-line, such as fan club memberships, video on demand clips, and store items that models upload and sell. This is important when a customer comes to see a specific model who is not on-line at the time, and it gives them another purchase option. Models have fan clubs which members can join for a rate that the model sets from $10 to $50 per month. Within each fan club, models can upload photo sets, videos, activate archived cam shows, update their diaries, or upload store items, that can be anything from their Snapchat subscription to custom content.

The fetish for used underwear (and bras, stockings, socks, and even items like soiled tampons) is becoming increasingly popular in the sex world. Sites like usedpantyportal.com, pantydeal.com, pantybid.com, usedpanty.com, LaceInYourFace.com and wornpanty.com are just a small sample, and include pictures, membership profiles for both buyers and the ladies whose panties are for sale, guides for success, forums, advice, and in some cases, videos to entice men into purchasing their (under)wares. Many of these sites serve as a kind of 'Lacebook' social network for panty fetishists

There has always been a market for women's used underwear, and the Internet makes it so easy to sell anonymously. Though it may seem weird to many people, there are plenty of men who will pay good money for panties, bras, hosiery, and lingerie items that have been worn by women. For the women who supply their used panties, selling underwear can be extremely profitable. It is perfectly safe and completely legal to make money selling used panties. As with camming, the only barrier to earning money is the models personal comfort level. For some, this just brings the sleaze-o-meter up to over 100, but everybody has their own tastes. Most models obtain a P.O. Box and a PayPal account, so that their personal info is completely hidden from buyers. Models employed by studios often have the PR staff help them set up their own website for full control, while independent cam girls would have to fork out for a freelance web designer to do that same. Others sell through one of the many third party fetish website. To be successful, it takes more than a quickly dashed off Craigslist post or a salacious eBanned picture. Establishing and maintaining relationships with patrons is an integral part of the sellers' success. Most patrons need to have a personal connection with panty sellers in order for them to want to buy their panties. Having a personal site really helps in this area. The demand for panties from honest, caring, attentive, alluring, creative women who are not focused solely on money is especially high. Most buyers want a personal connection to the person selling the stockings or panties. Knowing that the garments are used is enough for your average fetishist. The most successful sellers put a lot of work into crafting an on-line persona and usually offer other services like domme-ing or phone sex with it.

Pantysniffing as a fetish varies from person to person, but generally involves eroticizing a person's stained garments, and can include urine stains, vaginal fluid or mucus stains, menstrual blood stains, and even faeces stains. Many panty fetishists find the odour of the stains arousing, and having a visual aid makes the fantasy that much more realistic. As one fan relates, "The most erotic thing about used panties is the connection with the seller--having something she purposely wore just for me and masturbated in just for me, so I can have that intimate part of her. The smell is a very strong part of it, but for me the smell of her vagina is the best--I do not get off on pee or bum or anything else." Some panty sniffers like their panties to be as full as possible of what is known in the trade as 'grool' (girl drool also known as vaginal secretions) but there will inevitably be requests for scat, pee and even menstrual blood. There are fewer people into menstrual blood, but there are still requests for blood-soaked/stained panties. A vacuum sealer is must-have item for any seller to preserve maximum, uh, freshness when packaging. Try starting with an ad on Craigslist's miscellaneous romance and describe the scent as intoxicating, sweet and musky at the same time. As a rule, the more discharge and skanky ass stench embedded in the aforementioned garments the better. Panty perverts love big soft girl undies as they make for a smoother ride when being used.

When listing used underwear for sale, photos of the model wearing the underwear should always be included. This only need to be a below the waist shot. Photos will really help sell used panties more quickly. Have the model wear a matching shirt or bra and take a photo below the neck, or from behind. Any candid, inconspicuous, cotton-crotch panty shot will work but facedown/ass-up is always a great selling strategy. As long as the pictures are in focus and sexy, the perverts will come flocking.

Customers vary in their tastes; some men like lace or silk panties that have been worn during the day; some men like cotton underwear that has been worn while exercising. There is also a market for stockings, bras, or other pieces of lingerie. Men like lace panties for their look, and cotton panties for their scent. Cotton absorbs odours better than lace or silk, and most men who buy used panties really want the scent. Otherwise, they would just buy new panties at the store. Try to find underwear that has cotton in the crotch. Cotton underwear is cheap. To save money on silk panties, some models buy them at thrift stores. Others buy cheap cotton panties in bulk. After it has been worn for 24 hours, it is immediately sealed in a ziplock bag and stored in a cool dry place so that the smell is retained. The main expenses are underwear, plastic bags, and shipping supplies, all of which should cost less than $60 per month. Panties can then be sold for anywhere between $15 and $40 a pair, depending on how much the underwear costs, and how much demand there is in a particular month. Be warned that setting the price too cheap makes some buyers think they are getting lower quality.

Lots of men will request that photos be sent with the panties and this is something that can be charged extra for. Some men also like ripped underwear or used panties with stains. Buying worn underwear is not really that unusual. Most men seem to keep their fetish a secret from their partners, being convinced that they are 'sickos' or 'perverts,' and that their wives would leave them if they found out about their 'dirty little secret.' Society profiles these men as creepy and odd, the scum of society, but clientele in these niches are usually quite "normal." This lack of acceptance of such fetishes has a lot to do with the level of tolerance in society. In some ways it is extremely hypocritical that teenage boys are allowed to play hyper-violent, gore filled video games, while an older gentlemen who has developed a nose for natural female pheromones is immediately branded a weirdo. Fortunately, such values do change over time. Thanks to 'Fifty Shades' few people even raise an eyelid and a bit of light bondage or S&M. Music videos made leather and latex little more than an erotic fashion statement. Whatever the general consensus is, after you have worked enough demoralizing McJobs, hawking your dirty panties for $80 a pop can seem almost dignified in comparison.

Kay, a 21-year-old female college student from Singapore sells her used panties to help pay her college expenses but rises above the competition by engaging in physical meet-ups with her customers. This is perhaps feasible in a crime free autocracy like Singapore but in other countries, meeting customers in the flesh is a good way to end up as exotic upholstery. The country that brought us tentacle porn and Hello Kitty is originally responsible for introducing the Western world to the buying and selling of used panties. Burusera shops, which are still around in Japan and translate to bloomer sellers, stock the undergarments of Catholic school girls (often with a photo of the girl wearing the item, for authenticity). Up until a few years ago, you could even purchase used panties in Japan from vending machines, as documented by many perplexed and fascinated tourists on YouTube. Vending machines selling used schoolgirl panties were declared illegal in 1993, yet many people still see them around, some of them being converted cigarette machines that have been modified to accept 10,000 yen notes (about $80). Officials later attempted to curb the burusera fetish trade--in 2004, Tokyo banned the selling of used underwear from girls under 18, but as always with prohibition, the ban did not exactly work as intended. Burusera shops went underground and the black market price for panties increased fivefold.

Used panties can cost anywhere from $10 to hundreds of dollars, depending on how long they have been worn, and whether they are accompanied by photos or videos of the seller. Customers want to be sure that they are getting the 'Real Thing' and not the mass production from some Chinese seafood processor, where 'Specialist Technicians', use spray guns loaded with fish oils and pulverized anchovies to coat rejects from the ladies' underwear factory located right next door. Generally speaking the American ones are usually also much bigger. Panty trust is a member-run non-profit advocacy and verification organization for the used panties and fetish industry. The Panty Trust has been around since 2001 and offers education, third party verification, and dispute resolution services among other things. This also further reiterates the importance of having a buyer/seller connection. The verification process is necessary to weed out the many people that tend to run a scam, making a pair of panties smell as it were worn by a woman, but were not. So they get verified via Panty Trust, which is a one time $50 membership fee at the time of writing. If the girl is truly Pantytrust verified, you will see the seal listed on the girls site or page. The site is run by volunteer panty sellers who will answer all your panty questions. Apart from dirty panties, used thongs and worn knickers, panty trust also lists lingerie of all kinds, foot fetish items such as used pantyhose, smelly socks and shoes etc. It also accepts digital goods including photos, videos, camshows, chats, Skype calls, phone sex, etc, findom goods and services like domination and humiliation, slaves and mistress tasks, sissy assignments, etc. and even fetish accessories such as used sex toys, make up, collars, etc. In-person encounters and any type of bodily fluid on the other hand are both prohibited.

It is relatively easy for a webcam model to make well in excess of $10,000 over the course of a year with things that they would normally just discard anyway. Whether it is the scent, the material, the taboo, or the trophy aspect that used garment buyers find so enticing, it appears the industry will not be slowing down any time soon.

Other panty sites include Extra Lunch Money, which operates a credit system. 100 credits equals 60 - 65 dollars. So be sure not to undersell your worn goods. Factor in shipping price as well when selling. SellYourPanties is a completely free platform allowing girls to create a Kitty Profile, open their own shop and sell their erotic home-made specialities to customers (Cats) from all over the world. When they register, Kitties have the choice to be verified or not. All the girls with the "Checked Kitty" label have proven they are real and over 18 (showing a copy of their ID card). MyusedPanty store charges $25 for the year and deducts fees from the same payment. Pantydeal requires a $19 monthly fee to read emails to get connected to buyers. With all the free options, a model should build her clientele first and ask around before joining a site that she has to pay to be a part of on a monthly basis.

Perhaps the easiest place to sell fetish items is on Reddit. /r/FetishItems for example is a public subreddit forum with around 7,000 subscribers that has been around for more than five years, and caters for sales of and requests for hardcore fetish item sales and services. Categories listed include the following: Ass, bdsm, blood, boobs, clothing, cuckold, cum, erotica, fart, feet, femdom, food, girlfriend experience (gfe), jerk off instruction (joi), hair, lactation, masturbation, mature, oral, pee, role play, scat, smoking, spanking, sweat, toys and voyeurism. Sales posts must include at least one photo or they will be deleted by the moderators and linked media can currently only be hosted on imgur.com, gfycat.com, vid.me, sendvid.com, or videobam.com. Sellers are allowed to link their websites or personal subreddits to the bottom of their ads. This does not include third party sites, such as cam sites or studio sites.

Related subreddits include r/FetishSelling

/r/Sexsells
/r/KIKSnaps
/r/CamShow
/r/porncreators
/r/GoneInsane
/r/DirtyPantiesGW
/r/FFSocks
/r/Sexting for vanilla Kik and Snapchat
/r/Kiksnapsales for vanilla Kik
/r/RedditAmateurVids for vanilla videos
/r/GFEsells for GFE services
/r/UsedPanties for vanilla panties
/r/Panties4Sale for vanilla panties
/r/pantysellingca (for Canadian vanilla panties)
/r/SkypeShows for vanilla cam shows
/r/camshows for vanilla cam shows
/r/SexSellsBBW for everything BBW
/r/SexclusiveSelling for all of the above
/r/KinkyAussies (for Australian services)

The most successful sellers are entirely self-employed, thanks to panty-selling or writing custom erotica. While panties (worn, farted on, period-stained, you name it) remain the most sought after novelties (/r/pantyselling has nearly 20,000 users subscribed), some sellers also offer other bespoke fetish items, too, like sweaty socks, peed-in jeans, used lactation bras and pussy pops (yes, vagina-glazed lollipops). I even spotted a few listings for pussy-dipped cigarettes and cigars, too.

Personalized videos and custom cam-shows are also popular, a more appealing alternative to traditional porn. As one seller explains, intimacy and attention are what buyers crave, not just the sex. Buyers can request certain thematic elements (feet, smoking, animal role-play etc) or buy premade one-on-one clips. Cock ratings (read: dick pic reviews) are also heavily requested, and sellers usually charge about $10 for their feedback on a sampling of photos.

These are hardly the sketchy dives you would imagine. /r/SexSells, for example, with its 9,000 subscribers is an intentionally sex-positive hub run by a husband-and-wife team, who carefully screen and verify their sellers in an effort to prevent scamming, blackmailing, and stalking. Some sellers have encountered death threats, blackmail and the release of their (and their sellers') personal information, which is known as doxxing. The threat of losing on-line anonymity is still possible, but mods do their best to protect buyers and sellers alike. While sex work is still largely criminalized, its sellers are relegated to the dark outposts of the digital universe, where unsavoury clients moderate the forums and self-employed workers walk on eggshells just to keep their business afloat. But in a place where anonymity can be maintained, models can stay safe in a volatile industry without putting themselves at the mercy of people who recognize them. Until the laws surrounding sex work change, communities like Sex Sells are the last bastion of defense against the Internet's faceless antagonists.

/r/Sex Sells, and the many subreddits like it, play an Etsy-like role in

Reddit's burgeoning sex-work community. Buyers can browse pages of ads from people you might call independent contractors, occasional cam girls who go the extra mile and sell the used clothing you might see in their videos, then let buyers call the shots on what they wear, and take off, in private videos. Scores of women post ads for used panties, custom videos whose scope is limited only by the buyer's budget and personalized sexts on the messaging apps like Snapchat and Kik. By setting price tags that range from $5 to hundreds, the ladies are raking it in. No matter what the item, locks of hair, period-stained clothes, there are copycat sellers in triplicate. Even so, in an environment that values fetishes and anything exotic, it should be easy to find a unique angle.

Models can sell some adult content on eBay but there are many restrictions, and accounts need to be approved before they can start selling. Here are some of the rules and guidelines on selling adult content and products on eBay, examples of what is and what is not allowed. Adult films in the amateur genre must be produced by a legitimate studio where all actors were compensated for their performance, which seems to be a direct contradiction in terms. Hidden camera videos and amateur videos containing adult sexual activity are not permitted. eBay does not permit clothing listings outside the Adult Only category which contain adult or sexually-oriented images or descriptions, including fetish or other adult themed items. Clothing listings that contain nudity are only permitted in the Adult Only category, as are pictures of models wearing clothing that include sexual aspects, such as details of the genitalia. All used clothing items must include a statement that the item has been properly cleaned which is a deal breaker for most fetishists. This includes, but it is not limited to, boxer shorts, panties, briefs, and athletic supports. Art or images of full nudity (including photos of explicit sexual activity) are only permitted in the Adult Only category. Frontal nudity is allowed in Art categories when the item is considered fine art, such as Michelangelo's David, vintage pin-up art, Renaissance-style paintings, and nude cherubs. Other restrictions include used sex toys, services that include any sexual/adult activity, links to sites that contain adult items prohibited on eBay and any form of digitally delivered adult goods. eBay only allows members from the US and Canada to access items in the Adult Only categories. Even adult items that can be listed in the main eBay categories can only be shipped within the US and Canada. To make sure minors are not freely accessing adult material, eBay requires members to provide credit card information or alternative verification before they can view Adult Only pages. Ebay UK will not allow UK sellers to sell adult items which seems a little unfair as Americans and even Chinese can sell to UK. eBay is certainly not the most adult-friendly site for selling adult services. They also do not allow for selling services such as camming shows. All of this does not stop people from listing adult items and watching the emails flood in.

Sometimes guys will email asking about swimsuits and maternity bras. Maybe they can not find that perfect photo on the internet of a short haired Asian goth girl with a red mohican to jerk off to. Guys will ask for everything from recordings of a model gagging to used sanitary towels.

Selling your old (smelly and trashed) shoes on eBay can also be extremely lucrative. Expect lots of e-mails asking for full length photos of the shoes being worn, along with e-mails asking if they can buy toenail clippings and toe jam. Try selling a pair of used ballet shoes on eBay and you will soon have a torrent of foot fetishists engaged in a bidding war. Primark pumps cost around £3-£5 and only last about a month but will sell for anywhere between USD10 and USD50. eBay have some very strict guidelines about listing worn shoes and there are always the snoopy tattle-tales who love to look for and report such things. If your listing gets pulled then your policy compliance will lower, which ultimately means that eBay may place a listing limit on your account and when free eBay listing weekends come up, you will not be eligible to list for free. Therefore it is strongly recommended that you start up a new eBay account just for selling shoes. If your listings are taken down, eBay will not even have the courtesy to e-mail you, the listings will just vanish. Here are a few tips to avoid the same problems. Include as many photos as you can, sellers can now add twelve photos for free. If you are showing photos of the shoes worn, then photos must be below the knee only. Your listing needs to state that you will clean the shoes to both eBay's and the manufacturer's guidelines. You do not have to clean the shoes when sending them out, you just need to say that you will. Do not use the word fetish in your listing, or anything relating to it. Instead, mention that you wore them during summer, or in a job where you were on your feet everyday, etc. Ask buyers to e-mail if they have any questions. And keep e-mails between eBay's messaging system. When mailing old shoes, put them in a ziplock bag, bubble wrap and then package them discreetly. Make your auctions private, this is easy to do at the listing stage. Only leave feedback for your buyers if they are happy for you to do so, some may request that you do not leave them feedback, despite the auction being private. Offer international postage as 80% of the shoes will be internationally, with America being the favourite, closely followed by France. Charity shops and car boot sales are great places to pick up second hand shoes. One model has a deal with their local charity shop where the charity shop saves her all the shoes that are too gross to sell, in exchange for a donation made to the store.

Girls claiming to be air hostesses are also flogging their used shoes and tights to eager buyers on-line. There is a surprisingly active market for used flight attendant shoes on eBay. Listings claim to be of tights and shoes that are "well worn" by the cabin crew. One pair of tights was listed as, "Ladies cabin crew tights worn internationally. Size medium and worn by a tall woman. Can be sent washed or unwashed."

A pair of pretty feet has the advantage of selling any number of worthless items. One model specialises in special blend Princess Toe Jam Spread. To make it, she buys a big container of cheap jam, smears it all over her feet, and then scrapes it off into little four-ounce jars and sells them for $30 a piece. You probably think your grandma has the best recipe for jam in the world, but I bet she cannot sell a four-ounce jar of it for $30.

Some models have gone well beyond being panty-preneurs and have since discovered that there is nothing that comes out of them or grows off of them that cannot be harvested and sold to cyber-weirdoes all over the world. They make literally tens of thousands of dollars selling their toenail clippings, excrement, urine, spit, vomit, and just about anything else they can secrete from their pretty little orifices. If you view your models from the proper perspective, the profits will just pour out of them.

There is a subculture out there referred to as human toilets who become aroused by eating pre-packaged excreta. And you were just flushing all that poop down the actual toilet. One model claims to sell her poop for £2,800 ($5,000). When a man offered her £70 for a steaming pile, she obliged. But she got creeped out, so she hiked her price to £2,800, and he kept paying. It is likely that if you get into this business, some of the email will make you vomit. If this happens, be sure to catch it in a container as all the turdboy customers will probably pay extra for such a rare delight. You will be amazed at how much money can be made from the excessively masochistic. Some models even claim to sell rubbish from their bathroom bins.

This kind of activity is not at all new. It is especially popular in the rarefied realms of conceptual art where numerous similar examples exist. In 1961 for example Italian artist Piero Manzoni created Merda d'artista (Artist's Shit) by allegedly putting the fragrant fruit of his bowels into steel cans and welding them shut. The work consists of 90 tin cans, each filled with 30 grams (1.1 oz) of faeces, and measuring 4.8 by 6.5 centimetres (1.9 in — 2.6 in), with a label in Italian, English, French, and German stating:

Artist's Shit
Contents 30 gr net
Freshly preserved
Produced and tinned
in May 1961

Initially priced on par with their weight in gold, one of the tins recently fetched a record high price of 275,000 Euros at an August 2016 auction in Milan. At the time the piece was created, Manzoni was producing works that explored the relationship between art production and human production, Artist's Breath ("Fiato d'artista"), a series of balloons filled with his own breath, being an example. Artist's Shit has been interpreted in relation to Karl Marx's idea of commodity fetishism, and Marcel Duchamp's readymades. Manzoni's girlfriend Nanda Vigo, who helped him produce the cans, claimed the contents really were faeces. Sounds like a really fun date!

This kind of shock art has since become very popular. Damien Hirst's fascination with death has made him the world's richest living artist. It is hardly surprising that cam girls are keen to jump on the bandwagon.

Extreme fetish items are the most difficult to package. 'Toilet treats' like urine and excreta have to be sealed in airtight containers and be shipped priority mail so that they can be consumed as soon as possible. Saliva for example hardens after a day or so, but if sealed in an airtight container that screws shut, it can last twice as long. Tampons have the shortest shelf life out of anything. After just a few hours, menstrual goods will begin to brown and smell like syphilitic vagina puking up decomposing babies. There again, sometimes that will only increase the price. Always include a letter with every package, thanking or degrading the customer, whichever is most appropriate. This simple act will help insure future sales.

If you still need inspiration for product preparation, here are a few more examples of what others have successfully made money on. Allie and Lexie Kaplan, a pair of identical twins from LA, "sleep" with their action figures and then sell them for a whopping $333. They post highly suggestive photographs of the nights spent with the dolls on Instagram. The action figures, named "The Boys Toys," features seven fictional characters, Batman, Mario, Pikachu, Yoda, Chewbacca, The Hulk, and Darth Vader. Each 'Boy Toy' is signed on the tag and includes a Certificate of Authenticity sealed with kisses and a framed picture of the twins. The fact that the toys also smell like the twins is made very explicitly. I am confident that this could easily be replicated with all kinds of cuddly toys.

In 2015, Chinese student Long Yi made a small fortune selling quilts used by female students to their male admirers on campus. He was inspired by a graduate who sold her own quilt within minutes of posting it on-line. He did the maths and realized that the market was rife with buyers, so he spent his savings on dozens of old quilts belonging to female students who were graduating from Qinghua University, where Long was a junior. He posted all the quilts on-line and sold most of them in one day and raked in 10,000 yuan ($1,600). Demand was so high that he set up a stall on campus to complement his on-line sales. Believe it or not, lovestruck young men were lining up for the chance to cuddle with quilts that once belonged to the women of their dreams. It's such a bargain because they were used by the girl I have adored for three years, said student Xiao Lei, who spent over $100 on a quilt. Now that she's graduating, I'll have her quilt as a souvenir.

An underground sock trade has emerged in South Florida, thanks to a cadre of Latin women selling their dirty socks for $25 a pop on Craigslist. Even guys can get in on the foot fetish trade. A 31-year-old guy on Reddit, who goes by the name of TeamYMD put up his first ad in 2001 as a joke, saying his socks had been worn by a "hot college jock." Over the next three years, he sold hundreds of pairs of used socks and made $10,000

There is also a niche community of sexual deviants who get off on women farting. Clips4Sale is the biggest seller of short fetish videos on-line, and videos only need to be an average five to ten minutes in length. Some men like farting girls in underwear, some men only like white underwear farts, some like thongs, some hate thongs, some like farts through jeans, some like bare-bottom farts, some like women farting on furniture, like chairs, or couches or mattresses. There is even a fetish for farts and giggles. Rather than jumbo bean burritos, any candy that comes in a sugar-free form such as Worthers or Twizzlers, or sugar-free cough drops are the secret to monster whopper farts. These candies contain sugar substitutes such as isomalt, malitol and sorbitol which, if eaten in excess, can even go so far as to induce "wet" farts. Oatmeal has similar effects and is probably far more healthy. Raw cabbage will do it too, but who wants to eat raw cabbage? The appeal of female farting also may have a lot to do with the taboo aspect of farting and women. Farting is a man's world. Women are not allowed to excrete bodily fluids or fart; it is still unladylike for a woman to actually have bodily functions while men can create a veritable orchestra of multi-octave farts and be applauded for their amazing abilities.

In addition to camsites, there are a number video selling platforms and other sites that can help models to supplement their camming earnings and provide some passive income while off-line. Cam site traffic can have its highs and lows, so diversifying is important to maintain a regular income stream.

http://www.fetbido.com/
Fetbido is an adult themed auction site where people can buy & sell fetish related items. Used panties, used tights, gay related items, rubber & latex etc.

http://www.ebanned.net/cgi-bin/auction/auction.cgi
Ebanned is more like eBay than Etsy because there is an auction time frame and a "buy it now" option to put on it.

http://www.flirtbids.com/
FlirtBids is an on-line adult marketplace that uses tokens as currency. Tokens are processed through CCBill and require a credit card to purchase. 10 tokens are equivalent to $1.

Having a clear, high quality, detailed gif file is important in your marketing campaign. Always have a profile picture or preview pictures in gif form, which shows the highlights of the video and will make people want to buy it. Men are extremely visual and an ad with pictures is ten times more likely to catch your audiences' attention. A gif is basically an animated picture or a series of pictures put together to form what looks like an animation, that usually plays itself over and over. When looking at a host of pictures on one page, the one pic that is moving is the one that catches the customer's eye. This will result in more clicks, and in turn more purchases or inquiry that leads to purchase.

You should also remember to always add a watermark that either states your, Twitter tag, website, email or just your logo embedded in your video and on your gif as well as the video itself. Gif files can be made on-line at Gfycat, Imgur and EzGif. Alternatively you can download AVS Video Editor and can take snap shots from your video and use them to make a gif.

Do not fall for the lies perpetuated by the copyright cartels. No matter what precautions you take and no matter how much you threaten people, hardcore fans will always share your material with like-minded fans. Despite what intellectual property mavens claim, this is very good for business. If their claims about 'piracy' were true, then why are movie studio profits reaching record new heights every year. Despite constant claims of losing billions of dollars to "piracy", the North American box office closed out 2016 with $11.4 billion in ticket sales. That marks a new record for the industry, bypassing the previous record of $11.1 billion that was established in 2015.

Hollywood has been enjoying a streak of box office highs for the past several years. In short, "piracy" is not touching their bottom line. If anything, the ability to share these movies and the associated emotions has increased it. Word of mouth as the best form of advertisement. Who wouldda thunk it?

A file shared is not a file stolen. A file shared is not a copyright violated - no money exchanged hands for the "media". File sharing is not "pirating" - no sabres were rattled, no ships were stormed, no lives were lost. File sharing is not "theft" - the original source of the file still exists and still belongs to the owner. When will we, the people, kick our collective government representatives in the nuts until they wake up and stop listening to these Mafia-like entities, these black-mailing con artists who continue to make record profits while whining that they are not making more, all the time withholding payments to the artists, directors, actors, stunt-people, gaffers, mixers, computer artists, musicians etc.

While there are services out there such as Cam Model Protection who will use the latest technologies to locate and remove your pirated content quickly for a monthly fee of $69 per month, this is self defeating at best. Contrary to the lies of the music and film industry, my advice would be to get your name and sample material onto every torrent, tube and download site out there and watch the emails roll in. Remember that almost every music company in existence refused to sign the Beatles just as nearly every single publisher scoffed at J.K. Rowlings hand scrawled efforts. Do you really want to take business advice from these guys? Try uploading your clips to sites like NetPorn where they are shown for free. Use your email or website address as your watermark. If you are on twitter and instagram or just want to grow your followers, put your @yourinstagram or you @twittername so they can find you easily. Many of the emails will be barely written in full sentences, often without punctuation and full of spelling mistakes, although most are polite and funny and sweet.

Your models are self-made on-line celebrities and you should have no problem with custom videos being purchased at $100 a minute. Just make sure your models are different in some way, or that they are willing to do what other girls will not. This will make them worth the $100 a minute and at least $5 to $10 for per 3 pictures. Be sure to use high resolution, good quality sound, and bring something to the table that most of the other guys or girls in their category can not.

ManyVids
Payout: 60%
Fastest-growing video selling site that has primarily vanilla (non-fetish) videos, along with memberships, texting, Skype features, Fund me options, contests, store items, and more. Great support and an active community.

IWantClips
1st place ranking in Sexpose's 2016 Clip Store Derby where clip stores were compared based on content and user experience.
Payout: 70%
The site also offers a special Studio Account with the following features:
Manage separate model accounts from one central dashboard.
Receive one convenient payout totalling the earnings of your separate accounts.
Receive notifications for all accounts to one centralized email.
Receive and send all messages from one centralized message centre.
View the performance and earnings of all accounts from one display in your studio's dashboard.

ModelCentro
Payout: 75-85%
Best platform for cam models to create and host their own paid membership sites,

with a ton of features like video selling, Skype messaging and more. Best of all, it is absolutely free to join and no experience with HTML or coding is required.

Customs4U
Payout: 60%
Fetish-oriented customs and clip-selling platform. Models can also receive tributes from members.

YezzClips has been open since 2010, and publishes the following guidelines:
No under-age material - all actors must be at least 18 years old
No rape scenes - neither acted nor real - no non consensual or forced sexual contact of any kind
No animal sex
No drugs - no hard drugs at all - no soft drugs such as alcohol in combination with sexual contact - no intoxication - no chemically rendered unconsciousness
No necrophilia - neither acted nor real
No horror/snuff - no maiming or killing - neither acted nor real
No crushing of animals - no insects, lobsters, etc.
No blood

    Once a model learns how to maximize her earnings on sites like ManyVids, it is relatively easy to set up a camming passive income. When starting out, be sure to create a fun profile with a description, pictures and services you want to offer as well as uploading a minimum of ten videos. Link Twitter accounts to ManyVids to let them promote your on-line profiles while live on cam, since existing fans are the best customers. There are models that make up to $10,000-12,000 a month and payouts are bi-monthly through Payoneer, cheque and wire transfers. As for profitable videos, it is all about the performer. The girl can be relatively ugly, however do stuff that makes you go "huh?" and when compared to a super hot blonde who is like a dead starfish, the choice is obvious.
    Models receive a base MV Score of 750 points for creating a profile. This goes up (along with placement on the site) with a number of factors.
Dollar amount of sales (Most important factor)
Number of hearts on videos and profile
Volume of videos and store items created
Number of times your uploads get auto-tweeted by ManyVids
MV reviews (5 points will be added for each full review up to a maximum of 200 points)
The MV score is recalculated twice daily and is in effect for 45 days. After each 45-day period, your score is reset to the base score of 750 points, so it is important to remain active.
Try to take advantage of the many different services such as creating Fundme campaigns to raise money for an objective.
As you can see there are many different aspects to camming, all enabling models to make a living and earn money.

Of course, there are even more sideline opportunities such as phone sex through Niteflirt or similar platforms, Indiebill and other payment platforms for adult models and even license their names to adult novelty companies in return for a portion of the sales of their branded sex toys. For lots of other imaginative ideas, I highly recommend http://cammingwebmasters.com/

The Gay Cam Scene

While female models typically make much more money, there is still a market out there for male web cam models. Some such as Supermen.com are strictly gay sites, but there are guys that cater specifically to female customers and couples. If you are not aroused by men then it would be very difficult to perform, and to be honest you will soon find that much of the time, the male customers are not particularly nice. Being hetero myself, I am not really qualified to write about gay sites but I will talk a little here about the male webcamming experience.

As a male studio owner, you will probably be called upon to act as a stunt dick for those occasions where your models receive requests for a little m/f action. This might even be one of the perks of the jobs that you were looking forward to in the first place. From there, it is only a short step to doing a little camming yourself. Even if you decide that this is not for you and prefer to have a male webcam model on site to cater for such eventualities, it is still good to know a little about the world of male webcamming.

While most hetero males only accept female customers and couples, there will always be a fair number men coming into the free chat area looking for some male companionship. There will also be a lot of guys pretending to be girls (without turning their cam on) so that they can chat with the male models, but you will soon learn to spot these quite easily. Most of the customers for male webcam models are couples and the majority of them tend to prefer C2C. Women are more shy and usually it takes a couple of sessions before they will turn on their cam. As a model, you will find that it is always better to work cam to cam, as it makes it much easier to interact, to gauge their reactions and see what turns them on.

Contrary to popular belief, most of the female customers are not old boilers and battleaxes at all. Generally speaking they are in their late 30s and 40s, and usually are just lonely. Some models say that many of their female customers have a penchant for hairy chests but sexual fetishes seems to be far less prevalent among women than men. Most women prefer to spend time talking rather than anything else. One model reports that he is frequently asked to masturbate while standing up. Most of the customers are quite shy and just want somebody who can smile and flirt and make them laugh. Perhaps they do not have the opportunity to flirt with guys in real life or just too shy so a flirty conversation makes them happy. But generally, women are sensitive human beings who just want to be made to feel good about themselves. Making them laugh and giving them lots of attention seems to be the key. Well established male webcammers range from $1 to $4 a minute, some making as much as $150-$200 a night net, for about 5-6 hours work. Guys who just sit there with their dick in hand doing nothing else do not make any tips. There is certainly less competition, so it is much easier to stand out from the crowd by being different.

Of course, not all male webcamming is so easy. Back in 2015 Andras Vass was convicted of running a male prostitution ring of gay Hungarians in New York City and Miami. Three young Hungarian men helped dismantle an American gay prostitution ring that enslaved them, marking a victory for local prosecutors, but highlighting the difficulty in reaching and helping male trafficking victims. Such victims often struggle with their own sexuality and self-worth, and may find it hard to admit they are victims, while under pressure to meet certain standards of masculinity. More than 4,000 human trafficking cases were reported in 2015 in the United States but only one in ten involve men, according to the National Human Trafficking Resource Centre. Because trafficking typically refers to teenage girls, this formally encourages a stigma that men are weak and effeminate if they are a victim. This stigma attached to male victimization prevents many from coming forward.

Three male trafficking victims gave accounts of being raped, locked up in windowless rooms, and having their lives threatened. Sentenced to eleven years in prison Vass, was the first person convicted in Florida for trafficking gay men under the state's tougher human trafficking law, which took effect in 2012. The men told the court how they were lured to the United States with the promise of well-paid escort jobs and the chance to return home after a few months. Instead, they found themselves held as sex slaves for a website called GayRomeo.com, starved, sleep-deprived and abused on a daily basis.

Up to eight men lived and worked in the apartment where engaged in prostitution or performed sex acts in front of a webcam for 18-20 hours a day. Their travel documents were seized by one of the ringleaders who constantly wielded a sword, and frequently reminded them he was a policeman in Hungary. The captors threatened to kill them or hurt their families back in Hungary. Apart from using financial manipulation to keep them in constant debt, the captors rarely let their victims leave their shared apartment, and they were told it was because they could not speak English and they were not familiar with the area. This case just goes to show that even in the US there are studios involved in trafficking and abuse. Red flags might include girls arrested for shoplifting sexual lubricants or family disputes in which teens will not disclose to their parents how they got expensive gifts.

Teledildonics, Camfecting and Blackmail

Teledildonics refers to high tech sex toys that can be remotely controlled over the internet, enabling users to control a vibrator in San Francisco with a few taps on a keyboard in New York. Even more complex set-ups involve toys that are controlled by other toys, allowing one user to activate a vibrating masturbation sleeve by using a connected dildo. Each set of products has a sleeve (an electronic Fleshjack) for men and an insertable product for a receptive partner; the settings allow the vibrations to be coordinated between the two devices. In reality, long-distance relationships are not all that common and so manufacturers are jumping on the webcam bandwagon, marketing their products as an enhancement to cam shows. Competing teledildonics companies now make products explicitly for camming purposes which require an email address or at least a username to make the pairing process work. Makers claim that this is a way of getting more intimate with a person you would likely never be in the same room with (let alone inside of). Vibrators have now shifted squarely into the arena of commercial sex, with products from companies like OhMiBod, Kiiroo and We-Vibe helping cam girls up the intensity and interaction in their shows, and up the profits while they are at it. Among other features, the Kiiroo vibrator is able to send signals to multiple masturbation sleeves at the same time.

OhMiBod began this trend with the Club Vibe 2.Oh and the Freestyle G which are not teledildonics toys in the technical sense. Both products respond to local sound input, rather than remote inputs streamed over the internet but cam girls quickly hacked them to respond to the sound generated by customer tips. Babies put anything they can get their hands on into their mouth. Camgirls, on the other hand... The more tips a cam girl receives, the more intensely her vibrator responds, meaning the more viewers are willing to pay, the hotter a show they will become. Manufacturers obviously insist that higher tips equal stronger vibrations. Kiiroo CEO Toon Timmermans claims that these haptic devices take interactive intimacy to a completely new level and will play a large part in the future of on-line intimacy. There again, he would say that about his own products, wouldn't he?

Unfortunately, everyone is so focused on gadgetry and VR, that no one is thinking of simple things such as games that models and members can play together, more interesting contests, and parties. A large part of camming is about chatting and making relationships deeper with members. Camgirls really need tools to make this easier and more fun rather than more overpriced vibrators. There has been a lot of hype surrounding tip-controlled vibrators and sound-activated toys for use in cam shows. There has also been talk of them being a scam with girls faking their orgasms and lying about the strength of the vibrations from the tips they receive. It certainly does not help that deceitful marketing departments are fabricating cam girl testimonials along the lines of "The client has very direct, complete control over my vibrator," and toys tend to encourage rapid-fire and constant tipping from viewers.

DatingGold, the largest webcam affiliate is less excited about the current state of haptics, saying they have seen many devices come out over the last few years, but not many have stuck around or made any kind of lasting impression on any of its cam programs.

Every single advancement in technology has both positive and negative aspects. As we have already seen, webcams have provided valuable new income streams for some, while trapping others in the most loathsome, degrading conditions. While new employment opportunities are one thing, in the twenty first century information society, there is another important factor that needs to be considered. Data, especially big data has now become a very valuable commodity. While the adult industry might be somewhat of a latecomer to this field, sex is still one of the driving forces behind modern technology and as such generates huge swathes of data just waiting to be tapped.

An Illinois woman is already suing sex-toy company Standard Innovation, based in Ottawa, of consumer fraud, unjust enrichment, intrusion upon seclusion, and violating both the Federal Wiretap Act and the Illinois Eavesdropping Statute. Her $130 We-Vibe Rave smart dildo can connect to a smartphone for such activities as adjusting vibration type ("tease and please with custom vibes you create") and intensity ("build intensity"), not to mention allowing someone else to be at the controls from afar ("play together from anywhere in the world").

Thanks to a Defcon hacking convention talk she learned that her extremely personal usage was being scrutinized for marketing purposes by its maker. Chinese manufacturers are especially notorious for this kind of nefarious behaviour. It was recently revealed that Xiaomi, the Chinese smartphone manufacturer can silently install any app on your device using an absurdly shoddy factory installed back-door. In this case, a mysterious pre-installed app, dubbed AnalyticsCore.apk, that constantly runs in the background, checks for a new update from the company's official server every 24 hours and reappears even if you try to delete it. This also means Xiaomi can remotely and silently install any application on your device just by renaming it to "Analytics.apk" and hosting it on the server. Ironically, the device connects and receives updates over HTTP connection, exposing the whole process to man-in-the-middle attacks, which means it is easy for hackers to exploit this loophole. With Xiaomi's implementation, anyone between the target and the server can send the apk of their choice.

While this is probably at the behest of the Chinese government to monitor Chinese citizens, it does show how widespread the practice has become. Lenovo installs malware into its computers in the same manner but it should not come as a shock that Chinese hardware manufacturers with non-existent security build in back-doors and spyware. After all smartphones are little more than surveillance and data collection devices. Standard Innovation is not the only vibrator company that it is tracking just what customers do with their sex toys and how often. China has hundreds of manufacturers that secretly collect and transmit highly sensitive information including the date and time of each use as well as vibration settings. Do you really want your sex toys to come pre-loaded with state sponsored spyware?

To further investigate this trend, I spent some time at the Guangzhou head office of Lovense, a Chinese company that makes cheap teledildonic knock-offs from locally sourced products, and then marks them up by a factor of ten for an unsuspecting overseas audience. The company sells what are effectively ten dollar vibrators from their website at a 100 dollar mark up. These low quality toys have so many returns that they simply cannot hire enough English speakers to handle the volume of customer complaints. Last year, the company was receiving so many returns and complaints that they had to hire a creepy ex-English teacher to handle all the negative feedback. Having left the local foreign language university in very suspicious circumstances, this was the kind of guy that probably had numerous restraining orders prohibiting him from coming within three hundred yards of a school or kindergarten back in the US. He was very open about showing me how he matched the usage data with personal email address and geographical locations and credit card information. The fact that they were keeping all their customers' credit card details on file was a security disaster just waiting to happen. Any rogue employee or a hacker could bleed the system dry with very little effort. When I asked him about respecting consumer privacy rights, he simply sneered.

By coincidence this was quite close by to the Chinese firm Lianlian which gifted its single male employees with sex dolls instead of a more straight-laced and socially acceptable cash bonus. Women and married men were given spicy cooking sauce, sandals and dehumidifiers."Creative awards can express the company's culture," said CEO Wang Yuzhu in an interview with Chinese media. This is not the first time a Chinese company has given its employees year-end gifts of a sexual nature. Just last year, men at Beijing-based tech company Qihoo360 had the chance to earn a night with Japanese porn star Julia Kyoka.

Lovense toys use a mobile app that secretly siphons data on vibrator intensity settings, among many other usage stats. Custom written apps remotely control vibrators from an Apple or Android device via a Bluetooth connection. They also chronicle how often and how long consumers use the sex toy and sends that data to the company's servers, demonstrating a wholesale disregard for consumer privacy rights. One partner's phone connects to the toy over Bluetooth, then the other's phone connects to the company server allowing the vibrator to be controlled from the other end. Just by collecting the data in the first place, the manufacturers are opening themselves up to exploits where hackers could collect this data and use it to blackmail the company. Yet depending on where the user is located, the manufacturer could also be putting their customers in legal jeopardy: a number of places such as India, the Philippines and Alabama criminally punish the owners of sex toys. Of course, as a Bluetooth device, it also shares data with the user's neighbours, or any passer-by running a software sniffing program like Blue Hydra. This is an amazing data leak for any would be stalkers. Kids have it so easy nowadays. Back in my day we had to spend hours dumpster diving to see how many used D-cell batteries were in a woman's trash can to determine her preferences.

Seriously though, the only conversation should be between the device and the phone. If it is going over the internet, then it sounds like the marketing department is getting the real orgasm. I asked the Lovense CEO if he was collecting data in order to improve the performance and quality of his products but he seemed much more interested in finding ways to improve revenue, such as selling the data for advertising purposes. The opportunity to send spam marketing emails advertising new products to their most engaged users is extremely tempting.

Those data collection based surveys could get awkward real fast.

"Hi Sally, we can't help but notice that you tend to operate your dildo at maximum vibration settings, for extended periods of time. May we suggest you upgrade to our 'heavy-duty' model, if you desire even stronger vibrations than your existing unit can provide."

or

"Hi Sally. We have noticed you are using your device 20 plus hours a day. This device is not rated for such extended us. Please consider upgrading to our "Super Heavy Duty" model should this trend continue.

Or even

"Hi there, we've noticed that for the first month since activation, your device has registered an average temperature of 98 degrees F, but since then has registered an average of about 62 degrees F, but the usage has remained about the same. Remote diagnostics suggest the temperature sensor is working correctly, so we wanted to check with you about your current usage patterns. Click here to fill out a brief survey about how you're using the device."

What will they come up with next, loyalty awards? Points systems to unlock achievements? Can we look forward to a Mark III with a hidden mic and cervix cam, due to be released just in time for Valentine's Day 2018.

The Chinese CEO at Lovense was unwilling to discuss how much money the company is making from selling sex toys compared to how much they are making from selling the data they are collecting from the people foolish enough to use an on-line sex toy. The aggregate data is especially valuable to other on-line porn businesses This reminded me of the comments made by the head of the Stanford Medical School about visiting Chinese physicians. He rarely heard any administrators talk about how to improve care. Rather, they were all focussed on how to expand their hospitals, improve their reputations and increase revenue. Financial incentives lead to some very dubious business decisions. Who would have thought that programming a car to lie to the US EPA was a good idea? Dozens of engineers at VW, apparently. In fact, a lot of people at GM got away with it some years earlier, making the people at VW think they could as well. There was an expectation that it would not matter if they got caught.

I was also able to investigate the methods that Lovense used to connect their sex toys to users' smart phones. In contrast, data passed between my wireless mouse and my PC is never sent to Logitech or Dell nor is data passed between my phone and my Bluetooth speaker sent to Bose or Verizon. In contrast, lazy Chinese programmers at Lovense were using all kinds of short cuts to reach their goals. Admittedly there is an acknowledged IPv4 address shortage but rather than looking for a Multicast solution or investigating RFC1112or Ad-Hoc networking, their coders simply put everything through a third node with a fixed IP to make things easier. This means using a common meeting point - a server that is based in their office. The coders I spoke to had never even heard Tor or other anonymity systems such as HORNET or SCION. Any user can monitor the traffic with Wireshark and see that it is unencrypted and NAT (intermediate server needed). While I was in the office, their main server, went down on numerous occasions. It is said that there are only two types of organisations in the world: those that know they are hacked, and those that do not know yet they are hacked. 'Evil marketing' is only the tip of the iceberg if the company is hacked and the details released on the internet. Part of the problem here is that because of Chinese cultural norms, if these aberrations are reported as defects, nobody is willing to respond, as bug reports put the manufacturer in a bad light and that amounts to losing face.

I wonder how long before first news of 4chan trolls hacking into sex toys? I could see someone creating a raspberry pi (or similar) project that could turn a toy on dozens of times a day, at random times and duration. I would love to see the data analysts explain that. The day that Lovense gets hacked, your boss will know that the day you said you were home sick, you actually spent two hours on your rabbit dildo or that your toilet breaks are really dildo breaks. How long will it be before consumers are complaining that their internet enabled vibrator has contracted a rather nasty virus? The problem is that these companies simply cannot resist collecting all sorts of personal information, and usually do not have the expertise to properly secure the data and communications channel in the first place. This is a privacy nightmare, but the public still has not caught on. There are going to be many cases such as this one over the next few years. As yet, it is unclear whether for-pay teledildonics violates prostitution laws? Paying someone to remotely stimulate your genitals could certainly fall afoul of any prostitution laws which is why these services are currently positioned as live webcam services rather than 'telesex'. The US already has numerous victimless crimes on their books that are relentlessly pursued for corporate profit. Just think how much money they could make from webcam users, if they suddenly reclassified this activity as digital harlotry, with all the punishments that entails.

In the connected world, everybody that produces any software at all, uses it to collect every bit of data they can get their grubby mitts on. Most people do not care, which is why it continues. Any internet connected device that is not under BSD, GPL, or another free license, with an openly visible source code for everything, is likely phoning home constantly. Richard Stallman and EFF describe this as Treacherous Computing, and anyone who uses a so-called "smart" anything is a willing enabler. If you care about your privacy dump these parasites now. The only way to punish these companies is by voting with your wallet and rewarding their competitors. The Internet of Things was a utopian dream in the late 90s, with the possibility to connect everything with open protocols and giving users amazing options to control their electronic gear. Finally, the Internet of Things has arrived and it is a mess of proprietary protocols where all devices are not connected with each other, but with centralized databases of greedy manufacturers. There will soon be follow-ups to rule 34 and 35 along the lines of: If it exists, there is an ill-considered IoT device for it with security and/or privacy issues. If no such device exists, someone must design such a device.

They will only stop when people stop buying devices that phone home, and it becomes clear that doing it is a death sentence in the marketplace, while companies that respect privacy are rewarded. Right now, we do that exactly the other way around. We reward privacy violations and punish devices that are not "web-enabled". The only way to retain one's privacy is to fight for it, as the lady in Illinois is doing. It would be ideal if we lived in a society where the information about whether or not John or Jane Doe has used a vibrator at any particular moment is no more damaging or private than whether they have used a coffee maker. Unfortunately, that is not the case. The risk of damaging reputations of people that want to remain discreet is too high. In some ways it is ironic that this woman is afraid of her vibrator setting being saved, but not afraid of national exposure via her lawsuit. It will be interesting to see how many others are willing to come out of the dildo closet. Will we then see connected vibrators as part of massively multiplay contests. Could competitive on-line masturbation ever become and Olympic sport?

Just as I was finishing this book, Standard innovation, the Canadian manufacturers of We-Vibe, reached a $3.75 million class action settlement with users for collecting information about how often, and with what settings, the vibrator was used. In reality, the company is getting the deal of a lifetime, paying a knock down price for what is probably the most detailed study the industry has ever had. A team of market researchers would cost far more and yield far inferior results (even in anonymous studies, people lie and/or forget). Unfortunately, it is almost impossible to sue Chinese manufacturers such as Lovense, and so if you do not want your masturbatory habits put up for sale to the highest bidder, then avoid these products at all costs. In order to constantly cut costs, sex toy factories consistently use the cheapest possible motors they can and this kind of spyware is perfect for seeing how long a motor lasts under various usage. How long before it automatically connects to Facebook so it can update your status. There are plenty of jokes in here about back doors and security holes, but in reality these products leave users wide open to blackmail from husbands, crazy stalkers and shady adult cam site operators. Rather that passively welcome our new Chinese teledildonic overlords it is very important that users are asserting their rights to lock down rampant corporate over-entitlement.

Chinese cowboy manufacturers are not the only companies collecting data on customer sex preferences. Until quite recently, much of the data relating to our most intimate desires, was spread across thousands of sites, most of which were aggressively opaque, which maintained an air of discretion for customers eager to keep this one slice of their lives private. Profits were so healthy that porn economics did not even need big data. As certain parts of the industry are undergoing major decline, that attitude is changing quickly. YouTube clones focussed solely on porn such as RedTube, Youjizz, and YouPorn are already addicted to the ad revenue fix and almost every one now has complex tagging systems to optimise searches or to recommend videos based on viewing habits, 'trending video' pages, and some kind of program to push certain content via those channels that will draw more people to their sites for longer chunks of time.

One of the easiest pieces of data to mine geographic location. This has led to the discovery that Germans dislike interracial content while the Japanese are only really interested in Japanese porn. These are hardly insights worthy of a Nobel prize but they are having a very direct effect on the industry as a whole. When linked directly to profits, Big Data constrains choices. We only need to look at how the pursuit of the most loyal audience has already driven political websites and talk radio to polarising extremes, with vast societal implications. Human sexuality is increasingly being shaped by what kind of porn will still sell and the trend at the moment is preferentially guiding viewers toward extreme fetishes. Recent trends have included the promotion of very specialist fetishes such as fauxcest (incest role-play) videos on users who would have never sought them out, driving up interest and customer engagement. When this happens disproportionately for some fetishes over others, it makes certain proclivities more visible than others, and thereby alters our sexual reference points, all in the name of ad clicks. In turn, porn producers use the same data to guide the kind of content they create. This deliberately shifts the industry toward more extreme, more profitable genres. We have already seen how this works with the distribution of video and DVD porn. Just a few decades ago, anal was a relatively rare fetish. Today, it is the bread and butter of mainstream porn, and a routine element of everyday Americans' sex lives. The same thing happened with oral a few decades prior that. In straight sex scenes, performers are forced to do more physically taxing things, more often, and often for much less money. This impacts general tastes and can eventually lead to image problems. There was some discussion on the BBC recently, where they had some statistics showing that pubic hair removal is now the norm among university age women and very popular with men, with natural hair being openly mocked and described as "gross" and "disgusting". The main reason for this is because in porn, shaving is almost universal.

This unhealthy herd behaviour means that producers no longer have as much freedom to produce an ocean of diverse content. Instead, they churn out a disproportionate amount of content aimed at sexual niche groups that will pay more than others. This push to produce more extreme content in waves, catering to the highest paying customers' tastes, could soon grow even stronger as tube sites branch out of distribution and start creating their own videos. One firm especially, MindGeek runs most leading tube sites, and owns a range of key US production companies. The company currently operates or owns 13 tube sites, 10 production companies, and has ties to Playboy and other porn studios such as Really Useful Ltd and Wicked Pictures. For them, big porn data is a treasure trove just waiting to be scooped up.

It remains to be seen what will happen when they begin shovelling more and more hyper-fantasized, misogynistic snuff at us. Of course, if porn publishers were looking to make erotica with insight, empathy, originality and literary values, they probably would not be in the mainstream porn business in the first place. What we can look forward to ever more acts of extreme sexual behaviour. We have already seen dinosaur porn, Bigfoot porn and fauxcest, who knows what specialities we will be subjected to next. Just as novelty and sensationalism has brought down the media landscape to the level of the lowest common denominator, we will now see the porn industry using the same sensationalism and shock tactics to bring in ever more viewers. The media has learned quickly that there is no such thing as bad publicity and we are likely to see all kinds of barriers in bad taste come tumbling down around us. The fauxcest trend that I mentioned earlier will be a primary example. Paedophilia creates outrage amongst the kind of rabid red-neck mob that enjoys nothing more than a good old fashioned witch-hunt, preferably with a lynching or tyre burning as a conclusion. There was a time when interracial relationships and homosexuality bought out the same cross burning fundamentalists, but in today's 'protect the children' climate nothing generates clicks like a good sex scandal involving children. The tragedy is that the unwashed masses will soon become desensitised to the over-promotion of hebephilia, which will allow the truly dangerous paedophiles to operate much more openly than ever before.

Even if you never visit porn sites, there is no guarantee that you cannot be identified as being a member of the mailing list. Even if you live in communist China, where the Great Fire Wall rigorously blocks Porntube, Xhamster and hundreds of other porn sites, it will not stop these sites from sending you spam advertising at every possible opportunity. When the Brazzers forum was hacked, exposing the data of as many as 800,000 users, even those who never signed up to the forum also found their details included in the dump. Adult Friend Finder, suffered a massive hack that exposed the profiles of an estimated 3.5 million members, which generated international headlines by revealing thousands of high-profile kink-seekers on Capitol Hill, in Hollywood and higher education.

In a divorce-lawyer's wet dream come, almost every account password was cracked, thanks to the company's unbelievably poor security practices. The hack included 339 million accounts from AdultFriendFinder.com, which the company describes as the "world's largest sex and swinger community" and also includes over 15 million "deleted" accounts that were not purged from the databases. On top of that, 62 million accounts from Cams.com, and 7 million from Penthouse.com were stolen, as well as a few million from other smaller properties owned by the company. Ironically, Friend Finder Networks does not even own Penthouse.com any more. They sold the site to a new owner last February. The data accounts for two decades' worth of data and included usernames, email addresses, passwords and the date of the last visit, and passwords.

Almost none of these databases are being properly protected. It would be relatively easy to monitor all outbound traffic and then when a huge stream from the database server is seen heading out to somewhere it should not normally go, alarms and cell phones should would start ringing or maybe even a banshee scream that reverberates around the office. Unfortunately until the simple theft of personal information carries liability for the company holding the data, not just liability for the provable harm, nothing will change. After all, the development costs of a monitoring system would have to come out of this quarter's profits, and therefore this quarter's executive bonuses. Compare this to the executive downside of data loss... absolutely nothing. In addition, passwords are a terrible way of securing stuff. Human memory is too easy to predict and model, which is why even "good" passwords consisting of multiple words and numbers are relatively easy to crack these days, even with cryptography like SHA-1 protecting them. This situation will only worsen as AI continues to improve.

On both the "vanilla" AdultFriendFinder.com and the more explicit Alt.com, fakes are all over the place but very easy to spot, even in the old times without Google image search. Out of the 339 million accounts, cynical observers might suggest that but 338.8 million were fake accounts with pictures of large-breasted women all of whom who live near you and are eager to have sex with you this very evening. Even if you live in the middle of the Australian Outback or in a mediaeval monastery in the middle of the Tibetan Plateau. That would be like thinking Chaturbate was not watching who you tip Webcam site and studio operators are attractive targets for hackers/gangsters. While money laundering is obviously an issue, transparency in business operations is a liability for them too. Many adult oriented websites, some well known names, are routinely shaken down by cybercriminals. It is these kind of international gangs that would happily pay substantial amounts to a cowboy outfit like Lovense for all the data that is surreptitiously collects on its customers."Cam girls" are quickly becoming the new black mail. Scammers are setting up cam girls streams, which capture all kinds of personal information about a "client," as well as his actions on the other end, by hacking his web cam. The resulting session is then used as extortion, meaning the poor sap on the other end better pay up or his wife, kids, and boss will find out what he is doing at the computer late night. The fraudulent process of attempting to hack into a person's webcam and activate it without the webcam owner's permission has been called camfecting. In a 2013 case, the transmission of nude photos and videos via Omegle from a teenage girl to a schoolteacher resulted in a child pornography charge.

If you do not believe that this is already a common occurrence, then I would point you to a BBC report on the Moroccan boom-town where many of the scammers are based. One night, a young Palestinian man living abroad fell victim to an on-line scam, involving a web camera and a beautiful woman. Here Ahmed (not his real name) tells the story of how he was trapped.

"It happened when I was home alone. This girl added me on Facebook. I didn't think it was anything strange - I often get friend requests from old school friends who I don't know well.

The next day she sends me a message: "Hi, how are you? I saw your profile and I liked you." So I looked at her profile and, I mean, she was really hot.

With a girl like this, you lose your head

That night she starts messaging me via Skype. She says she's 23, her parents are dead, and she lives with her older sister in Sidon, Lebanon. She says she's bored because she doesn't study or work and that her sister is very strict. I ask her about her hobbies and she says she likes sex. She loves it, she says. "Hmm," I thought, "this is interesting." At this point I am curious but unsure, because it's strange how easily she's talking about sex with a stranger. But I was bored, my girlfriend was out of town, and didn't have anything to do. So I figured, "What the hell, I'll chat with this girl and see where it goes." Eventually she asks if I have a webcam. So I turn on my video and say, "Can I see you too?" She turns on her video and when I see her, you know, she is a really beautiful girl. With a girl like this, you lose your head.

We continue chatting, but only in messages, not actually speaking. She says she's afraid her sister will hear her. As we're chatting she tells me that talking with me is turning her on. I'm thinking because she lives with her strict sister, in the south of Lebanon rather than in a more open place like Beirut, maybe she's frustrated and looks for sexual encounters on-line.

Then she asks me to show her my penis. So I show her my penis. Then I say, "OK, your turn." She lies on the bed, undresses, and starts masturbating. I'd never seen anything like it. It was so easy. Too good to be true.

So I start masturbating too. She tells me to put the camera on my face because it excites her, so I move the camera back and forth between my face and my penis. After a few minutes she pretends to have an orgasm. Still naked, she comes back to the keyboard to chat with me. She asks me what I do, and I tell her I work in marketing in Milan.

"Oh, so you must be rich!" she says.

"Well, I get by," I say.

Then she says she hears her sister coming, so she gets dressed and signs off.

A half hour later I get a message on Facebook. "Listen," it says, "I'm a man, and I recorded a video of you masturbating. Do you want to see it?" He sends me the video. It's about five minutes of me masturbating.

"I have a list of your friends and family from Facebook - your mum, your sister, your cousins," he says. "You have one week to send me to send me 5,000 euros (£4,450), or I'll send them the video."

I was in shock. My first thought was to send him the money immediately. But I cancel her, or him, as a Skype contact and right away I get a message on WhatsApp. "I'm here," it says.

So I plead with him. I tell him I don't have 5,000 euros. He says, "Of course you do, you have a good job in Europe." "No," I tell him, "that was a lie, just to impress the girl, I'm just a pizza delivery guy."

Then I remember a photo I had sent her of me tiling my bathroom and I say, "Look, do you think if I were some rich guy I'd tile my own bathroom?"

He's sort of convinced by this and says, "That may be true, but I don't care. You have one week to send me 2,000 euros. Otherwise, I'm sending the video to your family."

I try to calm down and think rationally. If I send him money, what is to stop him from coming back and demanding more?

Then he sends me the link to the video on WhatsApp - I feel sick to my stomach Then it occurs to me that if he sends the video to my contacts - people he isn't friends with - it will go to a junk inbox that no-one checks. And even if they check it, I figure, who is going to open a video file from an unknown person? It could be a virus. So I have two choices: I send him the money and I have no guarantee he doesn't ask for more, or I refuse and hope no-one looks at the video.

The day comes, though, when he messages me and says, "OK, I'm about to upload the video to YouTube."

"Upload it," I tell him. "I don't care any more."

Then I change my privacy settings so no-one can post to my wall or tag me without my consent.

Then he sends me the link to the video on WhatsApp. I watch it again. It's me masturbating, on YouTube. I feel sick to my stomach.

Immediately I start reporting the video to YouTube for sexual content. I report it, close the page, reload the link, and report it again. Over and over.

He sends me a message saying he's about to send the link to my relatives on Facebook if I don't pay.

"Go ahead," I tell him, "send it."

When I asked why he was picking on a poor young guy like me he had said, 'You think I don't target rich guys in the Gulf states? Of course I do'

I couldn't pay him. First 2,000 euros, then perhaps 5,000. Where would it end? He was so upset. He starts sending me insults, telling me he'll send the video to my mother, to everyone I know.

I keep reporting the video. Each time I'm watching the number of views to see if anyone else has viewed it. After about an hour YouTube takes the video down. From what I can tell, all the views were mine, except for one. That could have been him viewing it after he uploaded it, or one of my relatives. I'll never know for sure, but I've never heard from anyone. Maybe a male relative saw it and never told anyone.

Can you imagine, though, if an aunt had seen it? She would have told another aunt, her husband, her kids, soon my whole family would have known. I have family all over the world, the US, Canada, Australia, Saudi Arabia, the Gulf states, Europe.

And what if my mum sees this? A video of me masturbating. I would have thrown myself out the window from the shame.

After the video was taken down I didn't hear from the guy again. I imagine he moved on to bigger fish. I remember when I asked why he was picking on a poor young guy like me he had said, "You think I don't target rich guys in the Gulf states? Of course I do. You're lucky I can see from your Facebook page you're not married, or I would be asking for a lot more money."

I think it's over, but every now and then I check YouTube to see if he's re-uploaded it."

The "23-year-old Lebanese girl" who seduced Samir on Skype was almost certainly a young man from Oued Zem - a small town in central Morocco that has become known as the capital of the "sextortion" industry. The Oued Zem scammers trawl Facebook for victims, and as soon as a man answers a video call - either on Skype or, increasingly, within Facebook itself - they activate software that shows the victim a pre-recorded video of a girl downloaded from a porn webcam site. They are so familiar with this video that they are able to chat-message their victims at exactly the points where the girl appears to be typing on the keyboard. Hundreds of young men in Oued Zem are running this scam. There are at least fifty international money transfer offices in the town. The manager of one of these offices claimed that they take in about $8,500 (£7,000) every day, and that the vast majority of that was blackmail money. There are German cars and Japanese motorbikes in the streets, and fancy cafe-restaurants that provide a front for families that need an explanation for their new-found wealth.

In the UK, Wayne May runs an on-line community, Scam Survivors, that offers advice and support to victims of the webcam masturbation racket. Since 2012 he has received more than 14,000 requests for help from victims all over the world, including the UK and the US. Many are young Arab men, he says, and about a third of all the scams originate in Morocco. But there is also a rising trend of scams that originate in China thanks to companies like Lovense. This is just one of many of stories looking at a new and disturbing phenomenon - the use of private or sexually explicit images to threaten, blackmail and shame young people, mainly girls and women, in some of the world's most conservative societies. I have already mentioned the popularity of slut shaming in China and this has prompted many computer graduates to get into the blackmail business.

Of course, it is not only scammers that are using digital sex technology to their advantage. Sexbots in the form of realistic animated 10-year-old girls are already being used to entrap internet users. A team of coders, animators, and researchers at Terre des Hommes in the Netherlands, recently announced that they had issued warnings to more than 1,000 on-line so-called 'casual' paedophiles in just ten weeks. Sweetie is reported to be an ultra-realistic 3-D CGI model of a 10-year-old Filipino girl that they say would fool even the most accomplished Hollywood blockbuster animator. The team claimed that the development of Sweetie took only six months and although the Amsterdam based team would not divulge the software or the coding language used to create it, it was more than likely rendered in Maya. Of course, no photos of Sweetie have been made available to back up their claims of ultra realism. If Sweetie's picture were freely available on the internet then she would no longer be any use as an AI honey-pot.

The researchers claim that a phenomena known as Webcam Child Sex Tourism, adults logging into sex-chat rooms with, is on the rise. They claim that tens of thousands of adults currently prey on children this way each day, and that the number keeps growing. Maybe that is because the more and more researchers are out there trying to entrap innocent guys who stumble across one of their creations. Inflating the statistics is a good way to guarantee their continued funding.

It has also been reported that the FBI has been operating thousands of Internet chat rooms dedicated solely Webcam Child Sex Tourism, communicating with minors in developing countries. Of course, the fact that they might be classed as minors in their own countries is conveniently ignored. Youngsters in these chat rooms are not just there for curiosity's sake, or just hanging out virtually with friends. These children are either young prostitutes working from Internet cafes or children who, forced by their parents or other family members, perform sex shows in front of a webcam from their homes in return for PayPal or Western Union Online payments. Going after the payment providers for enabling such transactions is a lot more challenging than the entrapment of single men, as was seen in the HSBC laundering of hundreds of millions of dollars for the world's biggest crime syndicate, where the only punishment was a fine equivalent to a pittance in its turnover. Executives not only got off but were promoted to higher service. Mexico's narco nightmare now counts 100,000 dead and some 20,000 missing while HSBC acted as the cartel's financial services wing, handling a staggering $376bn of suspect money. The bank was fined a record $1.9bn. But this was less than five weeks' income for HSBC's American subsidiary. Paul Thurston, the man in charge of HSBC Mexico, was promoted to become head of global retail on a multi-million dollar salary. Stephen Green, the chief executive of the bank throughout its service to Chapo Guzman's drug cartel, was appointed to the British government. Federal authorities chose not to indict HSBC for fear that criminal prosecution would topple the bank and, in the process, endanger the financial system. Interpol can be mobilised to go after international torrent sites that allegedly threaten the profits of large corporations but not corrupt bankers. Sites like Pirate bay, Kickass and Demonoid for classified as enemies of the state for enabling file-sharing but sites that enable forced child prostitution or money laundering are obviously not of the same importance.

The 'think of the children' paranoia that has now engulfed modern societies is completely out of control, and a new bogeyman has been manufactured so that police forces can now receive even more funding to support their constant militarisation in a war against, drugs, terrorists and now dirty old men.

An investigation into police sex stings conducted by Florida police found over 1,200 cases in which officers routinely entrapped innocent victims, stole their property, and destroyed their lives. Central Florida Internet Crimes Against Children (ICAC) task force purposely inflated arrest totals in order to increase their budgets. The ICAC task force is the beneficiary of millions of dollars in federal grants, and, thus, taxpayer money from the Department of Justice. Officers carried out arrests claiming men were looking for children on-line when there was absolutely no evidence to support such a claim. All of the cases examined showed the men were seeking adult company on-line, and it was the officers who acted as an adult with a teenage sister who was also interested. Even when the men stressed they had no interest in the under-age decoy, if they travelled to meet the adult they were arrested as sexual predators and charged with travelling to meet a minor.

During entrapment stings, detectives were not just using sites like Craigslist and Backpage, but also social media sites like Facebook and Twitter, as well as legal dating sites MeetMe.com, Fling.com, and SpeedDate.com. In most cases, detectives were posting pictures of adults looking to meet other adults, and would later introduce a child into the conversation or switch his/her age to that of teenager. These men who were arrested and publicly shamed during TV press conferences were not actually looking for children on-line like police suspected. Instead, they were looking for other adults when detectives started to groom and convince them to break the law. The majority of men arrested were in their early 20s or teenagers and were not considered a high risk to children. The detectives, however, were spending tens of thousands of dollars and hundreds of police hours on each sting, and the majority of the cases were thrown out of court. The task force was also using both enticement and entrapment to steal. Under Florida's Contraband Forfeiture Act, law enforcement can seize property as their own from anyone accused of committing a felony, even if charges were never filed. In one example, during a January 2014 sting, the Clearwater Police Department and Pinellas County Sheriff's Office arrested 35 men in a single weekend and seized 19 cars as their own. Law enforcement is using public sentiment, skewed arrest data, and the high conviction rate to justify continued funding for a problem that does not exist, and that is absolutely why Florida has a 73% increase in the number of sex offenders over the past five years as opposed to 23% for the rest of the country. I doubt that it will be long before this kind of chat bot technology will also be used to entrap political dissenters.

Sweetie was designed as a proof of concept application to inspire global law enforcement agencies and show them how many more innocents they can lock up in private run prisons and boost their funding for continued militarisation. The stigma attached to paedophiles is now total. Perhaps you can recall of the poor unfortunate who was discovered to have a number of scanned playboy images on his hard drive. The police mistakenly described them as kiddie porn and life suddenly became such a living nightmare that the poor guy was driven to suicide just days later. Child exploitation and human trafficking are serious issues that need to be addressed but not like this. We are entering into Orwellian or Minority Report "pre-crime" territory. Sweetie might be programmed to look like a ten-year-old girl but in reality it is just a piece of code. Is it really possible to commit a crime against a piece of code? The line between entrapment and really good investigation is whether the idea to commit the crime began in the mind of the accused or in the mind of law enforcement. This brings up issues much larger than overzealous cops trying to catch people who do not deserve to be caught. A person cannot be molested if they are encouraging you to do it.

It is ironic that the same media which stirs up this molestation hysteria is actually complicit by sexualising young women. One minute they are promoting Britney Spears dressed as a horny schoolgirl and the next minute they are saying that death is too good for anybody that harbours such fantasies. How many men would have even considered under-age girls until Matilda dressed up like her hooker mother and tried to seduce Leon? Is the fear-mongering having negative consequences that outweigh any of the supposed benefits? Most middle aged men will not even discuss this subject for fear of being labelled a paedophile. In confidence, they confess that they will no longer interact with any youngsters for fear of being mislabelled. I have spoken to many guys who will no longer consider careers in teaching, healthcare or children's entertainment, in case somebody thinks that they may have ulterior motives. Other discussions are now completely taboo. Is an attraction to minors really even that unnatural or current age restrictions cultural anomalies that do not reflect the natural order?

As a society we are caught up in "punish the evildoers!" mentality rather than thinking about how to cut down on crimes in the first place. This is very similar to the war on drugs. Putting large numbers of young people in prison on long mandatory sentences for petty, victimless crimes causes far more problems than it solves. Taking a financially disadvantaged teenager and locking them up for ten years with thousands of hardened criminals for smoking a joint is creating far more problems than it solves. Presidents who admit to smoking weed and snorting coke are obviously exempt.

Throwing people in prison is never a long-term solution. In fact, it is not a solution at all. "Out of sight, out of mind" is a toxic philosophy. Especially in the case of genuine paedophiles who's sexual preferences are never going to be changed by a sentence of perpetual rape and torture at the hands of fellow inmates. If we impose inhumane sentences and cruel and unusual punishment, then we are only sinking to their level of barbarity. The US judicial and prison-industrial complex falls way short of European standards. Actually it is not so much a justice system, but rather a harsh and vindictive revenge system. It is particularly bad for people with medical issues. The UK generally accommodates mental health issues in prison, with access to counselling and support. The US, on the other hand, takes a perverse pride in how terrible their prison system is. The public there expects, even demands that prisoners should suffer as much as possible. Administrators still refuse to address the situation because it would be seen as being 'soft on crime.' Prison rape is so common it is a subject for comedy, and that is the way the people like it. The emphasis is on punishment, not rehabilitation.

It is far more cost effective economically and socially to rehabilitate than to punish. Research could lead to better therapies as more recent studies show that this is a biological rather than psychological issue. As a society, we need to start addressing the problem, instead of straining resources hunting down symptoms. This should start with an open dialogue that includes both paedophile (pre-pubescent) and hebephiles (post-pubescent under legal age), where the public can see that these people are victims of sexual distortions no worse or better than most mental illnesses, and that they need help before they risk distorting innocent children. This will help others come out of the woodwork and allow them some greater sense of security when seeking help (many do not seek help out of fear, which only makes them more likely to act on their urges).

While hebephiles are lumped in with child molesters by the media, most studies show that paedophiles make up less than 10% of that much larger group. Hebephiles end up hating themselves, convinced that they are the same kind of monsters as those who hurt children. They end up destroying themselves by avoiding human contact and refusing to seek help, until they end up in a psych ward for suicide attempts and/or depression. This is exactly the same problem that schizophrenics, bi-polar and borderline people faced just a few decades ago, where they were so afraid of the stigma of being mentally ill that they forwent treatment and their situations only worsened. True sexual distortions, just like mental illness needs to be addressed, as ultimately their problem becomes everyone's problem when they eventually reach breaking point.

Further stoking the flames of paedophilia, Spanish researchers have developed a separate chatbot that poses as a 14-year-old girl. Called Negobot, it is claimed that the system will help authorities detect sexual predators in chatrooms and social networks. I wonder how long it will be before chat rooms are filled with nothing but chat bots trying to entrap other chat bots.

Maybe AI sexbots could be dispensed as a form of digital medication to pacify aberrant sexual urges in the same way that methadone is used to treat heroin addicts. There again. Maybe it would only serve to desensitise in the way that normal porn does. Whatever the case we had better start thinking about the issues quickly as it will not be long before sexbots find their way into video games and virtual porn.

We are definitely going to see more companies introducing connected sex toys to the marketplace. Watches, bracelets, earrings paired to an app that can easily be toyed with through the smartphone, or other pieces such as vibrating panties and massaging bras are all on the way. Unfortunately the risks of such items far outweigh the rewards. It is for these reasons that I would advise avoiding this temporary fad that puts both your customers and your business at risk. If you want to invest in toys for your girls, then by all means do so. Just try to avoid toys that report all their activity back to the manufacturer and possibly even their dictatorial government.

A good safe option is the Hitachi Magic Wand. This has been called the Cadillac of vibrators due to its strength, performance, and orgasm-power. It has a cord and a powerful motor (which makes it pretty loud, its only downside), but it puts all other cordless and battery-operated vibrators to shame. It has become an icon in the sex toy world and its plain white look is so easily recognizable. It recently went through a rebranding and is now called the Original Magic Wand with the Hitachi name now absent from the newer packaging; it is also now sold by Vibratex. So, with many Chinese fakes on the market, look for Vibratex listed as the manufacturer. Despite the name change, many girls still call it The Hitachi for short, no matter how much Hitachi wanted to separate itself from the product.

The Magic Wand has 2 speeds, normal and OMG orgasm, but if you want to be able to control it, you can do so by getting the speed controller version, which is really handy if you are more sensitive or want to be able to vary the speed. The original magic wand does not come with any attachments, but if you are someone who likes to experiment and likes insertable vibrators, there are attachments you can buy that fit right on top and take the Hitachi Experience to the next level. The most popular kit for the Hitachi has blue straight and curved G-spot attachments.

AR, MR and VR

VR Sex is one area where science fiction has been way off the mark. Either that or the scientists who were assigned to work on that project have not been heard from for years, being holed up in a secret underground lab in a state of perpetual orgasm. For decades, VR was little more than a pipe dream, relegated to fiction, Hollywood props and a few dread-locked hardware geeks. Oculus gained global attention back in 2012 by promising affordable, high-quality goggles. Facebook bought the company two years later for $2 billion. Unfortunately even at the 2017 Consumer Electronics Show, the world's biggest tech expo, there was little evidence of any serious progress. The main advancements needed to take VR forward -- better displays, wireless, and less bulky designs are still stuck on the drawing board. Marketing departments might be convinced that VR will revolutionize computing but consumers are simply burned out feeling that they must buy a gadget every year, whether it is the latest phone or a VR headset, especially when improvements are marginal. I am especially disappointed in the lack of progress as voice controlled VR would be fantastic for paraplegics and other less-abled users.

Virtual Reality remains, for the time being, a very expensive novelty. It will certainly continue to gain acceptance but it will do so slowly. Having it means that your studio will have all the bells and whistles, but it is a nicety, and will not be a huge money maker in the near future. Some larger studios are already stockpiling expensive equipment to be part of the Virtual Reality experience, but VR is still far away from becoming commonplace, and may be a profit-killing distraction in the meantime. When studios and cam sites look at the amount of revenue that continues to flow in from mobile users, few feel that VR has nearly as much potential as a superior mobile product does. VR camming might be on everybody's lips right now, but it will take time. The technology is still clumsy and difficult. VR webcams will only increase in popularity when the experience becomes better than a traditional cam show, and not just some expensive, cumbersome and buggy gimmick.

In the short term, high-resolution front-side cameras on smartphones along with their high-powered processors and software will allow the development of new apps that let the model broadcast her cam from her phone, just as it is happening right now with apps such as Periscope. Software such as the Wowza server technology now allows anyone to broadcast from anywhere, with fluid and crisp streaming onto any device, so that we can finally dispense with all that clunky and obsolete Flash Media Player that almost every webcam site in the world currently uses, and which only allows those sites to be used on a computer. More than 65 percent of internet consumption now occurs through smartphones, with five percent through tablets, and the remaining 30 percent via PCs, so this will be a very important step.

From a technical standpoint, the hardware and bandwidth requirements for VR are substantial to maintain. This gives a studio with the money to invest in the hardware a tactical advantage over the home-based cam model. Will the high bandwidth requirements of VR webcamming lead to distributed internet access and much greater levels of encryption? The initial outlay may be easier with the funding of a studio. In addition, VR cam sites will need to work very closely with cam studios to implement this technology because independent models will not invest the money and time in learning how to use it. Studios have the leverage on this topic due to the fact that are able to make higher investments easier than individual models and also have stronger technical knowledge through the people they employ. A VR room requires high technology which comes at a very high price, and which simply is not in the reach of the majority of models.

The main stumbling block to the uptake of VR cams is the price of the high-end camera arrays themselves, which are currently quite expensive. When the price of cams comes down to around $200 or less is when it will become more commonplace. Some manufacturers have begun to offer VR cameras on a rental basis for around $30 per month, which is a good way for a studio that wants to experiment with the innovative technology but does not want to be saddled with obsolete equipment. The technology will also need to be improved as well, before VR cams become mainstream. It currently costs around $10K to set up one model's broadcast room. Clearly this is very cost prohibitive, and it still only works across a limited number of platforms. Consider too that the suitability of many performer's home cam broadcasting infrastructure, while capable of streaming today's HD video, may choke on VR's higher data flow and more complex production requirements. While professional cam studios offer a viable option in select urban areas, this centralization inevitably lowers the pool of available performers to those who are able to use these facilities. An even more fundamental problem exists that will keep many cammers away from the VR realm. It is simply too much like hard work. VR camming requires more elaborate rigging of the camera, a more extensive set, and better lighting.

There are in fact a number of issues inherent in VR which may hold it back from widespread adoption. The experience of VR may be too immersive to be practical for most day-to-day applications. Total immersion in a virtual world requires total disengagement from the outside world. Even if you are watching a 360° video or playing a virtual reality video game from the comfort of your own living room, being completely immersed in the experience can lead to feelings of vulnerability as you are unable to see or hear anything happening in the real world around you. Many users of VR also report feelings of motion sickness or headaches after wearing a headset for extended periods of time because the immersive nature of VR confuses the brain. It is still unclear whether these issues can be alleviated by better design and continued exposure. Peripheral vision is more important than you might think, because it provides a wealth of information about speed and distance from objects. Central vision, despite the great detail it offers, gives you only a rough estimate of movement toward or away from you, based on changes in size or in the parallax angle between your eyes. VR can also be a strangely antisocial experience. This fact also hampers the practical application of VR in traditional office environments, where effortless collaboration is essential. Another barrier to the productive use of virtual reality is that it limits our ability to multi task. It is useful that we are able to glance at our phone while we are waiting for a game to load, or do work on our laptop while we are watching a movie.

The marriage of VR headsets and smart phones is driving screen resolutions up all the time. Mobile devices provide a tremendously low barrier to entry to the purchase of VR headsets, thanks notably to Google Cardboard's democratization.

Even medium-range headsets such as the Gear VR are still committed to using smart phones and provide a definite improvement in optical quality including resolution and field of view. The Gear VR being made available as a free add-on with any new Samsung S7 phone was certainly a major step forward, but the whole Galaxy scandal has set back Samsung as a whole in 2016. To make things even more complicated, everybody wants to be the first to market, in order to establish their market share. Unfortunately, in doing so, no one is sharing their technology with other companies. This leads to a handful of sites doing VR very differently, without any substantial. Without any standardization the entire industry suffers. Once standards have been established, more sites can start leveraging the technology, share it with others, and make improvements.

Cam star Ela Darling is the co-founder of VRTube.xxx, the world's first VR live cam platform available through Cam4. She has talked extensively about the technical challenges involved creating an entirely new stereoscopic VR webcam. Further discussion on this subject is available at Reddit's r/oculusnsfw.

I personally believe that VR can eventually be utilized in either of two ways. It can be used as an upsell, something to be layered on top of the normal platforms and websites, that will target an additional share of the users (ones who already own the headsets) and can bring new income for all of the players, from models to studios as well as cam sites. The second way is to make this a part of your general offering and have that competitive edge over your competition. But this can be done only if these technologies can be integrated in the right way, so that the user's experience is enhanced. If it is not done the right way, this could have the opposite effect. At the end of the day, cams will always be about the interaction between models and users. Technology can certainly improve this interaction, but will remain secondary for the time being.

Another technology that I do not see taking off is 4K webcams. A standard internet connection just can not handle that amount of data coming through it. Moreover, most cam models will not want to upgrade to a more expensive webcam when the Logitech c920 can do anything they need and then some. Terpon for example is already manufacturing cameras that will provide 4K resolution, but will not go beyond this to 8K because of compatibility limitations with the USB 3.0 bus. There are also the issues of image processing algorithms that run either on the camera itself or the computer prior to the audio/video encoding that will require dedicated hardware acceleration.

Far more important than VR will be AR. Augmented reality (AR) is a live direct or indirect view of a physical, real-world environment whose elements are augmented (or supplemented) by computer-generated sensory input such as sound, video, graphics or GPS data. Although prototype devices such as the Microsoft HoloLens are still very expensive (the developers' version of the headset was priced at US$3000, but this will quickly fall in the next few years. For a fascinating look at what the future holds, I highly recommend Hyper-Reality, (total runtime approx 6 minutes) is a concept film by Keiichi Matsuda, which is that is freely available on YouTube. Funded on Kickstarter, it presents a provocative and kaleidoscopic new vision of the future, where physical and virtual realities have merged, and the city is saturated in media in a world that has been overtaken by augmented reality. AR will bring full immersion experiences long before VR gains general acceptance. There are endless ways that this will bring ideas, creative ideas and thoughts to life.

According to industry forecasts, the number of Mobile Augmented Reality users is expected to reach 200 million by 2018. Without any doubt, will mobile devices play an important role in mass AR adoption. Based on the exponential growth that we have seen for smart phones, some experts are predicting that AR media will be consumed by more than a billion users by 2020. Huge figures like billions and trillions are thrown around rather casually these days, but bear in mind that print newspapers peaked globally at 450 million. It is important to note that while revenues for AR/VR are forecast to hit $150B revenue by 2020, it is AR that will take the lion's share around $120 billion with VR lagging far behind at just $30 billion.

Augmented Reality (sometimes referred to as Mixed Reality) superimposes graphics, audio and other sensory enhancements, over real-world environments in real-time enhancing a person's experience of an activity. The 2016 Olympic Games in Rio featured Augmented Reality throughout its coverage. Companies like Sportvision offer virtual lane markers and simulation cameras for sports like speed-skating, skiing, and diving. These visualisation tools are key to helping uninitiated audiences understand particular aspects of the sport they are watching.

2015 saw VR hit the peak of its 'hype cycle' with giants like Facebook, Google and Samsung publicly announcing their advancements in VR hardware. Virtual Reality completely removes the viewer from the real world and transports them to a simulated reality. Augmented Reality, on the other hand, enhances the way the viewer experiences the physical world. The viewer is actually encouraged to interact with the real world because these interactions become richer. A regular desk becomes a three-dimensional digital interface, an empty room becomes an interactive prototype, and the park at the end of your street is now full of Pokemon. The Pokemon Go phenomenon is a timely example of how AR encourages people to interact with the real world in ways they would not have otherwise. It is a running joke among players that walking around searching for Pokemon is actually making them fit. This stands in stark contrast to the isolation and disconnection of VR. In 2016 Augmented Reality (AR) reached an important coming of age. Or, at least, became the cool kid at school. We can compare the AR world of today to the internet world as it was mid 90s: new and cool, but very unpredictable.

We are still waiting for smart phones with dual camera set-ups that to allow distance calculations to become commonplace. This will kickstart AR until the hardware evolves in a hands-free optimized direction. This is when smart glasses will become the next generation of mobile devices. Wearable tech with much larger fields of view and rock solid tracking will be the start of an era that will usher in some of the biggest digital advancements we have ever seen on the face of the earth, through the birth of Mixed Reality. Mixed Reality is a hybrid of AR and VR. It combines the use of sensors, advanced optics and next-gen computing power to map and track your surroundings. MR allows users to overlay and interact with augmented 3D holograms within their environment in a manner that is often too difficult to distinguish from reality.

Any major city from New York to Shanghai is filled with folks walking around perpetually staring into the screens of their smartphones. There is even an iPhone app [type-n-walk.com] that now allows you to see what is in front of you while you are typing and walking. Tools like Amazon's UPC scanner are greatly helpful but we are still waiting for a truly disruptive app that allows users to be standing in a store and view items on the shelf through their phone with competing prices from nearby stores or on-line displayed in the air next to them. Technically speaking, AR recognizes a 2D image in 3D space, positions and orients it in that 3D space and then displays some 3D model/animation associated with that picture. Not a technical miracle, but the biggest marvel is not what it does, but the fact it does it cheaply (thanks to a smart phone's serious processing power) and does it well. Mobile devices are not going anywhere any time soon. Consumers spend more than three hours a day engaging on their device, and the least of that is talking. Marketers need to develop a 'small screen first mindset'. It will only take one killer app (probably not a game) and AR could be on millions of people's phones within a week.

The huge success of Pokemon GO put this technology on the map, but is only the beginning. Next board games, books and magazines. Twenty five percent of magazines and print material are expected to be using AR by the end of 2017. Imagine being able to hold your iPhone over your car manual and watch as a 3D diagram of a transmission explodes and reassembles itself. It will soon extend beyond advertising and retail and be implemented more often in scenarios like education, health or even tourism. Now that AR can be powered by the humble smartphone, the cat is well and truly out of the bag. Compare this to the friction that we are seeing in VR hardware adoption. This was the reason Pokemon Go exploded, as users were already armed with smartphones capable of powering the AR tech.

Google announced that the Pokemon Go game was for a time officially more popular than porn, previously presumed to be the Internet's favourite pastime. More people were searching for the new augmented reality game than were searching for x-rated videos. Pokemon Go showed a growth chart that made Candy Crush Saga look sluggish, usage that put Twitter to shame, and engagement that left even messaging apps far behind, all within weeks from launch. It was everywhere in the summer of 2016. The game's famous Pokemon critters virtually swarmed cities and landscapes across the world, using geographic localisation technology to position players and the Pokemon, which appear on the screen, with the backdrop of the player's actual surroundings. Rather than sitting on the couch playing a video game, kids actually went outside and walked around, exploring neighbourhoods they might not ordinarily visit as they simultaneously traversed the real world and the Pokemon world. We can conjure objects into our real world as if by magic with AR, and with Pikachu and friends earning up to $10m per day, R&D departments are desperately searching for the next phase.

Niantic designed a game that was inherently social, as you must have seen in the nearest park last summer, without asking you to link any social profiles or hand out a lot of data. They designed a game with close to no interaction that kept people in, without pushing a single notification. Niantic went against growth hacker's common knowledge in every aspect and kept engagement at levels that made Snapchat jealous. It also helped that 94% of players had a previous experience with Pokemon in one form or another. Pokemon video games are among the most popular in history, with 279 million copies sold before the launch of Go. Pokemon spawned an almost 1,000 episode long TV series (still running!), 19 movies, and tons upon tons of merchandise. Unfortunately the stratospheric growth was not enough to let Pokemon Go reach escape velocity. The gravitational pull proved too strong, strong enough to make 79% players from peak time abandon the game by mid-September. Pokemon Go barely had any end game, mid-game, or, to be honest, any game at all. Much has also been said about how Niantic neglected its community, turning fans into haters.

Despite the hype, Pokemon Go was never a true AR game. The first version of EyeToy, a twelve-year-old camera controller for PlayStation 2, offered more sophisticated AR than this. In Pokemon, AR is a promotional gimmick to feed virality, not a game play element and virality is time-constrained. In September, 45% of players were using the AR mode less than half of the time when playing. Only 22% never turned it off. For most people it became nothing more than a drain on their batteries.

Even so, Augmented Reality is a powerful, potent technology and much more than just a marketing gimmick. There are other far more successful uses of AR in consumer products: Snapchat with its filters and Faceswap and Google Translate, able to read and translate text from the camera on the fly. Or let's take the most promising ones: Magic Leap and Microsoft HoloLens, upcoming devices that will use AR as the primary interface. The common denominator for all these products is that they blend the digital part into reality, not just put it next to reality. With that in mind, think about how much more interesting AR would have been in Pokemon if they made it part of game play. If the 3D model of a Pokemon was not an overlay on the screen, but an element of the environment. If a pokeball could bounce off a table. If Magikarp could jump out of the water. Actual mechanics could be created around how the game elements interact with the physical world.

Pokemon's influence on augmented reality has been to make it much more approachable to the average person. It is no longer some overly technical or niche thing any more like Google Glass, and this is creating some serious anticipation for products like Magic Leap and Microsoft HoloLens. No longer confined to gimmicky smartphone apps and niche industry applications, AR has finally entered the mainstream. In many ways, the mixed reality world is set to become the ultimate computer when your entire field of view becomes an infinite display. For the first time we are seeing a completely new world within a world. Ad agencies are especially excited by AR as content is their bread and butter, and this new technology seems to be a perfect fit for many of their campaigns. This means that until someone invents an ad-blocker extension for AR it could become a nightmare of pop-up spam that makes down town Tokyo look like Trappist monastery. The addition of gamification, encouraging users to want a higher score or to at least maintain that score, will undoubtedly lead to some very self-destructive behaviours. For many users once their device is deactivated, the world will seem like a very dull and sad place without all the colourful 3D holograms. These people will likely become so addicted to the headset that they will never want to remove it.

Once the technology is capable of of facial/body/voice recognition, we could transform ourselves/our sexual partner in AR, allowing personal/partner holographic transformation. This could range from simple gender swap to full metamorphosis for yiffing furries. This will be Snapchat filters gone wild, not to mention voice filters.

Long distance sex will be suddenly be quite feasible, but will meat based boy and girlfriends be so popular once virtual/artificial sex partners become available. With a mix of digital overlay and haptic feedback we will suddenly have access to hentai tentacles, sex maniac poltergeists and even ghostly disembodied body parts.

One specific use case can be taking the users to remote events, utilizing the tech's possibility to connect people (e.g. through holograms) instead of individual entertainment. This will allow AR to snag a huge share in games and entertainment activities. Besides playing, maybe we will also start to attend seminars and parties virtually. In terms of webcamming it will allow models to appear in a users' own front room, posing seductively on their lazy-boy or rolling around on their bed. Existing games such as iStripper will be taken to a whole new level, with both mini strippers on your desk, all the way up to life-size and larger strippers. Body pillows and blow-up dolls will come with AR markings for motion tracking to know if she is on her front or back, etc. The possibilities are really endless with this stuff, we just need the technology to catch up with our imagination.

It will certainly beget more and more fantastical porn. After all why would anybody use this tech for the mundane kind of smut that is already all pervasive? With the aid of an AR device a user can walk into a club and every person in the place will be absolutely stunning. Many of them will probably not even be human, especially if there are AR NPCs walking around. Never had a gorgeous babe/hunk living across the street? Now you can. Think Shallow Hal on steroids.

Death of the Camgirl

Although the next internet megastar might well be a streaming camgirl, it is already clear that the days of pretty girls making millions merely by masturbating on-line are definitely numbered. Desperate young women from Manila to Malindi are already having the same effect on Western camgirls that sweatshop workers in Saigon and Sichuan have had on traditional manufacturing industries, but there is a much greater threat looming than cheap Asian labour. We are rapidly entering the age of artificial intelligence and technological advances are coming thick and fast. Virtual camgirls are already being used by government agencies and internet scammers. How long will it be before cam sites and studios start replacing their flesh and blood camgirls with AI digital avatars? For many, this trend first appeared in 1996, when Deep Blue beat the chess grandmaster and reigning world champion, Garry Kasparov. Machines have long played better backgammon than us. It is hard to know exactly when that happened, but it was somewhere between 1979 (BKG 9.8) and 1992 (TD-Gammon). In those days, systems derived their playing strength mainly from brute force computing power. Deep Blue was a massively parallel, RS/6000 SP Thin P2SC-based system with 30 nodes, with each node containing a 120 MHz P2SC microprocessor, enhanced with 480 special purpose VLSI chess chips. It was capable of evaluating 200 million positions per second and at the time, was ranked the 259th most powerful supercomputer in the world, achieving a speed of 11.38 GFLOPS. Today, some two decades later, a single A15 core inside a Samsung Galaxy S5 has more power (142 GFLOPS) than Deep Blue had across its whole system outputs. And the 192-core GPU on the Tegra K1 SoC produces an even more impressive peak of 364 GFLOPS. In terms of brute, number-crunching power, these mobile graphics processors certainly stand stronger, but most of that power goes towards determining the colour and intensity of each individual pixel every fraction of a second.
These days the average smart phone has more computer power than all of NASA back in 1969, when it placed two astronauts on the moon. In those days, multiple IBM System/360 Model 75 mainframes, costing up to $3.5 million could perform several hundred thousand addition operations per second, and their total memory capacity was in the megabyte range. As for the 70-pound Apollo Guidance Computer, which the Apollo 11 Command Module had on board, it was a machine that had 64 kilobytes of memory and operated at 0.043MHz. Several years later, in 1975, the legendary Cray-1 was capable of 80MHz. While used mainly for scientific projects, one of these behemoths helped render the CGI for the first Tron movie, released in 1982. The Cray-1's raw computational power of 80 million floating-point operations per second (FLOPS) seems laughable when the graphics unit inside the iPhone 5s produces about 76.8 GFLOPS, nearly a thousand times more.

The real breakthrough with Deep Blue was the programming. If someone could compile Deep Blue's chess software to run on a Tegra, it would run faster but it would not necessarily be any more intelligent. Even so, a 2003 documentary entitled Game Over: Kasparov and the Machine, claimed that Deep Blue's victory was little more than a ploy by IBM to boost its stock value. Although it was certainly an historic event, the triumph did not lead to any practical application or to any real world spin-offs. Indeed, IBM retired the machine soon thereafter. Deep Blue was only innovative in that it used specialized hardware for this type of search. The algorithms it used were well-established, and as there was no way to play it as a piece of hardware without great expense, there was no real reason to keep it around.

Today, in computer chess research and matches of world class players against computers, the focus of play has shifted to software chess programs, rather than using dedicated chess hardware. Modern chess programs like Houdini, Rybka, Deep Fritz, or Deep Junior are far more efficient than the programs during Deep Blue's era. Just ten years after Deep Blue, in a November 2006 match between Deep Fritz and world chess champion Vladimir Kramnik, the program ran on a personal computer containing only two Intel Core 2 Duo CPUs, but was still capable of evaluating only 8 million positions per second. Chess engines that you can run today, for free, on your own laptop, such as Stockfish or Komodo (the two strongest chess programs) are far and away better than Deep Blue (and any human), but still do not reach Deep Blue's raw speed.

It would seem that in the world of chess at least, computers are fast leaving humans behind. Chess proficiency is measured with an ELO rating system. This is named after its creator Arpad Elo, a Hungarian-born American physics professor. These days it is used in many sports from football to Scrabble, and even competitive video games such as League of Legends. The latest version of the Komodo chess engine is ELO rated at 3374 while Norwegian Grandmaster and current World Chess Champion, Magnus Carlsen has an ELO of just 2882.

Those with a taste for slightly less intellectual pursuits, will probably recall IBM's Watson trouncing Brad Rutter and Ken Jennings, former champions of the quiz show 'Jeopardy!' in 2011. Watson used advanced natural language processing to access 200 million pages of content, consuming four terabytes of disk storage, including dictionaries, encyclopaedias and the full text of Wikipedia. In total, the system had 2,880 POWER7 processor threads and 16 terabytes of RAM, and was capable of processing 500 gigabytes, the equivalent of a million books per second. The hardware alone cost about three million dollars, but its performance was rated at 80 TeraFLOPs, which nowadays is only about half as fast as the cut-off line for the top 500 Supercomputers list.

In 2007, the IBM team was given three to five years and a staff of fifteen people to solve the Jeopardy challenge. In addition, they drew extensively on faculty and graduate students from Rensselaer Polytechnic Institute, Carnegie Mellon University, University of Massachusetts Amherst, the University of Southern California's Information Sciences Institute, the University of Texas at Austin, MIT, and the University of Trento. By 2008, the developers had advanced Watson such that it could compete with Jeopardy! champions. By February 2010, Watson could beat human Jeopardy! contestants on a regular basis.

Although 'quiz show contestant' might have been the first job made redundant by Watson, the company sees a future in fields such as medical diagnosis, business analytics and legal research. Watson is based on commercially available servers that have been marketed since February 2010. A $1 million IBM Power 750 server is the minimum system requirement to operate Watson but IBM expects the price to decrease substantially within a decade as the technology improves. A number of companies are already working with IBM to create apps embedded with Watson technology. For example, Fluid is developing "The North Face" app for retailers, which is designed to provide advice to on-line shoppers. In the hospitality industry, GoMoment uses Watson for its Rev1 app, which gives hotel staff a way to quickly respond to questions from guests. Watson is even being used via an IBM partner program as a Chatterbot to provide the conversation for children's toys. According to IBM, the cloud-delivered enterprise-ready Watson has seen its speed increase 24 times over, a 2,300 percent improvement in performance, and its physical size has shrunk by 90 percent, from the size of a master bedroom to just three stacked pizza boxes.

Another important benchmark in the incessant march of artificial intelligence versus human intelligence was in March 2016, when Google's AlphaGo computer beat 9th-dan Go master Lee Sedol. One of the early drivers of computer Go research was the 40,000,000 NT dollars Ing Prize, sponsored by Taiwanese banker Ing Chang-ki, offered annually between 1985 and 2000 at the World Computer Go Congress. When the Google-owned company DeepMind finally created an artificial intelligence which could beat a pro, this was generally thought to be a feat that was thought to still be at least a decade away. It is interesting to learn that techniques proven to be the most effective in computer chess have generally shown to be mediocre at Go, partly because Go moves are not as limited by the rules of the game. The first move in chess is more restricted by the smaller size of the board and the way pieces are permitted to move. There are a total of sixteen possible pawn moves on the first turn plus four possible knight moves giving twenty total moves available. On the second turn, the second player is similarly restricted to twenty possible moves making the total number of chess board configurations after two moves to be 400. In computing, this translates into the branching factor. In chess, the average branching factor has been said to be about 35. By comparison, the branching factor for the game Go is 250.

Go (known as weiqi in China) is played on a 19 by 19 board, as compared to the much smaller eight by eight chess field, so Go players begin with a choice of 55 distinct legal moves, accounting for symmetry. This number rises quickly as symmetry is broken, and soon almost all of the 361 points of the board must be evaluated, which means that there are 361 by 360 or 129,960 possible Go board configurations. Some moves are much more popular than others and some are almost never played, but all are possible. The means that the search space for Go's game tree is both far wider and much deeper than that of chess. It has been estimated to be as large as 10^{170} compared to 10^{50} for chess, making the normal brute-force game tree search algorithms much less effective. To provide a little more perspective. The estimated number of atoms in the observable universe is only 10^{80}.

To operate AlphaGo, Google Tensorflow software uses a specialised Tensor Processing Unit (TPU), which it claims has advanced machine learning capability by a factor of three generations, the equivalent to fast-forwarding technology about seven years into the future. The company has been running TPUs inside their data centres for more than a year, and have found them to deliver an order of magnitude better-optimized performance per watt for machine learning. The TPU is tailored to machine learning applications, allowing the chip to be more tolerant of reduced computational precision, which means it requires fewer transistors per operation to use more sophisticated and powerful machine learning models. Actually, it should come as no surprise that a custom, purpose built ASIC is much faster at very specific tasks than general all-purpose chips. Similar chips have completely taken over other very specialised tasks such as Bitcoin mining.

AlphaGo evaluated thousands of times fewer positions than Deep Blue did in its chess match against Kasparov; compensating by selecting those positions more intelligently, using the policy network, and evaluating them more precisely, using the value network, an approach that is perhaps closer to how humans play. Furthermore, while Deep Blue relied on a hand crafted evaluation function, the neural networks of AlphaGo are trained directly from game play, purely through general-purpose supervised and reinforcement learning methods. Go is harder to write a bot for, because chess is more complex in ways that are hard for humans, while go is more complex in ways that are hard to program. Go is exemplary in many ways of the difficulties faced by artificial intelligence: a challenging decision-making task, an intractable search space, and an optimal solution so complex, it appears infeasible to directly approximate using a policy or value function. By using a new approach to computer Go that uses 'value networks' to evaluate board positions, and 'policy networks' to select moves we can now begin to anticipate that human-level performance can now be achieved in other seemingly intractable artificial intelligence domains.

Actually neural networks have been around for a while (since the 50s!) and they are essentially a decision-making black box. In Alphago's case, a 13-layer policy neural network started as a blank slate, with no prior exposure to Go. It then was trained on thirty million board positions from 160,000 real-life games taken from a Go database. That number represents far more games that any professional player would encounter in a lifetime. This is thanks to a complex cognitive neural architecture that was able to mimic certain kinds of child-level cognition with tiny amounts of training data.

Reinforcement learning was implemented years ago in neural networks to mimic animal behaviour and to train robots. DeepMind demonstrated this in 2015 with a vengeance when networks were taught how to play 49 different Atari 2600 video games, including Video Pinball, Pong and Space Invaders. Each time it played, the DeepMind network saw the same video game screen, including the current score that any human player would see. The network's output was a command to the joystick to move the cursor on the screen. It learned to move, to hit alien ships and to avoid being destroyed by them. And for most games, it achieved superhuman performance. Even so, the program runs on off-the-shelf processors.

Giving it access to more computational power (by distributing it over a network of 1,200 CPUs and GPUs) only improved its performance marginally. In a very magnanimous move, the developers openly described in exhausting detail the algorithms and parameter settings the DeepMind team used to generate AlphaGo. This further accelerates the frenetic pace of AI research in academic and industrial laboratories worldwide and is much better than publishing in Nature and other pay walled sites. Like you, I do not attend an expensive university, but I do still like to learn new things.

DeepMind's updated AlphaGo has since been anonymously vanquishing the world's top Go players on-line. With a streak of 60 wins and the defeat of reigning Go champion Ke Jie, DeepMind's AlphaGo has now made the same mark on the game of Go that IBM's Deep Blue made on chess. Go is a game that is very computationally difficult for traditional chess-style techniques. Human masters learn to play Go very intuitively, because the human cortical algorithm turns out to generalize well. If deep learning can do something similar, plus (a previous real sign) have a single network architecture learn to play loads of different old computer games, that may indicate we are starting to get into the range of neural algorithms that generalize well, the way that the human cortical algorithm generalizes well.

The next challenge is going to be independent learning. Human experts still supervise the learning process of all the best AIs. Once the need for the human adviser goes away, AIs are literally going to be everywhere. Your phone AI will recognize and react to your current mental state, as well as help you overcome everyday problems. The AI in your fridge could become a huge help in keeping you compliant with your diet plans.

If you are wondering how much humans will have to teach A.I. In the future, the answer is very little. DeepMind learned to beat the best go players in the world by teaching itself through trial and error. All the researchers had to do was explain how to determine success, and the A.I. can then begin playing games against itself on a loop while always reinforcing any strategies that lead to more success. Or, maybe, researchers will find that defining success in a more abstract way will lead to better results.

In terms of gaming we are now reaching some interesting limitations in terms of machine intelligence. Heroes of Might and Magic and other turn-based strategy games such as Disciples and even Walking Dead: No Man's Land are popular among strategy board game enthusiasts. It is interesting to note that even by the second release of Heroes, the AI was so good that it was no longer any fun to play and had to be dumbed down by the developers. This is actually a very common complaint about computerised board games: most are so skilful that they are no fun to play against. I love playing Scrabble but hate being thoroughly humiliated by Quackle or Elise, two of the current leading-edge scrabble programs. It is interesting that although software can be programmed to beat grandmasters and world champions, when it comes to playing an enjoyably challenging game with lower level opponents, the most commonly used strategy is for the program to perform at the same level with a few idiotic mistakes thrown in to balance things out.

Beating the Go champion might seem like an impressive AI milestone but humans have now begun devising games where they still have the upper hand. Arimaa for example has a branching factor of 17281, Connect6 is a 46000 and Nymbat a whopping 10^9. In the meantime, any game that involves Natural Language Processing (NLP), Syntactic Analysis (Parsing) and World Knowledge such as Diplomacy is still not really doable. This means that we still have plenty of time to worry about what academics term "the AI alignment problem" computerspeak for what most us know as "the Skynet apocalypse".

One result of the AlphaGo result is that a lot more Asians are now intrigued by the technology and the future of AI. Suddenly a great many Koreans, Chinese and

Taiwanese are suddenly afraid of losing their jobs because of advanced AI. Google's DeepMind AI now plans to take on StarCraft II, a Korean dominated bastion of modern eSports. Google and Blizzard are opening up the RTS (real time strategy) game to anyone who wants to teach artificial intelligence systems how to conduct warfare. Players fight against one another by gathering resources to pay for defensive and offensive units. It has a healthy competitive community that is known for having a ludicrously high skill level. How long will it be before Alphago asks its operator "Do you want to play a game? How about Global Thermonuclear War?" This newest development caused a deal of consternation on various technology forums with comments ranging from So it is fine if Google starts running bots, but if I do it, I immediately get a ban. They are really going to "teach artificial intelligence systems how to conduct warfare"? Do you want Skynet? Because that's how you get Skynet!

DeepMind A.I. has previously conquered complicated turn-based games like chess and go, where both players see the complete world state. Armed with that knowledge, it is easy to be systematic and deterministic. Games like Poker and Starcraft hide part of the world state from each player, forcing them to guess at the parts they can not see. And so a real-time strategy game makes sense as the next frontier. In fact, the best limit Texas Hold'Em poker player in the world is already a robot. Researchers at the University of Alberta essentially "brute forced" the game of limit poker, in which there are roughly 3×10^{14} possible decisions. Cepheus runs through a massive table of all of these possible permutations of the game, the table itself is 11 terabytes of data, and decides what the best move is, regardless of opponent. Even so, No limit Texas Hold'Em, in which any amount of bet in any dollar amount can be made, is by far the most popular. Limit poker has roughly 3×10^{14} permutations; no limit poker has 3×10^{48}, which is many orders of magnitude harder to solve.

Despite this, in the recent "Brains vs. AI" poker competition, an AI named Libratus created at Carnegie Mellon trounced its human opponents, who are four of the world's top professional players. One of the pros, Jimmy Chou, said he and his colleagues initially underestimated Libratus, but have come to regard it as one tough player. "The bot gets better and better every day," Chou said. "It's like a tougher version of us"... Chou said he and the other pros have shared notes and tips each day, looking for weaknesses they can each exploit. "The first couple of days, we had high hopes," Chou said. "But every time we find a weakness, it learns from us and the weakness disappears the next day." Unlike with games like Chess (best moves can be precisely calculated) and Backgammon (simple probabilities), Poker requires adapting to human behaviour, indeed varying your play depending on what you learn about your opponent.

These techniques are going to be applicable to a wide range of situations. For instance, AI will soon take over from humans to advise us on investment decisions. (In the past, the computer has been used for speed, and reacting to subtle market signals, but not so much for long term investment planning.) Basically, beating poker pros is the skill to con a human. I see great reprehensible applications in advertising, manipulation of elections and other fields of human-created evil. How long will it be before hackers use this kind of software to break an on-line gambling site. In theory, a user could just run this in their basement, simply babysitting the AI, acting on all the human-check captchas the sites deploy, and just doing what the AI decides? In this case, on-line poker effectively becomes gold farming.

Most of the attention around automation focuses on how factory robots and self-driving cars may fundamentally change our workforce, potentially eliminating millions of jobs. But AI that can handle knowledge-based, white-collar work are also becoming increasingly competent. One Japanese insurance company, Fukoku Mutual Life Insurance, is reportedly replacing 34 human insurance claim workers with IBM Watson Explorer, starting in January 2017. The AI will scan hospital records and other documents to determine insurance payouts, according to a company press release, factoring injuries, patient medical histories, and procedures administered. Automation of these research and data gathering tasks will help the remaining human workers process the final payout faster. Fukoku Mutual will spend $1.7 million (200 million yen) to install the AI system, and $128,000 per year for maintenance, according to Japan's The Mainichi. The company will save roughly $1.1 million per year on employee salaries by using the IBM software, meaning it hopes to see a return on the investment in less than two years, as well as improving productivity by 30%, Fukoku Mutual says. The company was encouraged by its use of similar IBM technology to analyse customer's voices during complaints. The software typically takes the customer's words, converts them to text, and analyses whether those words are positive or negative. Similar sentiment analysis software is also being used by a range of US companies for customer service; incidentally, a large benefit of the software is understanding when customers get frustrated with automated systems. The Mainichi reports that three other Japanese insurance companies are testing or implementing AI systems to automate work such as finding ideal plans for customers.

Artificial intelligence systems like IBM's are poised to upend knowledge-based professions, like insurance and financial services, according to the Harvard Business Review, due to the fact that many jobs can be composed of work that can be codified into standard steps and of decisions based on cleanly formatted data. But whether that means augmenting workers' ability to be productive, or replacing them entirely remains to be seen. Almost all jobs have major elements that, for the foreseeable future, will not be possible for computers to handle. And yet, we have to admit that there are some knowledge-work jobs that will simply succumb to the rise of the robots. The largest mistake mankind could make is underestimating the speed at which AI will prove it can do a lot of things better, faster, and more accurately than any human could ever do. Underestimating that speed will greatly reduce our ability to properly prepare for a world of unemployable humans. It is important that we do not underestimate the power of learning at damn near an exponential rate.

There are still problems regarding human language processing as slang, cant and argot change very quickly. Teenagers, in particular, will change the meaning of words, or create words, or even maul grammar to include or exclude others from their cliques. Irony and sarcasm are other bollards to progress for computers in this sense.

An AI can solve imperfect information games, it just is a lot harder. Since the game has aspects of randomness, it is impossible to win every single time, but in the long run, the AI plays as well as or better than any other player.

I personally would be really interested to see what would the results with DeepMind playing a Civilization type game, in which cooperation and soft-power are far more important than warfare strategies. While Civilization is little more than a glorified board game which bears only the slightest passing resemblance to reality, a much more in depth creation such as Buckminster Fuller's World Game might give us some hints on how to manage diplomacy/belligerence in a way that could lead to some interesting thought experiments in the real world.

Even so, the trend is now clear. A set of algorithms was able to outperform a human rival in a game that has many trillions of possible outcomes. In contrast, recreating a five minute fapping session will be childsplay.

We have now reached a technological point of convergence where a number of different media can recreate the telepresence of even the sexiest camgirl. In Hollywood movies, such lifelike CGI characters are quickly becoming common place. In Peter Jackson's The Lord of the Rings trilogy, Gollum is an entirely CGI character voiced and performed by actor Andy Serkis. The character was built around Serkis' facial features while the iconic "Gollum" throat noise was based on the sound of his cat coughing up hairballs. Using a digital puppet created at Weta Digital, animators created Gollum's performance using a mixture of motion capture data and a process known digital rotoscoping. Technically speaking this was an impressive achievement and won an award for Best Virtual Performance for the movie The Two Towers at the 2003 MTV Movie Awards. The category has since been reintroduced and has more recently been won by Scooby Doo, Kangaroo Jack, Dobby from Harry Potter and Yoda from Star Wars: Episode II. Gollum was shown as virtually naked, save for a loincloth and so the leap from 'my precious' to pixillated pornstar will not be that difficult to make. Augmented Reality and Digital Surrogates of porn stars performing with AI built in will be clearly the next logical step. After all, few hetero males fantasise about having a go with Gollum.

Hollywood studio hard-drives, are already filled with full body digital models and performance capture files of actors and actresses. When these 'perf-cap' files are assigned to any suitable 3D CGI model, an animator can bring to life the Digital Surrogate of the original actor. These are coupled with realistic skin rendering using Separable Subsurface Scattering (SSSS) rendering techniques and AI 'libraries.' The technology exists today, and better iterations will come about in the next couple of years. Wearing an Augmented Reality visor means that it would be possible to connect via the internet to your partner, and have their live perf-capture session captured to drive a photo-realistic avatar of your favourite pornstar. As AI algorithms improve, bordering on artificial sentience, the need for a human performance capture will become unnecessary. These days most coders rely on expensive hardware to ensure speed and smoothness, but we are going to have to squeeze as much performance out as possible if we want to see high level of visual fidelity on reasonably priced machines. DOOM 2016 for example, used the Vulkan API to push graphics quality and performance to new levels. John Carmack's technowizardry was a major game changer in the early 90s, when people wanted to play FPS games on computers bought for DOS spreadsheets. Since then, the 3D accelerator graphics card made much of the Id technology obsolete, but that may be changing once again.

Although there are now plenty of AAA games with comparable, if not better, graphics, the most impressive thing about Doom 2016 is the way that it runs silky smooth on relatively underpowered hardware, consistently achieving 60 fps at 1440p on even low-tier GPUs. Contemporary releases such as No Man's Sky are no where near as good in terms of performance across such a wide range of hardware. The algorithmic complexity of things such as texture atlasing, tiled rendering, mega-textures, and reflection computation... all the aspects of a modern game engine, are all going to have to be improved if we want to see continued 3D development.

Historically, Id Software is known for open-sourcing their graphics engines after a few years, which often leads to great remakes and breakdowns but whether this will stand true with Id Tech 6 remains to be seen. In addition, Carmack is now working at Oculus under the auspices of Facebook and so GPL releases are probably unlikely. Of course, some very solid open source engines have popped up on their own from hobby programmers, but big budget AAA video games do not come out of open source volunteers, whose only barrier is the graphics engine. For a long time now, the most difficult part producing modern large games has been the art assets and (to a slightly lesser extent) the game play code. The games that cost millions of dollars to produce, spend most of that money on an army of artists and a very small number of engine programmers in comparison. The good news is that digital sex bots are not going to require the vast virtual worlds that are expected of big blockbuster games. In a major release video game the complex setting and fantasy milieus are de rigeur. In porno, the backgrounds are almost irrelevant.

All over the world, small software start ups are already working on creating their own million dollar cam girl and you have to be extremely naive to believe that painstakingly programmed porn stars are not just around the corner. In fact, they might already be here. How can you be sure that the all the girls on Livejasmine are actually flesh and blood humans? If a selection of those sexy little starlets are in fact digitised avatars, then the company is certainly not going to admit it publicly. Consider for a moment that effects genius Stan Winston was making realistic looking dinosaurs for James Cameron more than two decades ago. In that time computer power has increased by a factor of thousand or more, and so it is hard to believe that we still can not make a bangable looking chatbot. Winston's creations were considered characters rather than special effects and this is what is needed to create a really convincing camgirl. A great innovator and hugely influential artist, Winston bridged the gap between the pleasantly unrealistic stop-motion creations of Ray Harryhausen and Jack Pierce-style monster make-up, to the CGI extravaganzas of Michael Bay. Among Winston's other triumphs were the Alien Queen in James Cameron's Aliens, the endoskeleton of the Terminator's robots, the Predator and the talking teddy from A.I. Artificial Intelligence. It's about you being able to relate to them, he once said. You could see something in the language of those creatures.

Movie dinosaurs have quickly gone from dressed up piglets and costumed iguanas in Raquel Welch's heyday to a 9,000lb Tyrannosaur constructed out of sheets of metal and powerful hydraulics that could be controlled and adjusted live on set. The two T-Rexes in The Lost World weighed twice as much as their predecessor thanks to finer machinery, and the Spinosaurus was bigger again, at 44ft long and 25,000lbs. 'Even though I created this thing, I got so caught up in it that I suddenly didn't see it as a machine, but rather as a real animal." This is the kind of approach that we need to see with both digital and physical sex bots.

Before his death in 2008, Winston was working with Jon Favreau on the first Iron Man's robotic suits. These have since become almost as ubiquitous as storm trooper outfits. Anybody with a vacuum forming table in their garage can now knock out realistic looking outfits like this. Suspension of disbelief is key. "Special effects, by themselves, don't mean diddly squat in a movie, said Winston. If the characters I created can't perform, can't act and aren't interesting, it isn't going to work. It's not enough to give something more. It has to be more real." This is the kind of can do attitude that we need to create believable sex bots and functional gynoids

As usual, it is the Japanese who are leading the field in this area. In the studios of downtown Yokohama, X-rated cartoons are freed of the body's physical limitations and animated porn stars can fulfill any type of taboo desires. Japanese hentai has always been the domain of kinky fetishes such as tentacle rape and thinly disguised paedophilia. Now that it is entering the realm of hyper-realistic 3D animations, things are only getting weirder. Hentai is actually short for hentai seiyokuto, or perverse sexual pleasure. It is not at all a new phenomenon and the genre has long been an outlet for kinky perversions. A woodblock from 1814, called The Dream of the Fisherman's Wife, depicts a woman with her legs spread wide, getting pleasured in all her orifices by a very obliging octopus.

3D Hentai by itself is unlikely to kill the human porn star. Repeated video loops of naked bodies are simply not enough to cut it in a world where interaction is becoming more important all the time. Hentai is rapidly transitioning from two dimensions to three, and unlike the frozen faces of their 2D counterparts, the computer-rendered porn stars of 3D hentai look positively fleshy. The biggest difference between 2D and 3D hentai is the latter's hyper-reality. Even though computer-rendered cartoon porn aims to look lifelike, its real appeal lies in the fact that these massively endowed stars are actually superhuman, therefore more virtual, more expressive, and more pliant than their human colleagues. Their eroticism does not lie in looking completely human, but rather in their surreal strangeness. Mainstream video games, CGI films, and even advertising have long been aiming for OCD-level attention to detail. Cartoon porn is just catching up. As the adult film industry grinds to a halt, it is easy to see why these digital avatars could easily replace frail, disease-prone adult actors and awkwardly faked orgasms.

Japanese high school girl Saya made headlines around the world in 2016, after it was revealed that she did not actually exist. The girl was, in fact, a 3-D computer-generated model with an incredibly life-like appearance that fooled everyone into thinking she was a living, breathing student. Self-taught computer graphics designers, husband-and-wife team Yuka and Teruyuki Ishikawa, created stunning skin tones that had an incredibly realistic texture. The amazing details extended to the reflection in her irises and even the flyaway strands of hair on her head. Unfortunately, as an animated 3D character, Saya is still lumbering and clumsy. This is true for a great deal of 3D porn. Ironically some of the main problems in recreating realistic avatars is that they look far too realistic, too professional to be real. Very few human beings are perfectly photogenic. Even the most beautiful people are imperceptibly flawed, but flawed they are. This instinctive kind of inclination is something that is very difficult to capture. It is relatively easy to make a T-Rex or a terminator look 200% lifelike, mainly because none of us has ever seen the real thing, and have no real world frame of reference to which we can compare. Fellow human beings on the other hand, we see every single day and much of our observation is done at the unconscious level. We can all tell the difference between a Westerner and an Asian at fifty yards simply by their gait, but I would challenge you to put that difference into words. We all know immediately if a child is even slightly retarded but what is it that makes it so clear? Most guys can tell the difference between a ladyboy and a real girl long before it is too late to back out but very few of us can explain what gives it away. Perhaps we will need to understand these minor details in much greater detail before we can replicate fully the female form in all its glory.

The other problem is that modern pornstars are now so far removed from reality, that for many men, their sense of attraction has been significantly altered. Silicon implants, unnatural skin tones and endless surgery mean that the average adult starlet is now significantly different to the average woman on the street. This goes some way to explain the ever increasing popularity of ladyboys, from Bangkok to Lagos to Las Vegas. If your fantasy female no longer resembles a real world version, then it makes perfect sense that you would choose a clever fabrication.

Second Life, the on-line community where user-generated cartoon porn has long proliferated, had its adult community confined to a red light district in 2009. While Hollywood aims for picture perfect recreations, it is hobbyists that are pushing the envelope in realistic digital porn. Umemaro 3D for example is a Japanese doujin circle that has been involved in 3DCG animated pornographic work since 2002. Doujin, is a Japanese term for a group of people or friends who share a common interest, such as a manga fan club or even a sewing circle. These days, the term is usually used to refer to amateur self-published works, including manga, novels, fan guides, art collections, music and video games. Some professional artists participate as a way to publish material outside the regular publishing industry. Despite westerners' unfamiliarity with the term, it is a multi billion dollar business.

Literary circles first appeared in the Meiji period such as the Kenyusha society of literary writers that first published collected works in magazine form in 1885. After World War II, manga doujin started to appear in Japan. Manga artists like Shotaro Ishinomori (Kamen Rider, Cyborg 009) and Fujio Fujiko (Doraemon) formed doujin groups for artists to make a professional debut. This changed in the coming decades with doujin groups forming as school clubs and culminated in

1975 with the Comiket in Tokyo. A portmanteau of "Comic Market, the largest doujin convention covering more than over 20 acres on a twice yearly basis, and attracts in excess of a million attendees each year. Doujin creators who base their materials on other creators' works normally publish in small numbers to maintain a low profile and avoid litigation, which makes them highly collectible.

Over the last decade, the practice of creating doujin has expanded significantly, attracting thousands of creators and fans alike. Advances in personal publishing technology have also fuelled this expansion by making it easier for doujin creators to write, draw, promote, publish, and distribute their works.

A major part of doujinshi, whether based on mainstream publications or original, contains sexually explicit material, due to both the large demand for such publications and absence of restrictions that official publishing houses have to follow. Indeed, often the main point of a given doujinshi is to present an explicit version of a popular show's characters. Such works may be known to English speakers as "H-doujinshi", in line with the former Japanese use of letter H to denote erotic material. The Japanese usage, however, has since moved towards the word ero, and so ero manga is the term almost exclusively used to mark doujinshi with adult themes. As in fanfics, a very popular theme to explore is non-canonical pairings of characters in a given show. Another category of doujinshi is furry or kemono, often depicting homosexual male pairings of furries and, less often, lesbian pairings, sometimes described as Futanari, a term for female characters that are generously endowed with male genitalia.

Most of Umemaro's works centre around seemingly mundane places such as colleges, hospitals, and your typical regular Japanese households. Despite the unusually standard locations, the sexual acts performed in all of them break all kinds of social taboos. Sex between high school students, student-teacher romance, S&M relationships, and medical professionals engaging in lewd acts with their patients, these are just a few of the themes explored in Umemaro's brand of erotic productions. Lately, with the more story-driven projects such as Twin Succubus, the 3D artist has also introduced some supernatural motifs, such as demons and ghosts into his work. In an attempt to put the "joy" back in joystick, the studio has also released two full-featured, text-based adventure games, OMEGA and OMEGA 2. Umemaro 3D then expanded into non-animated comics with the release of The Chiropractor in December 2014, which was distributed in both PDF and JPG formats.

The interactivity aspect of Umemaro 3D movies is not the only thing has improved over the years. One only needs to take a chronological look through their expansive portfolio to notice immense improvements in rendering style, animation, sound design and body jiggle physics. Later releases featured new camera angles, point of view shots, interactive CG galleries, sex scene speed selections and more. Each new Umemaro release is marked by some major improvement, further solidifying the creator's ever-increasing appeal. Even so, the works are not without their flaws. While sex movements are often very realistic, more everyday motions such as standing and walking are stilted and unnatural.

The artist himself has a personal preference for needlessly large breasts and wide hips which often look distinctly out of place on otherwise petite Japanese characters. The faces of his female protagonists are strikingly beautiful but the males incorporated into the storylines are far less appealing, often bordering on cartoon caricatures. Other problems include unrealistic weight displacement that results in lumbering and lurching, which looks completely out of place on what are supposed to be petite Japanese schoolgirls. Another repeated criticism is that the creators include far too many different camera angles. This unintentionally gives it away that this cannot possibly be real. After all this is a porno, not some Ridley Scott masterpiece. Sex movie directors usually stick with the same predictable shot that focuses on the action. Only art house auteurs go for the unusual angles and multiple cut-aways in order to exemplify their craft. Porn flicks on the other hand, change angle much more infrequently, keen to give viewers chance to focus very carefully on their fantasy.

The credits for every release since Twin Succubus identify Umemaro as the 3D animator, Hirobon as the system programmer, and Akiwo Watanabe as the scenario writer. Umemaro has been working in the 3DCG industry for most of his professional career. His pre-Umemaro 3D work was with Forester, a 1990s 3D CG eroge company. He uses LightWave 7.5, Adobe Creative Suite 3 (specifically Photoshop, Premiere, and After Effects), Real Flow 4, and FiberFX. He regularly makes lengthy technical blog posts where for example, he complains about background flickering problems in Radiosity and FiberFX. He explains that he uses three PCs for network rendering with 200 frames taking about thirty minutes to complete. The area lighting feature improves quality, but the actual number of lights exponentially increases the rendering time. Two lights doubles the workload and three quadruples it, even without Radiosity.

Starting from Lewd Consultation Room, all of Umemaro 3D's movie collections have been subtitled in English, and two of them (Lewd Consultation Room and Twin Succubus) have even been professionally dubbed in English. The circle's work is available for purchase at DMM and Dlsite. Popular streaming sites include Hentaimama, Hentaistigma and Xvideos which feature some of the leading artists in the field such as Nishikawa Takashi and Doublesoft Cream although like most Japanese porn much of it is still censored with genital pixellation. Forums that discuss the field include LewdGamer and Hongfire.

Once the first Ashley Madison type chatbots are combined with Umemaro type graphics (probably at low resolution for mobile phone users), the result will quickly start putting webcamgirls out of work. It will not take long before it has a knock on effect, making life harder for all kinds of strippers, dancers and even hookers. Although secrecy is paramount at the moment, there are already numerous companies working on similar projects. Even when a porn production company like Brazzers launches a product like Oversnatch (an Overwatch porn parody), this is still pushing the very same tools that are required to create a computer generated cam girl. Occasionally there are hints dropped in the dark recesses of adult webmaster forums such as GFY.com but the potential market for this is in the trillions and nobody wants to give away their competitive advantage.

How many people two decades ago would have said yes, they would regularly jerk off to lighted up pixels on a screen transmitted across a series of tubes? Hell, how many people would admit that now? From less than half an inch away, even the hottest pornstar is nothing more than millions of pixels containing one yellow dot, one red dot and one blue dot. Even when your brain knows this to be true on a logical level, it makes little or no difference. When the illusion is strong enough - the evolutionary instincts kick in, and the brain is all in.

Male sexuality is much more visually focused than female sexuality, and we see this throughout the history of porn. Women have had dildos since time immemorial. A disembodied penis and an imagination being just fine for their masturbatory fantasies, but men have endlessly pursued images to fire up their fantasies.

This will be the cybersex of the new generation. There are so many sexual subsets out there, that we will quickly see a proliferation of characters that will stretch far beyond the female form that we are used to. It will not be long before elves, green Orion slave girls and devil women are all on offer. Not to mention the market for Otherkin, who simply put, are people who believe they are something "other" than human, be it a vampire, elf, fairy, dragon, or the like.

Unfortunately, porn because of its very nature, receives little academic attention. Open discussion of Japanese porn in particular has been driven even further underground. Because of its violent, and taboo themes, 3D hentai is already facing all kinds of censorship. Even specialists like Professor Mark McLelland, a sociologist and cultural historian, specialising in Japanese sexuality, gender theory and new media are unwilling to discuss these subjects. Although he has published titles ranging from 'Japanese Cybercultures' to ' Male Homosexuality in Modern Japan,' he refuses to elaborate on his research, saying that in Australia, where he is based, even talking about this stuff is potentially illegal. Sweeping these subjects under the carpet will not make them magically go away. If we have learned anything from the twentieth century it should have been that prohibition is never a satisfactory solution and usually makes matters far worse than they would have otherwise been.

Three Documentary Recommendations

Sex Lies And Rinsing Guys

This documentary chronicled the rinsing habits of three beautiful young women, whose prey consists of men who are daft enough to donate gifts and cash to them, in return for minimal effort on their part. That is what rinsing means, getting stuff for nothing. Mugging, really; certainly the men who fall for it are mugs. The show follows the tactics of three gold diggers as they manipulate horny and very wealthy men, relieving them of their cash and nothing else. It featured the lives of Jeannette Worthington, Danica Thrall and Hollie Capper who make a living rinsing rich guys.

This was a fascinating documentary about three young women who, by dint of their glamorous appearances, are able to solicit expensive gifts and cash from wealthy men in return for nothing more than, say, a friendly tweet, a phone call or the chance to treat the girl to dinner. Indeed, their businesses are based on cultivating friendships with these men, who are then expected to pay for the privilege of attention from these modern-day sirens. But make no mistake: these women are not prostitutes, and sex is strictly off the menu. After all, as Jeanette from Liverpool said during the programme: I do nice things for my friends and do not expect to have sex with them. Basically these girls are hookers with out the happy ending. But the girls insist they are doing nothing wrong. They do not engage in sex or force men into giving gifts, just hint at what they want on social media. If they are lucky they might get a thank you Tweet or a chat on Skype, priced at £50 for 10 minutes, provided they do not talk about sex. And, astonishingly, the brazen model claims she is the one being exploited by her fans. She said: Never have I felt an ounce of guilt. I'm just using what I'm good at to gain money, just as nurses do.

Danica charges up to 50 quid for ten minutes of scintillating conversation about what she ate for dinner over Skype, while up in Mansfield, Hollie receives 200 pounds for six minutes of financial dominatrixing via webcam. "The last deposit you made in my bank account was pitiful, pig," she faux-rages. "You're going to have to do better."

This sheds some much needed light on the weird world of financial domination and the psychology of the individuals involved. Hollie realises that there is a submissive sexual element to it all too, which she takes full advantage of, castigating one of her financers for being fat, poor and pathetic during a web-chat. Yes mistress, said the chap time and again, enjoying her derision. Financial domination, or findom as it is known in the trade, is clearly a viable business.

Meanwhile, blonde glamour model Jeannette demands trips to New York and designer handbags via the medium of Blackberry Messenger. Apparently it does have a name though, 'damsel in distress' syndrome. Because nothing says 'buy me a dyson' like a lost little woman standing in Debenhams like a bewildered fawn carrying a dachshund. The girls themselves seem to believe that they are pioneering in some form of feminist campaign whereby women bleed blokes dry in the name of the sisterhood. "Girls should feel well more empowered," Hollie advises us. She sells stuff she gets on eBay, with help from her mum, who must be very proud. But their ambition to level the playing field in terms of power is tragically misguided and their pursuit of motherfuckers to pay the bills is likely to have done little to inspire another generation of bra burners. The ladies themselves insist that they are smart business women, using what they have to make ends meet, but their subjugation of the opposite sex (and unwittingly, themselves) sees them pegged back to the same level of your average posh female escort of the Victorian era.

This investigation into the insidious world of using-good-looks-to-steal-from-lonely-men attracted almost 50, 000 tweets and some pretty vigorous debate. If there is one thing to take away from the show, it is that lots of men clearly have more money than sense. Or perhaps more accurately, more money than sex. The ladies realised that a lot of these men are lonely and took full advantage of the fact, charging them hundreds of pounds for a brief chat on Skype. Of course, the girls professed to find the situation strange and spent most of the show belittling their wealthy, besotted patrons. Muppets, mugs, suckers, that is how these men were described by the girls, but it did not stop the chaps from showering them with gifts. The ladies attempted to explain this by hypothesising that some men get an ego boost from knowing that their donations have enabled girls to wear glamorous clothes or sport expensive make-up. However, the ladies' callous, materialistic and amoral attitudes seemed to stem not solely from greed, but from bad experiences earlier in life: Jeanette and Hollie both claimed to have been bullied for being 'ugly' while they were at school, and Danica reported having been sexually exploited during her time in the glamour industry. Two of the girls were single mothers, and all the women insisted that they were not looking for romance in their lives, that they had almost given up on the idea of finding happiness with a man. Anybody who has worked in a strip clubs understands that men are easily lead and stupid to come in and pay ridiculous money on girls that are just blatantly taking the piss.

Whether it is to gain a pair of shoes or to get a bloke to do the washing up, it has been happening since Noah was a lad. There have been other terms used for such practices in the past like Gold Diggers or having a Sugar Daddy, but are we now living in the Age of Mr Grey where all types of relationships are based on strange power games?

At its most basic level these girls are con artists, and all of this is technically illegal but hard to enforce as victims rarely press charges. The rinsers are clearly involved in deception and emotional manipulation for financial gain. This is very similar to fortune teller scams. They also share similarities with the West African 419 internet scams whose goal is to squeeze the most money possible out of their victims. They use social networking, lots of lying and Machiavellian, emotional manipulation. This rinsing is a form of fraud and I do not see how anyone can celebrate this in good conscience. The guys who are victims, often young, have very poor models of how male female relations actually work. They may be following a deeply flawed Disneyland/Hollywood idea of romantic relations. This would make them easy marks for rinsers.

Even more interesting than the show itself was the response that the "rinsing royalty" received on social media. Danica cashed in on the gold-digging documentary to demand another £7,000 worth of luxury trinkets and triggered a barrage of on-line abuse in the process. She was blasted for posting her wish-list on Twitter hours after the Channel 4 screening. Hollie has called in the police after receiving a string of death threats following her TV appearance.

One person tweeted "F***ing slag I'll slice your throat."

Other entertaining comments included the following:

"I've had baths deeper than these vapid, ugly on the inside, vultures."

"I am willing to place money on one of those girls going missing one day. They'll accept a ticket to Russia over BBM, piss off the wrong person and never return, I guarantee it."

"An great example of the female role model du jour! I want to be just like that when I grow up!!! Pathetic and sad. Have a bit of self respect girls, and be a better role model for your kids!!!"

The Truth About Webcam Girls

BBC Three's investigation into the world of on-line sex/striptease shows covered everything from the grim functionality of squeezing in a game of X-Box between punters and managing to strip off when you have still got your leggings and everyday socks on, to the dark underbelly lurking beneath webcam sex - the financial lure of hardcore porn and escorting. The Truth About Webcam Girls from director Chris Atteshlis was an admirably unsalacious and untitillating hour about three of the women who make up the panting, pouting army of thousands earning money by getting naked or semi-so in front of their computers for an equally heavily breathing army of one-handed typists at home.

While the documentary managed to maintain a light tone - "Whips, latex, baby oil, dog lead, nipple clamps, anal beads?" the show did not shirk its responsibility to unearth the most grim parts of their lives. The beginning of the documentary veered head first into titillation, pushing the viewers into the position of the punter, getting a full-frontal display of bending, teasing and smutty talks. As we got to know the girls, unravel their pasts and their insecurities, anyone leering over the show must have been left feeling pretty grubby. While some of the revelations may not have been too shocking, it certainly lifted the lid on an industry without an ounce of glamour.

From the scarred former porn actress Sammie ("I would never do that again. I would never do movies like that again. But I would beat up some guys for money.") to the lonely singleton Carla, who is happy to take on pretty much any request (naked except Ugg boots with cooking oil - why not?), but can not find a man, to 21-year-old Olivia, who currently covers her modesty on-line. But how long can she avoid the lure of much more cash. Sammie has starred in over 100 adult movies, but her experiences in the industry have left her emotionally scarred. She is desperate to leave a troubled past behind and hopes that she can make enough money on the webcam to return to college. Sammie's tales of her previous career in hardcore porn, "I pushed myself to limits I didn't want to" were genuinely upsetting. She seemed much happier working in this environment. So that is something.

The 25-year-old works from her Birmingham flat and has opened up her life to a different sort of camera. Sammie, who lives with her girlfriend, says: "I know these men are teachers, policemen and judges, who hold positions of authority but who want to be submissive to me. They want me to tell them to walk around with drawing pins in their boxer shorts, or put on dog leads and be used as an ashtray. They want to worship my feet or be tortured, to have their life controlled and be put through pain and humiliation. I'm happy to sit there with my clothes on while they walk around in their wife's panties! It's easy money." More worrying was the quote, "The webcam stuff is better and I like doing the dominatrix stuff, where I insult them, because I've formed a hatred for men through my job. This is my payback."

Ambitious 21-year-old glamour model Olivia thinks webcamming can boost her career, hoping that it would be a way of helping her make it big in the world of glamour modelling. Unlike other webcam models she will not go fully nude, but with competition fierce, just how far will she have go to achieve her success? We also met Carla, whose acumen in this field seems unrivalled. She has managed to attract niche crowds, who will pay £2 a minute to watch her cook dinner in her knickers. She once made £300 in one night from people watching her play XBox. A state of affairs that makes one ponder both the state of mind of the punters and also the value of an education. Carla seemed the most robust, although her apparent self-confidence did not stop her taking up with the deeply unlovely Rob, who would not accede to her requests for an evening cuddle on the sofa. "I sleep next to you. Don't you think that's e-fucking-nough?" he snarled. In the end, though, she decided he was not a keeper and returned to her more distant but appreciative admirers.

It was hard to know what to make of all this. What fascinated me was the banality of the interaction. The whole thing seemed as sexy as grouting. The women, though, seemed fairly happy with their lot, viewing the work solely in transactional terms. The men? God knows. Thankfully, we only saw one side of the camera.

Cam Girlz

Directed by Brooklyn-based film maker Sean Dunne, Cam Girlz unfolds as a series of behind-the-scenes stories from women in the business, that include Sophia Locke, Aella, Steph Brooks and Ginger Meadows. Some are married with children while others are barely over 18, and one by one they explain how they got into camming and describe what life has been like since joining what they call the community. In the space of just over an hour, the film featured a total of 39 girls. It shows us young single girls paying for college with their cam money, a professional career woman using cam time to express herself, a stay at home mom who helps support her family, a middle-aged widow who fills a sexual and emotional need with her cam time, and several women who have turned their back on the conventional norm to live a free spirited lucrative cam life.

While the documentary managed to focus the attention on the cam girls, it also shed a light on the guys who pay to watch these girls. The male fans in the movie often said they came to camming sites as a way to fulfill emotional needs. They said it's not like a strip club, Dunne explained, it's like a community and you feel it when you're in these chat rooms. It's a community and entertainment that goes very far beyond sexuality. Dunne said the most accurate analogy was going to a bar. While some think camming operates as a virtual strip club, and some women do dance on cam, Dunne thinks it is more like a number of men showing up at their local pub to interact with one another and flirt with the attractive bartender.

One of the women describes herself as part therapist, part sex object; many women who sell sex will tell you the same. The women on the other side of the camera are very clear they do not want real relationships with their male viewers, it is the men who are confused, unable to separate fantasy from reality, despite the fact that we are told repeatedly, as feminists, that porn is just a fantasy and has no impact on real life. These men, some of whom are featured in the film, very clearly do not know how to connect, emotionally, to real human beings. They believe they are experiencing intimate moments and building meaningful relationships with the cam girls because they listen to and dote on the men.

One unnamed cam user in the movie said he also viewed the girls as therapists. These girls have helped me out tremendously, giving me self-confidence I did not know that I had, empowering me, like, 'Look, you're an attractive guy, you're a smart guy, you're a decent guy,' he said. I can use this tool when I want to and it will satisfy my need. It does give you that warm, fuzzy feeling for the next couple of days afterwards where you know that you had an intimate moment with somebody else. This poor guy misguidedly believes he is accruing genuine, intimate connections. That is, sadly, the major fallacy. For the girl, it is an act, a chiefly invented personality; they are paid to be enthusiastic about their erotic endeavours. In a real life situation, they would certainly behave differently. The degree of anonymity (as evidenced by suggestive screen names), as long as it exists, is the only protection, and also the catalyst for more dangerous follow-ups. Yet this predicament is only touched upon by a single model, with just a couple of sentences.

Apparently, no one is getting hurt. But, of course, that is the most controversial aspect: is someone involved being abused or exploited? Or is this all genuinely harmless? As long as they are doing it by their own design and desire, what is the problem? Surely, those that partook in "Cam Girlz" did so of their own volition (not everyone in the industry is a product of emotional and sexual abuse), but decidedly more nefarious entities and victims certainly populate the world of monetized sex streams, though that is sadly absent from the scope of this documentary.

Dunne cast the film mostly through Twitter. One cam girl in particular, Sophia Locke, runs the Cam Girl Mansion event in Las Vegas, which is essentially a number of women who perform on cam while all hanging out in a mansion. Dunne was able to cut a trailer after his invitation to Cam Girl Mansion, then used

Kickstarter to fund the rest of the film. Most of the footage is snippets of the shows (pole-dancing, masturbation, showering, fondling), which, when devoid of narration, are mere sexual images for the sake of sexual images. This is a fascinating subject, but executed with a distinct lifelessness, a lack of technical and editing verve, a tonal flatness, and a failure to movingly illustrate the various personas that frequent the picture. It is more than the uninspired standard of talking heads, but it is nevertheless wanting for depth and potency, regardless of the compelling nature of the issue.

Furthermore, the plodding pacing, with its focus on visuals over a more philosophical debate on the topic, diminishes the potential for a truly inspirational analyzation. Few breakthroughs or eye-opening viewpoints are scrutinized, succumbing instead to generally trivial blurbs of individual ideals on achievement and emancipation from the entry-level employment rat race. So many of the cam girlz both in the movie and out of it pretend they are there for friendship, but when they talk highly about the positives of this industry, the top of their list is always the freedom they get, the money, the lax working hours, the lifestyle, not having a boss, and doing whatever the hell they want because they have boobs.

In reality the dynamic is simple, women and men are struggling to survive in this economy, and women have something that is in demand, it is called a vagina. There is no discussion that this might be a dangerous economy which leads to no tangible productivity for our society and transfers usable, workable wealth (i.e. cash/tokens) to the opposite gender only to support the globalised beauty industry. It is little more than a voyeuristic peek into the titillating lives of some uneducated women who take advantage of the droves of stupid/poor/sick/lonely/sad/unmarried/married men who are a slave to their biological urges. Would women think so favourably if the tables were turned? I doubt it.

Cam Girlz shows the world of webcam sex workers who find economic freedom, empowerment, intimacy and creative self expression from the comfort of their own homes. Only very briefly does it show how many women who do this suffer from low self esteem and depression. One of the girls talks about being on the verge of a psychotic break down, when her web cam business takes a financial dip for a few weeks. Several discuss how being a cam girl is a chance to be exactly who you are, while others express feelings of leading a double life, or even being bipolar, because of what they do for a living. It was interesting to note that no matter what background and how different each girl's show was, every girl seems to incorporate spanking. How this reflects our society was unfortunately not discussed.

The director feels that he has made a documentary about women who challenge social norms but in reality this is film about women as masturbatory tools for men, reinforcing the socially acceptable, patriarchal notion that women exist for male pleasure. As a man who has not been made to believe his entire purpose in this world is to be fucked, to look pretty, to turn men on, it would be confusing as to how yet another medium that reinforces this norm could be harmful. Naturally, Dunne has no gendered analysis of pornography. When asked, by Vice, whether or not he looked into male camming, he said there was really no such industry, not in any notable way, in any case. Though there are certainly cam sites that feature male and trans performers, Cam Girlz sticks to its namesake and only features female performers. Nor is there any acknowledgement that outside of his little documentary bubble there are cam girls that are forced to do this work, often in horrific, third world conditions.

It was perhaps a mistake on my part to have previously watched one of Dunne's earlier offerings, entitled American Juggalo. This is a complete freak show where the subjects are all repulsive, profane, incoherent or stoned. If they are not naturally unattractive they break out the studs and tattoos and weirdo garb to become that. As the title suggests, the Juggalos are a bathetic antithesis to the slickness and suave of Richard Gere in American Gigolo. I mistakenly thought that this was going to be the work of Sam Dunne, who has created an excellent series of rockumentaries including Rock Icons, Metal Evolution, Rush: Beyond the Lighted Stage and Iron Maiden: Flight 666.

It is unlikely you will learn anything you do not already know and the hour long documentary is really just a more-naked extension of the trailer. Watching the camera pan up and down women's bodies, focusing on bruised asses and pierced nipples only serves as an extension and reinforcement of the objectifying gaze Dunne tells us is revolutionary. Dunne calls camming, the democratization of pornography, but is probably more aptly described as a democratization of misogyny, free and available to all. They are just regular women. Regular women who are responding in a pretty unsurprising way to a capitalist patriarchy that commodifies everything, in particular, women's bodies and sexualities.

More Resources

There are many forums for cam models where they can discuss hints, tips and of course, share war stories.

Sex-workers are really supportive of one another and will help each other out and answer questions. There is always power in collective consciousness. One of the most active sites is the Stripper Web Exotic Dancer Community where there is some discussion about technical issues but much of it is just venting or socializing.

There are some useful resources in the sidebar of /r/camming but compared to other sub reddits, it is not especially active. Much more popular is Ambercutie's forum but there are also forums at WeCamgirls and webcamstartup.com. gfy.com is short for gofuckyourself.com and is a really active forum but it is mostly about affiliate marketing, webmastering, white label sites etc. Not too much about the things we are going through to get a brick/mortar studio up and running. Studio managers keep it pretty close to their chests.

There are a number of books on Amazon concerning panty selling, but most of them are less than ten pages long and therefore best avoided. The only half decent book on the subject is Sex in the Cloud: The Savvy Entrepreneur's Guide to Selling Used Undies and Other Fetish Items in the Online Underground Marketplace by Viktoria Glasse but at only 33 pages do not expect anything earth shattering.

There are large numbers of books explaining how to be a cam model, but again the content of most is freely available on relevant websites. A better read is 'Confessions of a Webcam Model' by L.K. Watts.

More useful in this instance is Ho Tactics: How To MindF**k A Man Into Spending, Spoiling, and Sponsoring' by G.L. Lambert. Written along the same lines as The Power of the Pussy: Get What You Want From Men by Kara King this book is mainly about the soft spots in a man's psychology that any woman can exploit. There are chapters on flirting, phone sex, and asking for gifts in the proper way, all useful info for an aspiring cam girl. The second part of the book builds on the first twelve chapters and signals an advanced stage where those women who don t mind going the extra mile sexually can master things like on-line dating and The Kardashian Effect. This is especially useful for building up confidence, identifying the tricks men use on women and how to beat them at their own game. Useful for those women who have been way too nice to guys and allowed men to manipulate them.

Slightly less controversial but just as useful is Confidence on Camera: 7 Steps to Present Your Power on any size screen by Lottie Hearn. Webc@m girl by Natasha Davies is an entertaining and true to life look at the I-Net industry and the many characters that manoeuvre within it.

Another third-party service catering to the cam community are trade events such as CamCon, which usually coincides with the XBIZ Miami event. According to CamCon promoter Clinton Cox, the popular show offers a truly comprehensive platform that unites models with their fans and the industry.

The models who attend learn how to create more money for their business, learn about other products to build their brand, and on 'Fan Day' meet the fans who they have been interacting with all year, while creating lifelong friendships

with other models. The industry gets to be exposed to true
career models and newcomers, all wanting to learn how to make more money in this segment, as well as meet the gamut of fans, from the highest calibre 'whales' to the curious local. Cox says that fans benefit by meeting their favourite models at CamCon and by enjoying a true Miami VIP experience, while other attendees benefit from receiving a positive perspective on the cam industry and where it is going.

About the Author

Darby Jones first began writing as a teenager, when he quickly displayed an early talent for penning sensuous erotica and hard-core porn. For many years he was a prolific contributor to UK magazines such as Mayfair, Fiesta and Knave, as well as a host of lesser known but equally popular titles. After a short stint at Viz Comics, he left England to become the lead contributor of an infamous but long out-of-print travel opus, entitled Sex Havens for Tax Fiends. This was a strictly limited edition, leather-bound gazetteer commissioned by the now defunct Scope Publications. It was published as a follow up to their extremely popular PT (Perpetual Traveller) titles, including as The Passport Report, The Honorary Consul and The Invisible Investor. Each volume immediately sold out and remains highly collectible to this day.

For the last three years, he has been enjoying forced early-retirement after an extremely stressful eighteen months smuggling Chinese-made arms and munitions to the various rebel groups in Eastern and Northern Myanmar. He was forced to spend nearly a year in Malaysia recuperating from a near-fatal gunshot injury, which was sustained in a shoot-out on the upper reaches of the Mekong. He is currently in an undisclosed Asian location working on his latest book.

Please feel free to contact me at travellingman@zoho.com

Other books by Darby Jones

Fifty Shades of Sexual Fantasy- Borderland Press
Mandarin Optional - Borderland Press
Mandarin Preferred - Borderland Press

Forthcoming in 2017

Football Coaching Careers in China
Automated into Oblivion
Mandarin Essential

Disclaimer

First published 2017 by The Borderland Press
This electronic edition published 2017 by The Borderland Press, an imprint of
Sino-Worldwide Publishers Limited
ISBN 978-1530358786
Library of Congress Cataloguing-in-Publication Data
Jones, Darby., 2017, Adult Webcam Studio 101 - A Money Making Guide for E-
pimps
p. cm.

1. Management, Philosophy.
2. Business opportunities, Public opinion.
3. Computers (General)
4. Success in business.
I. Title.
HD30.19.R67 2016 658, hd22 206049010
ISBN-13: 978-1544293394
ISBN-10: 1544293399

Disclaimer

www.ingramcontent.com/pod-product-compliance
Lightning Source LLC
Chambersburg PA
CBHW051705170526
45167CB00002B/539